Anna Komnene

Onassis Series in Hellenic Culture

Onassis
Foundation (USA)

Anna Komnene

The Life and Work of a Medieval Historian

Leonora Neville

OXFORD
UNIVERSITY PRESS

OXFORD
UNIVERSITY PRESS

Oxford University Press is a department of the University of Oxford. It furthers
the University's objective of excellence in research, scholarship, and education
by publishing worldwide. Oxford is a registered trade mark of Oxford University
Press in the UK and certain other countries.

Published in the United States of America by Oxford University Press
198 Madison Avenue, New York, NY 10016, United States of America.

Library of Congress Cataloging-in-Publication Data

Names: Neville, Leonora Alice, 1970– author.
Title: Anna Komnene : the life and work of a medieval historian / Leonora Neville.
Description: New York, NY : Oxford University Press, 2016. | Series:
Onassis series in Hellenic culture | Includes bibliographical references and index.
Identifiers: LCCN 2016001467 (print) | LCCN 2016009353 (ebook) |
ISBN 9780190498177 (hardcover) | ISBN 9780190939892 (paperback)
Subjects: LCSH: Comnena, Anna, 1083– | Princesses—Byzantine
Empire—Biography. | Historians—Byzantine Empire—Biography. | Byzantine
Empire—History—Alexius I Comnenus, 1081–1118.
Classification: LCC DF605.3 .N48 2016 (print) | LCC DF605.3 (ebook) |
DDC 949.5/03092—dc23
LC record available at http://lccn.loc.gov/2016001467

For Robert and Beth Neville

{ CONTENTS }

{ ABBREVIATIONS }

My citations to the *Alexiad* are to the book, chapter, and paragraph number, as they appear in the edition by Reinsch and Kambylis. The lines of the Reinsch and Kambylis edition are numbered within each book from 1 to 95 and then starting again from 1 to 95, irrespective of the chapter and paragraph breaks. The *Thesaurus Linguae Graecae* database includes the Reinsch and Kambylis edition, but numbers the lines sequentially within each paragraph. Where I include line numbers, they refer to those of the TLG, which I believe to be more widely available. The translations are mine unless otherwise noted.

Alexiad	Reinsch, D. and Kambylis, A. eds., *Alexiad*. Corpus Fontium Historiae Byzantinae. Berlin: De Gruyter, 2001.
Choniates	Van Dieten, J., ed. *Nicetae Choniatae historia, pars prior.* Corpus Fontium Historiae Byzantinae. Berlin: De Gruyter, 1975. Citations are to the page and line number.
Zonaras	Büttner-Wobst, T., ed. *Ioannis Zonarae epitomae historiarum libri xviii*, Vol. 3. Corpus scriptorum historiae Byzantinae. Bonn: Weber, 1897. Citations are to the page number of volume three.

Anna Komnene

Introduction

Anna Komnene began life surrounded by royal purple, born in a pavilion in the Great Palace of Constantinople lined in ancient purple porphyry stone, in which the wives of the emperors had been giving birth for centuries. Birth in this purple room, the *porphyra*, gave Anna the exclusive title *porphyrogennete*—born in purple. Her mother, knowing that Emperor Constantine the Great had founded Constantinople to create a new capital for a revived Roman empire, doubtless saw herself as in continuity not only with all the imperial women who had given birth in the *porphyra* of the Great Palace in Constantinople, but also with the empresses of old Rome on the Tiber. Anna's father was the Emperor of the Romans, and would have been quite confused by the modern scholarly habit of calling his people "Byzantines."

Anna differed remarkably from the long line of imperial princesses born in the *porphyra* by becoming one of the leading intellectuals of her generation and one the greatest historians of the middle ages. Emperors' daughters were literate and some enjoyed refined rhetoric and classical texts. Yet Anna's education was on an entirely different order of magnitude. She delighted in ancient philosophy, commissioning commentaries on Aristotle. She read Attic tragedy and comedy, making meaningful allusions to the plays of Sophocles. She studied mathematics, astronomy, and enough medicine to argue forcefully with her father's doctors. She knew Homer so well that, when she took her hand to history, she wrote another *Iliad* to tell the deeds of her father. Of all that she wrote, it is this history, the *Alexiad*, that remains as a testament to her authorial abilities as well as to her father's adventures. The *Alexiad* is a masterpiece of vivid historical narrative to which we owe much of our knowledge of the history and politics of the eastern Mediterranean in the twelfth century.[1]

This extraordinary intellectual career took place within the confines of a fairly normal life for an imperial princess. After the birth of Anna, her parents, Alexios Komnenos and Eirene Doukaina, went on to have eight other children: Maria, John, Andronikos, Isaac, Eudokia, Theodora, Manuel, and Zoe. Anna's brother John was crowned co-emperor when he was five.[2] The fundamental shape of Anna's family suggests that her parents enjoyed a devoted marriage. A historian of the mid-twelfth century accused Alexios of affairs and lack of interest in his wife.[3] Yet the great number of children that Eirene and Alexios produced indicates that Alexios had some interest in Eirene. Children six through nine, at least, testify that Alexios took his marriage far more seriously than other Byzantine emperors whose mistresses enliven the pages of history.

Anna's life was affected by her father's need to strengthen his own political position at the start of his reign through the choice of her marriage. Beyond all the normal joys of parenthood, Anna's parents were pleased by her birth because she was able to assist in the larger project of increasing Alexios's power by reconciling former rivals. The birth of a child in the porphyry pavilion was a necessary first step toward establishing a stable dynasty. At the time of Anna's birth, on December 1, 1083, her father's dynasty was hardly stable. Alexios Komnenos had seized power in a violent coup d'état on April 1, 1081, during which his troops had plundered Constantinople. The emperor he deposed, Nikephoros Botaneiates, had himself come to power through a revolt shortly before in March of 1078. During Botaneiates's short reign, *seven* other generals revolted in hope of becoming emperor themselves. The previous emperor, Michael VII Doukas, had weathered eleven revolts in six years.[4] The question everyone had for Alexios was whether he would be able to bring the destructive infighting to a close and create the political stability that would allow the empire to deal more effectively with its vigorous foreign enemies.

To the probable surprise of many of his contemporaries, Alexios succeeded in staying on the throne, despite numerous early rebellions against him, and gradually strengthened his control over the empire. By the time he died of natural causes on August 15, 1118, he had ruled for nearly forty years. He was succeeded by his oldest son, John II Komnenos, who also enjoyed a long reign, dying in 1143.

As a step toward creating this stability, Alexios betrothed Anna shortly after her birth to Constantine Doukas, the son of one of the previously deposed emperors. Constantine died from illness soon after 1094, before he and Anna were married.[5] As a consequence of her engagement to Constantine, Anna went to live with Constantine's mother, Maria of Alania, when she was seven. Aristocratic Byzantine girls were normally betrothed soon after age

FIGURE I.1 *Hyperperon of Alexios I. After decades in which Byzantine emperors minted increasingly debased coins in order to pay their bills, Alexios initiated a reform of the coinage in 1092, minting new gold hyperperon "highly-refined" coins that had nearly the same gold content as the nomisma gold coins used from late antiquity through the eleventh century. On one side Alexios stands in imperial regalia while the hand of God reaches down from the upper right to bless him. On the other side Christ sits enthroned, raising his hand in blessing [BZC.1947.2.114.A2011.N66.76.3].*
© Dumbarton Oaks, Byzantine Collection, Washington, DC.

seven, and were married at adolescence. It seems that they would move into the household of their future husbands' families near the time of betrothal so that their future mothers-in-law could raise them and help prepare them for their marriage.[6] Maria certainly had a palace in Constantinople, where Anna may have lived, but she also had estates outside of the city. Anna mentions two estates Maria owned in Christoupolis (modern Kavala) on the northern coast of the Aegean.[7] Constantine had his own estate near Serres, named Pentegostis.[8] Anna would only have lived in Maria's household for a few years, however, because in 1094 Maria was implicated in an extensive plot to depose Alexios.[9] Constantine apparently did not take part, and it is possible that Anna's betrothal to him ended only when he died.

After the death of Constantine, Anna's parents arranged a new marriage for her. Nikephoros Bryennios was the grandson of one of the rebels that Alexios had defeated shortly before his own coup.[10] The Bryennios family continued to have great influence in Adrianople and the surrounding regions. It is possible that Anna spent some time living with Nikephoros's family prior to their marriage. In her history she mentions in passing that she had seen the great walls of Philippopolis (modern Plovdiv), farther up the royal road to Belgrade from Adrianople.[11] She may have visited Philippopolis with her husband's family, or when accompanying her father on campaign.[12] Anna married Nikephoros Bryennios around 1097, when she was fifteen and he a few years older.

Anna and Nikephoros had at least two daughters, Eirene and Maria, and four sons, Alexios, John, Andronikos, and Constantine.[13] Alexios and John were married in a lavish joint ceremony that took place sometime after the death of their grandfather Alexios Komnenos in 1118.[14] Young Alexios's bride was a daughter of King David II of Georgia.[15] John's wife was named Theodora.[16] They were led in the marriage procession by the reigning emperor, their uncle John.[17] One of Anna's daughters was already widowed at the time of their wedding.[18] This sister is probably Eirene, who, after Anna's death, became the protector of the women's monastery founded by Anna's mother.[19] The role of protector of a monastery involved legal and financial control, but not spiritual oversight or joining the monastery. Anna's sons Alexios and John had prominent military careers, as did Eirene's son, Alexios Doukas.[20]

Anna's other children, Maria, Andronikos, and Constantine, seem to have died young. A text, written sometime in the 1120s, mentions both Anna's daughter Eirene and another unspecified daughter as living.[21] If this second daughter is Maria, it would seem likely that she lived at least through early childhood and perhaps through adolescence. Of Andronikos and Constantine, we know only the days on which their deaths should be commemorated. In the preface to her last testament, Anna describes herself as the mother of many good children. She is thankful for her marriage from which she had "most beautiful and perfect children of both sexes, of whom some have exchanged their perishable life (this was God's will) and some are still alive."[22]

While Anna's marriage to Nikephoros was politically advantageous, in that it connected the interests of the Bryennios and Komnenos families, he was also a good match for Anna because they shared strong intellectual interests. By the time Alexios and Eirene needed to make a new match for Anna after Constantine's death, she may well have begun displaying the keen interest in classical learning that was to be such a significant part of her life. Nikephoros's own intellectual interests may have recommended him as a suitable match. As adults, Nikephoros and Anna were known for their extraordinary levels of learning and intellectual accomplishment. Anna and Nikephoros were both skillful writers who patronized intellectuals and rhetoricians. Their major surviving texts are classicizing histories. Nikephoros wrote a history of the aristocratic civil wars of the 1070s that ends, unfinished, just before Alexios's revolt in 1081. Both Nikephoros and Anna wrote letters that were highly praised by leading rhetoricians of their era.

Nikephoros's history is a well-constructed and thoughtful piece of historical writing, but it is far less artful than the *Alexiad*. Nikephoros deserves to be considered an accomplished intellectual, but his wife was playing in a different league. Her history is one of the best pieces of writing of the twelfth century, and, if the funeral oration for Anna is to be believed, her history was an afterthought in comparison to her work on philosophy.[23] It cannot have escaped Nikephoros that his wife was the intellectual star.

Anna's participation in a circle of scholars studying classical philosophy and ancient literature was made possible by Nikephoros's respect for her and trust in their marriage. Nikephoros probably enjoyed some of the philosophical conversations that took place in his household, but he also must be seen as genuinely supportive of his wife's intellectual interests. It would have been acceptable at any point for Nikephoros to say that he did not want his wife talking with a lot of strange men and bar them from his household. Yet his wife debated leading scholars with his full knowledge and acceptance. Nikephoros's approval of Anna's interactions with other men interested in scholarship was crucial to her intellectual work.

In addition to his literary activities, Nikephoros served both his father-in-law and brother-in-law in military capacities. Nikephoros helped defend the walls of Constantinople during the tumultuous passing of the First Crusade.[24] His letters indicate that sometimes he worked "in the east" on behalf of John's government.[25] Anna relates that he was campaigning with John in Syria in the 1138 when he contracted his final illness.[26]

After the death of Nikephoros, Anna continued to be an active literary patron. It was in the later stages of her life that she took up history writing. We know that Anna was working on the *Alexiad* after the mid-1140s because in it she comments obliquely on the politics surrounding the Second Crusade (1145–1149).[27] A funeral oration for Anna describes her as becoming ill as she tended to her sister Maria as the latter was dying. Anna had enough time to put her affairs in order and take a monastic vow before her own death shortly thereafter.[28] The precise year of Anna's death is unknown but probably took place sometime in the 1150s.

This story of Anna's life differs from standard versions by making no mention of Anna's supposed political ambition or efforts to supplant her brother John as ruler. A more common understanding of Anna's basic character is reflected in the poem composed by the great Alexandrian poet Constantine Cavafy in 1920:

> "Anna Komnini"
>
> In the prologue to her *Alexiad*,
> Anna Komnina laments her widowhood.
>
> Her soul is all vertigo.
> "And I bathe my eyes," she tells us,
> "in rivers of tears. . . . Alas for the waves" of her life,
> "alas for the revolutions." Sorrow burns her
> "to the bones and the marrow and the splitting" of her soul.

> But the truth seems to be this power-hungry woman
> knew only one sorrow that really mattered;
> even if she doesn't admit it, this arrogant Greek woman
> had only one consuming pain:
> that with all her dexterity,
> she never managed to gain the throne,
> virtually snatched out of her hands by impudent John.[29]

Cavafy's portrait was inspired by his reading of early twentieth-century scholarship on Byzantium in which Anna was depicted as prideful, haughty, and consumed with frustration at her inability to rule as empress. Both Cavafy's poem and scholarship of his era acknowledged that Anna was an author of history, but presented her primarily as a failed conspirator. Cavafy begins with the laments that open Anna's history, but the poem is about her frustrated ambition, arrogance, and hypocrisy rather than her authorship.

Most people studying medieval history know that Anna wrote the *Alexiad*, but Anna is famous for wanting to be empress and unsuccessfully disputing her brother's right to the throne. She is known more for her thwarted political ambition than for her authorship. It is commonly believed that, after nursing imperial ambitions since her childhood, she twice attempted to install her husband Nikephoros as emperor instead of her brother John. Soon after the first attempt at the death of her father in August 1118 failed, she tried to have John murdered. When these efforts failed, she was forced to enter a monastery where she lived, consumed by hatred and jealousy, until her death. In Charles Diehl's dramatic portrait, first published in 1906, after her second coup failed, Anna "was only thirty-six years old, but her life was over."[30] She wrote the *Alexiad* in the later years of her life, when the standard narrative holds that she was imprisoned in consequence of her failed ambitions.

This conception of Anna's life makes it impossible to identify her primarily as an author and intellectual. In Diehl's view, Anna was rhetorically already dead before she began to write history. Her time spent writing history is not celebrated as a wonderfully creative and intellectually engaging period of her life, but negated as something she did to pass the time after her life was over, sitting in prison and stewing in hatred.

Authorship is empowering. Authors of ancient and medieval Greek histories, who decided which of men's deeds to record for posterity and how those deeds ought to be remembered, exercised a particularly robust version of authorial power. Anna's culture held strongly negative views of women who grasped after power because power was considered as naturally appropriate for men: good women upheld male authority and bad women threatened male authority. No surprise, then, that women did not write history in Anna's culture.[31] In fact, she may have been the only woman to write a history in Greek prior to the twentieth century.[32] That Anna is primarily remembered

FIGURE I.2 *Hyperperon of John Komnenos. John and the Mother of God together hold the imperial scepter. On the other side Christ sits enthroned [BZC.1948.17.3393. D2012.r.JohnII.bw, and BZC.1948.17.3393.D2012.oJohnII.bw].*

© *Dumbarton Oaks, Byzantine Collection, Washington, DC.*

as a woman who desired power, but did not get it, rather than a woman who exercised authorial power successfully, raises questions about lingering discomfort with powerful women among the generations of scholars who constructed the modern narrative of her biography.

Power, gender, and authorship lie at the heart of my interpretations of Anna's life and her historical work. My first goal in this book is to understand how Anna sought to negotiate her novel position as a woman who wrote history. Less effort than one might expect has gone into thinking seriously about how Anna's gender affected her writing process and her end product.[33] I interpret Anna's responses to her culture's conceptions of appropriate female gender as driving forces behind what are perceived as the idiosyncrasies of her text. The vast majority of Anna's long history adheres to the conventions of Greek classicizing historical narrative. Yet occasionally her text departs from standard practices of historical writing in unusual and unexpected ways. These departures, I believe, are places where Anna is working to shape her character in the text so that her audience would see her as a good woman, as well as a reliable historian. Anna seems to have been well aware that writing history as a woman could cause discomfort for her audience and bring accusations of inappropriate behavior on herself. She attempted to counter these potential accusations by presenting herself in the text as acting in ways that her culture considered feminine and in ways that were designed to humble Anna and elicit pity. In some passages Anna adopts an exaggeratedly feminine persona of extreme emotionalism, or deploys other strategies intended to evoke a positive and kindly emotional response among her audience. Anna seems to have tried to get her audience to sympathize with her by adopting a posture of piteous suffering. The first half of this book is devoted to understanding Anna's authorial persona and exploring how she endeavored to respond to the challenges her culture's conceptions of proper gender created for her historical activity.

My second goal is to understand the origins and development of the story that defines Anna's life by her thwarted political ambition. In seeking to understand how Anna flourished as a woman historian in the twelfth century, and how she has been received as a woman historian in the eighteenth through twentieth centuries, we are called to think about the interactions of gender, power, and authorship in both medieval Constantinople and modern academic culture. Twelfth-century Byzantine culture and eighteenth- to twentieth-century academic culture had different conceptions of appropriate behavior for women, different ideologies of power, and different conceptions of history.[34] Modern historians' ideas about gender, authorship, and power have been different enough from those of Anna's culture that, for the most part, they have completely misunderstood how Anna was endeavoring to respond to her culture's ideas about appropriate female behavior. Yet there are enough points of commonality, if not continuity, that Anna's status as a woman writer of history remained problematic well into the twentieth century.

On the one hand, Anna's performances of medieval feminine emotionalism were seen as marring her historical dispassion and objectivity in ways that caused distrust and discomfort for her modern readers. When Anna was perceived as acting like a woman, for example when she lamented, modern readers instinctively see her as lacking objectivity and not acting like a good historian. Charles Diehl's early twentieth-century opinions about women's natural inclinations guided his interpretation of the *Alexiad*. He describes the *Alexiad* as significantly affected by Anna's gender in ways that make it less valuable as a history:

> We must not forget that she was a woman, and consequently had a liking for the decorative, for exterior magnificence, which sometimes concealed from her the true heart of things; that she was a passionate woman, consumed by hatreds and resentments, and lastly, a learned woman, a literary stylist in love with fine phrases. All this, though it may diminish the strictly historical value of Anna Komnene's work, does not by any means make it less interesting.[35]

Diehl's conception of what female authorship would look like is fueled by Anna's emotionalism and literary extravagance in the *Alexiad*. There are some places in her writing where I believe she was enacting femininity, as it was perceived in her culture. Some of these feminine performances, such as emotionalism, continue to be perceived as feminine by readers such as Diehl, but he also interprets as feminine other aspects of her style, such as "fine phrases," which were not considered girly within her own culture. It is the commonalities, but also the differences, between the medieval and modern conceptions of gender, authorship, and authority that make the *Alexiad* such a puzzle.

On the other hand, passages in which Anna makes herself into an object of pity have sparked efforts to give her life a predominantly political reading as a way of explaining her expressions of misery. I believe that Anna's lamentations were designed to allow her to display the emotionalism considered natural for a woman and to mitigate the arrogance of her authorship by provoking pity and condescension among her audience. Scholars now can recognize her humbling strategies as fairly conventional ancient and medieval literary tactics.[36] Yet for Anna's eighteenth- to twentieth-century audience, her expressions of suffering did not evoke sympathy or pity. These readers rather concluded that something must have been drastically wrong with her. The story of the failed coup supplies a backstory that helped modern readers make sense of Anna's piteous self-presentation. Once Anna's authorial persona is better understood, the evidence for an attempted coup suddenly becomes far less compelling. The second half of this book reviews the evidence for Anna's life, tries to work out what can be known about her, and traces the development of the modern narrative of her thwarted ambition, which fuels Cavafy's portrait of the arrogant Greek woman.

Medieval texts have often been interpreted in light of what we believe we know about the authors' lives. Given the paucity of evidence, it is also common to get much of our information about an author's biography from his or her writing. This process can be problematically circular.[37] Using biographical information extracted from an author's text as a tool for the interpretation of that text largely assumes that authors are straightforward and honest about how they present themselves in their texts. This mode of reading assumes that if authors say that they feel something, it is because they really felt it. For many medieval texts, it seems more likely that authors said what they thought would draw out the desired emotional response from their audience. In some devotional texts, the "I" in the text is not the author at all, but the reader, who uses the text as a script to practice the performance of particular emotions.[38] Learning how to present oneself in such a way as to provoke the desired emotional responses from one's audience was part of basic education for Byzantine authors.[39] Byzantine authors paid attention to how their writing would make their audience feel, both about the subject of the text, and about the author. We can understand Byzantine texts better when we think about how they are trying to get us to feel.[40]

In the case of Anna, key details about her biography, such as her birth, education, betrothal, and marriage, have been derived from the *Alexiad* itself. Although the *Alexiad* contains no trace of a coup attempt, Anna's sorrowful emotional state in the text is used to corroborate the story of her failed attempt to depose her brother John. Anna's bitterness expressed in the *Alexiad* becomes some of the key evidence for her involvement in the coup. Circularly, Anna's failed coup of 1118 looms large in our understanding of twelfth-century history in part because that political disappointment is used as a tool for the interpretation of the *Alexiad*. The story of Anna's political failure and internal exile is used to explain Anna's expressions of sadness in the *Alexiad*. Curiously in this process, the story of Anna as politically disappointed has been used to refute Anna's testimony about her own emotional state in the *Alexiad*: while she says she mourns her husband and parents, she is *really* upset about the failure of her political ambitions. The failed coup explains the vehemence of her emotions, which have been taken as truthful, but only by assuming that her own explanations are lies.

What drives both the distrust of Anna's text, and the politicization of her life, I believe, is a discrepancy between the intended emotional impact of her writing and the feelings it in fact raises among modern readers. While Anna seems to have intended her cries of misery to evoke sympathy and condescending goodwill toward a poor old widow, to Diehl they were a sign she was "consumed by hatreds and resentments."[41] Rather than provoking sympathy, Anna's emotionalism made her the object of lurid fascination and an urge to discover what *really* happened to her. For Cavafy, the lamentations opening the *Alexiad* need both explanation and denial. Her tears are false, and to explain them he seizes on "the truth" that Anna had one consuming pain, "even if she doesn't admit it."[42]

The next few chapters try to show what Anna was hoping to achieve through the authorial persona she created: why she cried in her text, why she boasted, and why she doted on her father while loudly proclaiming her own impartiality. The consideration of the affective responses she was trying to provoke in her audience can free us to better understand both her text and her life. Byzantine conceptions of gender, authority, and history writing are outlined in chapter 1, establishing a set of cultural circumstances to which Anna was responding when crafting her self-presentation. Chapter 2 explores Anna's efforts to prove both that she had the skills and training to write history and the modesty and humility expected of women. Chapter 3 looks at her struggle to be both a properly devoted daughter, zealously maintaining her father's honor, and an impartial historian fairly and dispassionately narrating both Alexios's successes and failures. Chapter 4 turns to those points in her history where Anna seems to adopt a more feminine persona, endeavoring to understand what prompts these moments and how they functioned. Anna's efforts to convince her audience of the high quality of her research, without transgressing the boundaries of appropriate female behavior or being in any way self-aggrandizing, are treated in chapter 5. Throughout these chapters we see Anna facing contradictory cultural and intellectual imperatives. She does not resolve, or gloss over, these contradictions, but rather holds them in deliberate tension. She makes her responses to the competing imperatives patent, allowing her audience to see the taut fabric she is weaving. When the *Alexiad* is read with an eye for the cultural difficulties of the task Anna set for herself, those elements and passages that have made it seem like an odd or deficient history become places where we see her artistry in creating the authorial voice of a virtuous woman historian.

The new understanding of what Anna says about herself in the *Alexiad* changes how we can interpret other medieval evidence for her life. The second half of the book explores how Anna is portrayed in narrative histories, court rhetoric, and other texts of the twelfth century, focusing especially on the transfer of power from Anna's father Alexios (1081–1118) to John II (1118–1143), without the presuppositions of the standard modern narrative or the need to explain Anna's emotions in the *Alexiad*. Slowly over the course of the eighteenth, nineteenth, and early twentieth centuries, the story of Anna's life turned into a tale of the endless rage as she became Cavafy's "power-hungry woman." Chapter 10, on how Anna was presented in histories of Byzantium in the eighteenth–twentieth centuries, shows how modern conceptions of the proper relationship between women and authorship changed over time, and varied among authors. Both the commonalities and differences between medieval and modern conceptions of gender, authorship, and power worked to predispose modern historians to choose a version of Anna's biography in which she is characterized more strongly by her anger at political disempowerment than the empowerment of her authorship.

PART I

A Good Historian and a Good Woman

Why Didn't Greek Women Write History?

Think of a Greek historian. Chances are good that you just thought of male Greek historian. You may have chosen a contemporary Greek woman, but if you thought of an ancient or medieval Greek historian (I bet you picked Thucydides or Herodotus), you almost certainly thought of a man. That Greek women did not write history is one of those historical facts that we all know, but rarely consider.[1] What made it so difficult for women to write history? The exception to this rule is Anna Komnene.[2] Why was she able to do it? I think ideas about gender, history, and authorship in ancient and medieval Greek culture combined to make history writing extraordinarily difficult for women.

History writing in the Greek tradition was a masculine form of expression. Anna's history, the *Alexiad*, has often been considered an odd history, but we have not recognized how Anna's vigorous efforts to look like a good woman while participating in a male activity are responsible for most of the strangeness of her history. In attempting to write history as a woman in her culture, Anna was being fundamentally transgressive. Yet she strove, I believe, both to write history and to remain an admirable woman according to the norms of her culture. While modern people may applaud women of other eras who refused to play by the cultural rules of their societies (Anna gets a chapter in *Uppity Women of Medieval Times*), Anna's goal seems to have been to create an authorial persona that was a fully good and praiseworthy woman, according to her culture's ideas about morality, and simultaneously a writer of authoritative history.[3]

The idea that men ought to be dominant and women ought to be entirely submissive was extremely strong in Byzantine culture. On the other hand, we have evidence for women acting with remarkable degrees of authority and autonomy, given that prevailing ideology. Some women in Byzantine society were able to act with considerable self-determination; we see them active in trades, as business owners, landowners, and monastic leaders.[4] Ruling empresses are among the empire's most famous citizens.[5] There was no danger that someone would barge into Anna's room and take her pen away. Yet her writing is full of evidence that she was deeply concerned with being perceived as a good woman who conformed to the gender norms of her culture. As we shall see, there were a number of standard techniques Byzantine women used to act with self-determination while simultaneously upholding their culture's gender ideology. Anna employed all of these strategies in the *Alexiad*. These means of gaining autonomy while going along with the dominant gender norms had the double consequence of enabling women's activities and reinforcing those norms.

Byzantine conceptions of appropriate gender seem strongly connected to issues of authority and control. Among the most pervasive and foundational cultural values of Byzantine society was that authority naturally resided with men, and that support for masculine authority contributed to the proper and natural social order. Systems of moral, religious, legal, and political power worked to reinforce the tight linkage between maleness and authority. Maleness in medieval Greek culture was displayed by a man's ability to control his passions and sexual impulses; men expressed their masculinity through control of themselves and others. Power and masculine gender were hence deeply intertwined in Byzantine culture. Just as masculinity was defined by the ability to control oneself and others, virtuous femininity was expressed through submission to masculine authority.[6]

Virtue for women consisted in behaviors that supported masculine authority. As men should express authority, women should be demure. Women were praised for displaying what were considered natural feminine characteristics such as patience, sweetness, compassion, or emotionalism. Women were considered evil when they disrupted or challenged male authority. The main fear expressed by the male authors about women was that they would sexually incite men, causing men to lose their self-control. Because medieval Greek culture conceived of control over the passions as a defining element of masculinity, by tempting men to give in to sexual passion, seductive women undermined the proper social order. The pervasive worry about evil women was based on fear of women's ability to disrupt the proper order of social relations.

Sexual sin was seen as caused by the evil nature of women that tempted men to lose their self-control. Christian moralists within Byzantine culture demonized female nature as laying snares for men, drawing men into sin through lust. Within Byzantine hagiography "the notion that women by nature continue the work of Eve is ubiquitous."[7] Evil women used to their beauty and seductive powers to excite men into sin and lapses in control of their passions.

Virtuous women, on the other hand, employed extreme modesty, which helped uphold the natural order by enabling men to control their passions. Modest women helped men maintain their self-control by policing their own bodies and deportment. Women's speech could be an entry point for seduction, and hence virtuous women were described as carefully controlling their speech, as well as the gaze of their eyes and their bodily movements. Virtuous women carefully avoided any potentially seductive movements or glances.[8] Women's attention to demure and modest deportment was seen as protecting their own virtue, but also functioned to support masculine self-control.

The complete seclusion of women, and removal of opportunities for men to see them, was considered ideal. Aristocratic women of Anna's era were not supposed leave the privacy of their homes, except for religious observances. The value of a girl at betrothal was seen as correlated to how rarely she had been seen in public.[9] An eleventh-century advice book recommends men not to let a friend stay in their houses because the guest would be able to look at their women.[10] Women were banned from testifying at trials on the grounds that their presence and speech in a public forum was inappropriate and disordering.[11] In practice, only wealthy women were able to maintain their seclusion, and so the ability to avoid going to the marketplace became a marker of high social status.[12] The association between the marketplace and loud, raucous shouting and talking contributed to making it an inappropriate place for a good woman, because good women were silent.[13] For women of Anna's social class, complete seclusion was a possibility.[14]

The cultural ideal that virtuous women should be unseen and silent is an aspect of Byzantine society that shows deep continuities with ancient Greek culture. Anna's contemporaries could easily nod in agreement when Thucydides had Pericles praise most the Athenian woman who was spoken of the least.[15] Yet medieval attitudes about the virtues of seclusion and silence for women are not a matter of lip service to ancient ideals, or a cultural affectation of classicism, but rather are connected to the fundamental structures of Byzantine culture. Christian moral theology, which considered women as sources of temptation for men, added new and powerful justifications to ancient androcentric attitudes. The late antique and medieval reconceptualization that masculinity was expressed not so much by sexual activity and power (as it had been in the ancient world), as by control over sexuality and other passions, strongly reinforced the cultural logic that men needed to dominate women.[16] The ideal that women should remain in the domestic sphere had lasting strength because it was connected to deep structures of authority within medieval Byzantine culture.

The system of gender just described was a matter of pervasive ideology within Byzantine culture. The existence of that ideology does not mean that women were in fact always disempowered, passive, and subordinate to men. Yet women seem to have wielded authority more by upholding than disputing the dominant gender ideas of their culture. Ideals of female subordination to men were reinforced by depicting particularly virtuous women as having overcome the problems inherent in their femaleness: some women could be good because they became like men. Women were invited to practice the masculine virtue of self-control and hence to become, through training, more like men. Early Byzantine stories about women saints said that holy women were amazing because they were good, even though they were women, and hence naturally bad. Since women were naturally emotional and subject to passion, they had a more arduous journey toward the monastic ideal of dispassion. Fourth- and fifth-century stories about saints saw each holy woman as an exception to the norm who transcended expectations for women to become "an honorary male."[17] By labeling every example of a virtuous woman an exception, "the image of women as a whole remained unredeemed."[18] Through mental efforts women could become more like men, but their nature was always weaker.

In secular contexts, women could also be depicted as gaining control over their passions, and natural emotionalism, through the exercise of reason, prudence, and masculine strength. In a speech he wrote for Empress Theodora (1055–1056) the courtier and rhetorician Michael Psellos has Theodora declare that she is able to address the assembly because her noble birth and study of scriptures allow her to go beyond her female nature.[19] A woman would not normally be able to speak in such a setting, but Theodora has special strength because of her nobility and intellectual efforts. By showing that they were more fully in control of their emotions and themselves, particularly virtuous women could become more like men; it became a high compliment for a woman to be "manly."[20] Anna's mother, Eirene, was flattered for ruling her own passions as well as she did the empire.[21] Anna herself was praised for acting with masculine authority when she discussed medicine with the doctors during Alexios's death.[22] Women were not expected to be competent in medicine, but Anna's exceptional moral and intellectual strengths allowed her to be masculine enough to do it.

We see the same strategy in legal sales documents where women's participation is enabled by their ability to overcome the limitations expected of their female nature. In medieval Greek records of sales and donations, women routinely swear that they are not acting under the influence of "female simplicity."[23] In order to make their agreements legally binding, women needed to exercise the sound judgment and reasoned deliberation their culture associated with men.[24] Women did undertake significant financial transactions, but like the female saints, each woman who signed the deed of sale exhibited exceptional masculinity. The cultural ritual of having women swear that they were not acting like women when doing business enabled women's financial autonomy while simultaneously upholding and reinforcing the fundamental gender ideology of their society. In both the hagiography and legal documents dealing with women, women were depicted as able to act like men through deliberate effort. By nature, they remained emotional and subject to passion, but they were able to transcend this nature, to an extent, through practice.

A second significant way Byzantine women could exercise power was to act helpless and needy, which pushed men to help them. By performing the neediness their culture attributed to women, they encouraged men to display their authority and power by helping them. By being needy, women called on men to be provident. For example, in 1112, a woman named Eudokia employed a posture of helplessness and poverty to circumvent legal restrictions on selling her dowry.[25] While it was illegal for a woman to sell part of her dowry, she could do so in the case of extreme need. To get approval for her sale from the governor, Eudokia argued that her family was completely indigent and that it would be uncharitable and merciless for the governor to block the sale. Eudokia's petition emphasizes her extreme poverty and humility before the greatness of governor, addressing him with terminology normally applied to the most revered of religious leaders. In begging God to guide his judgment, and in her adoption of an attitude of piteousness and helplessness, Eudokia was acting in the well-established role of the prayerful, piteous woman asking for help.[26] Other parts of her deed let us know that Eudokia and her husband were people with both titles and property, even after the sale. The monks to whom she sold her property clearly feared her ability to dispute the sale later.[27] Her self-presentation as utterly helpless and indigent was a role she took on in order to provoke the desired response from the governor.

In appealing to the governor in this way, Eudokia did not give him much choice. He could act charitably and mercifully—like God—or he could be hardhearted and merciless, like those God condemns to eternal punishment.[28] Unsurprisingly he chose to authorize the sale of her land. However much wealth and social status Eudokia indeed had, by presenting herself as a poor woman in need of help, she constrained the governor to help her. Her agency in making her sale was enabled by her performance of an exaggerated form of female weakness. Her piteous petition to the governor was quoted verbatim in her deed of sale, in which she elsewhere abjures acting with "female simplicity" and performs the masculine sound judgment needed to make a binding legal transaction.[29]

Another example of a woman getting men to help her by performing female helplessness occurred on the island of Skyros in the early eleventh century. There, Glykeria appealed to cultural conceptions of female weakness in order to overturn her sworn act in which she had previously donated her property and her church to her bishop. In her new donation document, Glykeria tells a grand tale of woe: a first-person narrative of her travails in which she endeavors to elicit sympathy by depicting herself as a helpless, childless widow struggling alone against the oppressive and tyrannical power of the bishop.[30] Glykeria's self-presentation as a childless widow, an utterly unprotected woman, allowed her to claim that her previous donation had been made under coercion, and therefore could be legally overturned.[31] Like Eudokia, Glykeria's ability to determine what should happen with her property was enabled by her performance of an exaggerated female help-lessness. Also like Eudokia, Glykeria was not actually without resources. Glykeria had the social status to assemble a group of prominent landowners from surrounding islands and a high official from one of the empire's great-est monasteries, the ecclesiarch of the Great Lavra of Mt. Athos, to witness her new deed. Both Eudokia and Glykeria fundamentally circumvented the laws of the Roman empire.[32] They were able to get away with it, with the back-ing of their surrounding communities, by enacting a behavior that required the men in those communities to support and protect them. Their perfor-mances of weakness appear to have elicited the performance of supportive behavior from men, which in turn permitted the women to achieve their desired goals. The posture of piteousness turns out to be a major strategy for female self-determination in Byzantine culture. It was the weak woman, rather than the strong woman, who was able to constrain the behavior of her male neighbors.

Some of the women who acted with the greatest degrees of public power in Byzantine history were similarly depicted as weak and needy. Eirene, who ruled as regent for her son Constantine VI (780–797) and a sole empress (797–802), was described by the historian Theophanes as having been given power by God, so that the restoration of icons could be brought about through a widow and her orphan son.[33] In Theophanes's story, Eirene is not an ambi-tious woman who seized political power, but a pitiable widow who is sup-ported by God. Theophanes's ascription of power and authority to God casts Eirene in the more culturally acceptable and meritorious role of a demure, meek, and humble woman. Theodora, the wife of emperor Theophilos (829–842), who after his death ruled as regent for her son Michael III from 842 to 855, is similarly portrayed by her hagiographer as a demure woman, too defer-ential to speak up, even to dispute her husband's heretical iconoclast religious views. While she was ultimately considered a saint because of her support for icon veneration, she was portrayed as never arguing with her iconoclast husband. Throughout her period as ruler, she is depicted as continuing to exhibit the female virtues of deferential humility and reticence.[34] The endur-ing meekness of Theodora's behavior cast her supporters into the good and powerful roles of men who providently cared for weak women (rather than in the comic role of weak men ordered about by women). It was the men helping her in the midst of her weakness who acted to end iconoclasm. At least in her hagiographer's description, the legitimacy of her regime was strengthened through her assumption of a disempowered posture.

Byzantine women seem to have exercised self-determination by working within the norms of their culture. Both the women who entered into legally binding transactions by denying their natural female weakness, and implicitly claiming the ability to act like men, and those who appealed to their female helplessness to circumvent the laws, reinforced the cultural stance that women, by nature, needed male authority. No matter how many women were considered to have the exceptional ability to act with masculine self-control, since each was an exception, the norm remained that women lacked self-control. Empowerment for women seems to come through their willingness and ability to play along with the cultural expectations of their nature. When we look at Anna's strategies for authorship, we shall see her both claim an exceptional ability to think in a rational masculine fashion, and perform exaggeratedly female roles in her text. Both postures seem aimed at making it more culturally acceptable for her to write history.

Beyond these fundamentals of Byzantine gender, certain aspects of the Greek tradition of history writing made it an activity for men only. The underlying ideas about the purposes of ancient and medieval history writing were markedly different from modern historical practice.[35] The proper subjects of history in the Greek tradition were the great deeds of men, and the words they spoke, in war and politics. Ancient and medieval Greek history writing focused on the deeds of men in war and politics because the primary purposes of history were to preserve the memory of great deeds from oblivion and to provide models of action for emulation. The topics covered in histories were wars, the causes of wars, the conduct of men in war, and the deliberations of men about war and politics. History sometimes included excurses on ethnography, geography, or other digressions. But the fields of social history, economic history, women's history, cultural history, literary history, and others would have been simply confusing to authors of ancient and medieval Greek history. It was not the case that money, food, or poetry were considered unimportant, but that these matters were not classified as pertinent to the writing of history. Historians of the tenth–twelfth centuries maintained the tradition of narrating deeds of men at war and politics.[36] For the most part, the classicizing histories of the eleventh and twelfth centuries adhered firmly to the conventional topics of ancient history.[37]

In the Greek tradition, historians wrote on the basis of their personal observations and research. The experiences of the author were a central part of his qualifications for writing history. For most classical Greek and Roman historians the best history was based on reporting personal observations about events that the author witnessed, or had discussed in detail with living witnesses.[38] Most of the men who wrote history in the Greek tradition had at least some experience of war and politics. Polybius argued that personal experience was a necessary qualification for historians, even when they derived their information from the questioning of witnesses, because without personal experience about "battle order or siege or sea battle" one could not "properly understand those telling the details."[39] While few historians spoke so clearly about methodology as Polybius, the value of political and military experience for the writing of history remained unquestioned.

Many Greek histories were written by men with military careers, whose field experience and firsthand knowledge of the events gave their testimony weight. Xenophon and Thucydides were generals and wrote about wars in which they had at least some personal participation. The position of the general's assistant was developed into an authoritative historical stance by Polybius in the second century BC, Procopius in the sixth century, and Attaleiates in the eleventh century.[40] In the medieval period, history continued to be written by male political actors.[41] In the eleventh and twelfth centuries, history was most often written by judges: men with extensive legal education and long careers at centers of power in Constantinople.[42] In the early twelfth century, Anna's husband, Nikephoros Bryennios, revived the classical ideal of the soldier historian, compiling his history in between campaigns.

The character of the author was considered a key factor in determining a history's reliability. If the man writing the story was considered trustworthy, just, and perceptive, as well as experienced, then the history would naturally be considered more reliable. A man of poor character would be more likely to misrepresent what had happened or inaccurately evaluate the moral significance of events. Historians needed to convince their audience that they had the authority and character necessary to be reasonable and trustworthy narrators of events.[43] Historians therefore had to construct an authorial persona that their audience would perceive as morally upstanding.

The historian's role as a moral guide was significant because he necessarily became the judge and evaluator of the actions of men. The historian decides which deeds are great enough to rescue from oblivion, which deeds to celebrate, and which to condemn. The historical narrator "employs an 'artificial authority' by which he interprets the events in his work for the reader, and explicitly directs the reader to think in a certain manner."[44] History writing is therefore tremendously self-aggrandizing in that the historian claims the ability, not only to organize information about the past, but to tell the audience what to think about it. Historians often wrote with explicitly didactic purposes of educating young men in the history of the past so that they could improve their own political fortunes.[45] In those histories with explicitly didactic intent, the historian tells the young whom they should admire and emulate, and whose behaviors they should avoid. The historian sets himself up as arbiter of morality and character, as well as success and failure. In so far as the purpose of history was to teach the current generation proper behavior, historians were arbitrators of morality and connoisseurs of character.[46]

How would this conception of history interact with Byzantine conceptions of gender? As a form of writing about the public sphere, which Byzantine cultural values maintained was for men only, history was simply inappropriate for women. Within the Byzantine cultural system, women were supposed to remain exclusively within the private, domestic sphere. Any efforts by women to influence openly affairs in the public sphere were viewed with deep suspicion.[47] Although this cultural theory did not entirely correspond to reality, it did have strong impact on how women and men conceived of their proper roles. The strong focus on men's public actions as the core subject of history is a sufficient explanation for the scarcity of female Greek historians.

The connection between an active political and military life, and the ability to write a reliable history, made the historical genre particularly ill-suited to female participation in a culture that prized the seclusion of women. Women in this culture were not supposed to have conversations with men who were not their close relatives. If a woman wanted to write a history, how would she have access to the male witnesses she needed to interview in order to undertake historical inquiry? One of the reasons women did not write history was that they had no access to information about the kinds of deeds that were thought worthy to be noted in a history. The events of the domestic sphere were not commemorated in histories. If a woman did manage to gain access to information, how would she be able to convince her audience that she had the judgment born of experience necessary to understand what her witnesses told her, when she herself had been shielded from the public arena?

The problem of a woman's access to historical sources amidst expectations for seclusion is evident from Byzantine descriptions of the first-century author Pamphile of Epidaurus, who wrote a *Miscellany of Historical Notes*. The ninth-century intellectual Photios described her text as valuable and containing "a large number of essential historical facts; there are also some witty sayings, precepts of rhetoric, philosophical ideas, thoughts about poetic style, and other matter of the same kind." Less attention is given to describing Pamphile's work than to explaining her marital status and how she accessed her information:

> She was married, as she notes in the preface to the work. Having lived since she was a young girl with her husband, after thirteen years of marriage she began to put together these notebooks. She put on record what she learned from her husband, with whom she had lived without interruption during those thirteen years, not separated from him for a day or even an hour; to this material she added whatever she heard from her husband's visitors—and many people with a name and reputation for their culture frequented the house—and in addition everything that she read for herself.[48]

The interest in her marriage from an early age, and her constant accompaniment of her husband, reflect a desire to present her as a morally upstanding woman, properly chaperoned and protected by male authority. She is described as learning from her husband, from notable men who came into her house, and from books—not from any experiences that she had outside of the house. It is probable that Photios was repeating elements of Pamphile's self-description from her preface. For both of them, her ability to gain access to the information she repeats in her collection needed explanation, and the preferred explanation upheld her as a woman who stayed under the constant guidance and supervision of her husband, not leaving his side for even an hour. For her writing to be acceptable, Pamphile needed to present herself as an entirely virtuous woman.

By choosing to write a miscellany of anecdotes rather than an historical narrative, Pamphile did not set herself up as a judge or arbitrator of men's actions. She did not need to have the judgment to discern how to best present information in a coherent narrative. Rather she took the stance as an inquisitive admirer, arranging her anecdotes so as to create a diverting text:

> All this material, whatever she thought notable and worthy of record, she compiled into a miscellany, not assigning each item to a particular category, but putting facts together at random as they occurred to her; not that she thought it difficult to classify according to subject-matter, but she reckoned that a mixture with its variety would be more pleasant and agreeable.[49]

Surviving anecdotes attributed to Pamphile confirm Photios's description of her text as a compilation of episodic data.[50] While Pamphile's achievement certainly should be admired, by declining to impose her authorial vision on the material and craft it into a narrative history, she fought less vigorously against the prohibitions Greek culture created for women writing history. Her decision to write an admittedly random collection of anecdotes fit better with her culture's expectations for what she would be able to do. Even with the less assertive task of compiling a miscellany, Pamphile's authorship was often attributed to her husband, and Photios explains that her simplicity of style and thought is what one could expect of a woman.[51] Pamphile's choices illuminate the challenges Anna confronted.

Clearly one of the key problems facing Anna's historical endeavor was convincing her audience that she had access to information about war and politics. As we shall see, her efforts to prove the reliability of her sources are deeply interlaced with her efforts to present herself as remaining safely within the woman's sphere. Some of Anna's most highly feminized writing sits close beside her claims to have the skills and sources needed to write a history of men's deeds. The valorization of women's seclusion made history difficult for Anna both because the standard means of gathering historical information were inappropriate and because women were not supposed to have the personal experiences considered necessary for sound judgment about what that information means.

The requirement that a historian possess exemplary moral character made even slight transgressions of ideal women's behavior problematic for Anna.

In order to get her audience to believe her history was reliable, Anna needed to remain morally above all reproach. Since leaving the female sphere would diminish Anna's character, as judged by the standards for elite women of her culture, any steps taken to conduct historical inquiry through the questioning of witnesses could potentially weaken her claim to have the good character needed for history writing. If she remained properly cloistered, she could be a worthy woman, but hardly a historian.

Another obvious bar to women's participation in the Greek historiographical tradition was that they did not normally have the classical education necessary to understand that tradition. The education needed to read Thucydides went far beyond the basic literacy in which it seems elite twelfth-century women were trained. While Anna certainly managed to obtain an extremely fine classical education, that was both unusual and unexpected. Anna excepted, history was a male genre because it required the kind of education only given to men. Anna would need to overcome the expectations of her audience that she would not have the necessary intellectual background to compose a proper history.

Beyond these fairly practical matters of access to information, political experience, and education, far deeper structures of Byzantine society rendered women's participation in authorship unexpected. Female gender was tightly linked to emotion in Byzantine culture:

> Byzantine psychology . . . conceptualized the submission to and expression of affect as a typically female trait, either congruent with the nature of women or a clear sign of feminization for men. After all, the very condition of pathos, namely passivity (the most basic meaning of the word *pathos*) was associated with femininity in premodern Greek writing, whereas men and "manly" women were supposed to master pathos. . . . Ultimately, rhetorical practice styled excessive expression of emotion . . . as a trait of female nature.[52]

Within this cultural system, a man who was subject to extreme emotion was acting in a feminine manner, while a woman capable of restraining her emotions exhibited masculine self-control. Emotional self-control was a necessary characteristic of a male public discourse, and particularly history writing. It was fine for a speaker to describe a character in a narrative as expressing emotion, or to attempt to provoke strong feelings in his audience, but the expected practice was that he would not become subject to emotion himself.[53] The author needed mastery over his own feelings in order to be in control of himself and his speech. When an author conjured up an image of a character beset by emotion in the course of a narration, he maintained authority over his creation and endeavored to control the emotional effect on his audience.

The cultural understanding that women, by nature, tended to be subject to emotion thus created a barrier to their participation in any kind of public discourse. So long as authors were required to be dispassionate and lacking emotion, women, who were perceived as naturally subject to emotion, could hardly be authors. Women would need to be seen as overcoming the essential emotionalism of their nature to be able to effectively participate in any manner of public discourse. This problem would of course be more acute in the case of historical writing, in which the detachment and emotional impartiality of the author were of paramount importance. Anna needed to exhibit exceptional masculine control over her emotions. Like the women who undertook legal transactions, she needed to convince her audience that she was not acting like a woman.

In addition to the tight connection between femininity and emotion, female authorship was complicated by the role of authors and texts in moral formation in Byzantine culture. Authors had especially important roles in Byzantine conceptions of character formation because character was both learned, and expressed, by modeling one's behavior on ideal patterns, which were often encountered in written texts. In the Byzantine conception of ethics, an individual's character was both created and expressed through patterning one's own behavior on idealized types. People learned how to behave by hearing examples of good and bad behavior in Bible stories, hagiography, hymns, and Psalms, and then trying to pattern their behavior on the good models.[54] Basic education involved composing and performing first-person speeches of stock characters in particular situations, with assignments such as "what Achilles would say seeing Patroclus's body." This practice involved learning how to be expressive by imaging oneself as another.[55] History was another such genre that provided models of behavior to either emulate or to avoid. We have already seen this behavioral modeling working in the records of women's financial transactions. When Eudokia, the woman who claimed poverty in order to sell her dowry land, took on the role of the poor woman crying out for help, she was modeling her behavior on an established role. She may have learned this role from the Psalms, or liturgical hymns, or other women in legal contexts, or other moments in the life of her community. When elsewhere in the course of her transaction Eudokia declared that her free will was not compromised by being a simple woman, she was expressing herself through a different model, that of the manly, reasonable woman. In both cases she was aligning her behavior with ideal models and simultaneously using those models to express herself.

The formation and expression of character through modeling on ideal types greatly empowered authors of texts, because they presented most of the models for emulation. Given the exalted role of written texts in the development of moral character, writing was expected to have an ordering, stabilizing function in twelfth-century society.[56] In some sense, the author was to present oneself as a model for others. Authorship was thus naturally self-aggrandizing, since authors implicitly asked audiences to be like them, or at least be like the models they presented. For Anna's historical writing to be accepted, she would need to be perceived as a positive moral model.

Authorship was also somewhat self-aggrandizing because the simple act of asking an audience to patiently listen to what the author was saying created an imposition upon the audience. This principle held for ancient Greek culture as well, in which "both speaker and listener knew, of course, that to put anyone into the position of listener was to some extent to exercise power over him, to constrain his activities in terms of one's own behavior."[57] In that authors ask others to quietly listen to them talk, they were open to simple resentments.

To counteract these aggrandizing aspects of authorship, late ancient and medieval Greek authors emphasized their own humility. The strong cultural concern to avoid the appearance of arrogance led to a "discourse of modesty" and the denigration of forceful self-presentation within Byzantine culture.[58] Byzantine authors commonly claimed that they would write plainly, in an unadorned style, and that they were humble, rustic, and unrefined. Such claims should never be taken as indications that these men were in fact poorly educated, nor was this false modesty, but rather "a rhetoric of longed-for humility."[59] The humility of the author became a central element in the development of Christian authorship.[60] Statements of authorial modesty were necessary in a culture where self-promotion was inherently suspected. Byzantine writers tended to speak of their authorial choices as originating outside of themselves, inspired or provoked by external considerations.[61] Anything that directed attention toward oneself ran the risk of being seen as self-aggrandizement, driven by a distasteful personal ambition and lack of humility.[62]

The problem of authorial humility was strongest when authors felt called upon to talk about themselves: "Greek rhetoric and Christian ethics demanded that one speak and write about oneself with considerable restraint, if at all."[63] Talking about oneself was generally avoided in favor of projecting an air of humility. In classical and late antique Greek culture, talking about the details of one's own life with people outside one's family was distasteful.[64] Plutarch taught that self-praise is tolerable only when defending oneself against a false accusation, when one has been insulted, or when one has been unfortunate.[65] Twelfth-century texts repeated the idea that talking about oneself was obnoxious.[66]

At the core of the Greek distaste for talking about oneself was the fear of provoking jealousy among the audience.[67] The profound concern with avoiding accusations of boasting is grounded in a long-standing cultural emphasis on the problem of envy. In medieval Greek culture, envy (*phthonos*) was not an abstract concept but a malignant agency, often simply synonymous with the devil.[68] Envy was not a trivial problem in this culture. Boasting, which could call out retribution, was fundamentally dangerous as well as distasteful.

The most common and long-standing method for talking about oneself without being annoying was to tell a sad story about one's sufferings. Self-description was more acceptable when framed with talk about the ills and troubles one had experienced. The audience could not as easily get mad at a speaker for talking about himself while they were feeling sorry for him. By making an audience listen to him talk, the speaker was putting himself above them, but by telling them how miserable he was, and how much he had suffered, they pitied him. This pitying condescension put the audience above the speaker and so balanced out the power relations of the encounter. The "tale of woe" became a standard technique of rendering self-disclosure and self-description more acceptable.[69]

The Byzantine preference for authorial humility interacted in particularly unfortunate ways, for Anna, with the simultaneous cultural need for historians to be perceived as authoritative. Historians gained the trust of their audience largely by demonstrating the reliability of their sources (optimally gathering information through autopsy and interrogation of witnesses), their insight gained through personal experience, the quality of their education, and their knowledge and understanding of history. Historians were further trusted when they were perceived as honorable individuals; and hence their moral character was an important factor in establishing their credibility. Good women in Anna's culture were expected to studiously avoid participation and discussion of events in the public sphere of politics and war, to avoid conversation with men to whom they were not closely related, and to attain only minimal levels of education. Certainly it was possible for Anna to achieve a stunningly good education, and to learn about public affairs through detailed conversations with men who had participated in her father's wars. Yet how could she let her audience know that she had participated in these immodest, even transgressive, behaviors and still maintain a reputation as a woman of high moral character? If she was entirely humble in her writing, no one in her audience would believe that she had the access to the information, the training, and the judgment to write history. The more she worked to prove her skills and capacity for accurate history writing, the more she opened herself up to accusations of arrogance and lack of humility.

Anna thus confronted significant cultural constraints that challenged and undermined her ability to be considered a persuasive and reliable historian. The oppression of these constraints was not so great, however, that Anna was physically prevented from writing history. If Anna had been dealing with more extreme repression, she would have written under a pseudonym, or not at all. She chose rather to write in her own name, trying to be, as she said, both "woman and historian."[70] Female historical authorship was a challenge, but one she embraced, and her ability to take up that challenge speaks to the significant social standing and power she enjoyed. Anna fundamentally had the autonomy and freedom, as well as the skills, necessary to write a history.

Anna responded to the cultural constraints she faced by writing with great tact and consideration of how to soften the impositions her activities made on her society's expectations for women's behavior. The following chapters try to trace the various strategies she used for writing sensitively and graciously as a woman participating in a strongly masculine activity. Her efforts to be tactful were essential for the preservation of her good character and honor. Additionally, since an audience's perception of the character of the historian affected whether they believed the history, Anna's maintenance of a gracious and admirable female character was essential for enabling her history to be persuasive, and hence successful.

Qualified, and Modest about It

Writing while female in medieval Constantinople was thus a challenging endeavor. Anna's responses to these challenges take a number of forms as she tries to present herself as capable of participating in the masculine genre of history while remaining a virtuous woman. Anna needs to clearly stake her claim to the ability to write history in the first few lines of her work. But she must also humble herself before her audience so she would be considered a woman of good character. In her prologue Anna creates a self-presentation that closely mixes authorizing, masculinizing claims with humbling and feminizing ones. To be trustworthy she must be both authoritative and modest. As we shall see, her claims to possess the education and access to historical information that justify her abilities as a historian prompt humbling and self-abasing statements at every turn.

It was standard practice for Byzantine historians to insist on their inadequacy for the task of history writing in their prologues while simultaneously displaying their erudition and credentials.[1] Denigrating their skills was a normal response to the problem of authorial self-aggrandizement.[2] In the midst of claiming humility, history writers also staked claims for their skills and education in their prologues, either explicitly, or by using artful and high-style writing. Historians also routinely made claims that they would adhere to the truth and write in an unbiased fashion, showing praise and censure where due. They frequently expressed the fear that their work would be criticized because they had spoken the truth. Often historians would explain the reasons that compelled them to write history, establishing an external force that pushed them, reluctantly, into the position of history writer. The standard medieval historical prologue was thus a mixture of authorizing and aggrandizing claims—to literary skill, to education, to access to information, to virtue in devotion to truth—with humbling expressions of fear of criticism, reluctant authorship, and inadequate style. The authorizing claims were necessary to establish the author's credentials as a historian, and the humbling claims were necessary to mitigate the arrogance of the act of writing.[3]

Anna's prologue includes most of these expected elements as she deals with the standard problems. Yet Anna's identity as a woman endeavoring to write history makes these problems more acute. The connection between the writing of history and an active career in politics and war made history the genre perhaps least open to female participation. Since she did not have a political or military career, Anna would need to explain why she was in a position to know enough about her subject to write a history. In order to remain a modest, and hence virtuous, woman, Anna would need to show that she learned about political and military events while remaining in her appropriate domestic sphere. Anna needed to assert her credentials more forcefully than usual because such intellectual activity was unexpected in a woman. She necessarily broke with tradition by not denigrating her writing style or education—as a woman she ran the risk that if she said she could only write in a simple style the audience would actually believe her. Yet all of the factors that pushed male authors to enact humility also applied to Anna. Indeed, the centrality of modesty to the Byzantine construction of virtuous women made this point far more decisive for her. Immodest women were identified with harlots who led men to sin.[4] So while the need to substantiate her authority was acute, the simultaneous cultural imperative for women to be humble made her need to combat accusations of boastfulness extreme.

Anna's prologue shows that she was keenly aware of what she was up against in her efforts to undertake female historical authorship. Her prologue contains most of the standard elements of the medieval Greek historical prologue, but treats them in ways that tactfully lay the groundwork for her unique female historical authorial persona as both an authoritative writer of history and a modest and good woman. Her innovations and departures from the normal patterns of Greek historical prologues are places where she drew on new strategies of self-abasement and historical authorization.

Anna's opening sentence both signals her adherence to the conventions of history and hints at how her project disrupts them. She opens with a complaint about the destructive force of time that compels her to the task of writing history:

> Time, moving eternally with its uncontrollable streams, sweeps away and carries off all things in creation and plunges them into deep obscurity, whether these matters are not worthy of mention, or great and worthy of memory, and, according to the Tragedian, "first draw fourth from darkness then bury from light."[5]

As a complaint against time, this is an entirely conventional sentiment within medieval historical prologues. Yet she incorporates into this convention a reference to Sophocles—the Tragedian—which hints that her history will not fit into conventional patterns of historical writing or gender. Anna quotes the first line of a speech by Ajax, in which he tells the chorus and his concubine, Tecmessa, that her arguments in favor of reconciliation with his enemies have persuaded him. While Anna makes Sophocles's words fit her description of the destructive effects of time, Ajax's topic is not time so much as the vagaries of human events:

> All things the long and countless years first draw from darkness, and then bury from light; and there is nothing which man should not expect: the dread power of oath is conquered, as is unyielding will. For even I, who used to be so tremendously strong—yes, like tempered iron—I have been made female by this woman's words, and I feel the pity of leaving her a widow and the boy an orphan among my enemies.[6]

Ajax's point about time is that sooner or later everything is bound to happen and nothing should be unexpected. The sentiment that nothing should be surprising is one Anna could easily have wished upon her audience as they begin hearing the prodigious narrative of a history written by a princess—a princess who had studied philosophy no less. Ajax elaborates that in his particular case the marvel, which ought not be surprising, is that the strong man is made female through pity. Anna alludes, therefore, to a statement that even changes in gender should not be unexpected.

Modern classicists call this Ajax's "deception speech," because while Ajax goes on to say that he will submit to the authority of Agamemnon and Menelaus, he in fact kills himself rather than participate in such a reconciliation. The speech provides a strong reminder that what speakers or authors say they feel is not always what they do feel. Anna may here put her audience on notice that a literary expression of a feeling does not necessarily reveal a genuine experience of that emotion. This is hardly a point of which her audience would have been unaware, but placing a reminder in the first sentence of her history may call attention to the potential artificiality of writing that ostensibly reveals the self.

Anna's allusion to Ajax's statement that he has become female is immediately followed by her most masculinizing sentence in the *Alexiad*, in which she states her name and lays claim to a level of education that put the vast majority of her contemporary elite men to shame:

> Having discerned these things, I Anna, daughter of the emperors Alexios and Eirene, born and raised in the purple, not without some share of learning, but rather having studied Greek language in full and being not unpracticed in rhetoric and having read through well

the Aristotelian treatises and the Platonic dialogs and having crowned my mind with the Pythagorean terms of mathematics—for it is necessary to betray these things, and this is not bragging; how much nature and the zeal for learning gave and God above granted and opportunity supplied—I wish on account of this to tell in writing the deeds of my father not worthy to be passed over in silence nor carried away in the stream of time as into a sea of forgetfulness.[7]

The prominent statement of the author's name is not something that sits comfortably with the twelfth-century poetics of anonymity, but it places Anna firmly in ancient traditions of historical writing in which the name of the author is the core element of a history's opening:

> This is the display of the inquiry of Herodotus of Halicarnassus, so that things done by men not be forgotten in time, and that great and marvelous deeds, some displayed by the Hellenes, some by the barbarians, not lose their glory, including among others what was the cause of their waging war on each other.[8]

> Thucydides, an Athenian, wrote the history of the war between the Peloponnesians and the Athenians, beginning at the moment that it broke out, and believing that it would be a great war and more worthy of relation than any that had preceded it.[9]

In imitating the great old histories by placing her name and birthplace so near the start of her history, Anna boldly joins the company of Herodotus, Thucydides, and all the other historians who have emulated them.

Anna also explicitly testifies to her extreme education. The description of her study of Greek language, rhetoric, philosophy, and mathematics lays claim to a highly elite and unusual educational background. As described, Anna's education goes far beyond the normal study of classical rhetoric. Anna was educated not only in classical Greek language and rhetoric that would allow her to understand classical texts, but in the philosophical discourses that use that language for substantive discussions of significant moral import. Classical philosophy appears to have been somewhat more widely studied in the twelfth century than it had been in the eleventh, when Michael Psellos claimed to have single-handedly revived its study.[10] Yet it had not become a normal part of the Byzantine educational curriculum. Even basic literacy was uncommon among Byzantine women.[11] George Tornikes's funeral oration for Anna presents her desire for education as highly unusual for an elite woman. He describes Anna as acting secretly, against the wishes of her parents, in her efforts to study. Given the low levels of education among other aristocratic women, Anna's statement that she had studied not only classical Greek, but also Aristotle, Plato, and Pythagorean mathematics was a stunningly strong claim. Anna does not merely say she is educated, but that she was among the best-educated people of her era.

Anna's assertion that she studied Aristotle and Plato may have been designed to place her in the exceptional company of the celebrated female philosophers of antiquity. Elsewhere in the *Alexiad*, Anna attributes an aphorism on modesty to the ancient Pythagorean philosopher Theano, clearly expecting her audience to know who she was.[12] When Anna was remembered in a late twelfth-century funeral encomium for her grandson, the author mentions Theano as a precedent of a philosophical woman and claims that Anna's education rivaled that of the Alexandrian Neoplatonist Hypatia.[13] It seems that the existence of female philosophers in antiquity was remembered in Anna's era.[14] Her emphasis in her prologue on her own philosophical training and expertise may have worked to cast her as their successor.

Anna does not explicitly claim to have read the great works of Attic tragedy and comedy. She makes her knowledge of these texts clear however, by quoting Sophocles's *Ajax* in the first line of her prologue, and through the vocabulary and textual fabric of her writing. Anna's ability to make an illusion that interacts meaningfully with Sophocles's text displays her deep reading and understanding of classical Attic texts. Beyond the meaning it imparts to her text, the allusion functions to demonstrate her deep classical learning. The allusion signals that the authors Anna explicitly says she has read, Aristotle, Plato, and Pythagoras, are not the sum of her ancient learning; the Tragedian goes without saying.

Anna further asserts her ability to write history by following the major conventions of a historical prologue. Anna includes "most of the conventional elements of historiographical introductions (the need to resist time, the elaboration of topic, reference to an unbiased composition and fear of criticism, the use and adaption of classical sources and, to a lesser extent, the direct appeal to the public)."[15] By including most of the standard elements, she displayed her knowledge of the genre. Her one notable omission was of any claim that she would write in a simple and unadorned style. This standard expression of authorial humility was problematic, I believe, because Anna needed to strongly argue for her unexpected rhetorical skills. As we shall see, she deployed other, far more striking and elaborate, strategies of self-abasement. By treating so many of the expected elements of a prologue in a creative and inventive way, Anna further displayed her skill as a rhetorician. The quality of the writing in the prologue in itself makes a forceful claim for Anna's skills as a writer.

At first, Anna's emphasis on her relationship with her imperial parents in the opening of her prologue seems an act of self-exultation strikingly at odds with the normal practices of authorial humility. It is motivated, in part, by the need to present Anna as having reasonable access to information on her topic. Anna's status as the daughter of the emperor makes her believable as a knowledgeable source of information about the history of Alexios. Anna's emphasis on her relationship with her father is a necessary part of her claim to firsthand knowledge, and hence the ability to write history. The authority of some ancient historians was validated by their assertion of close proximity to those in power and hence special knowledge of the inside story.[16] Privileged access to those in power, however, created problems for historians because it left them open to accusations of bias or favoritism.[17] Anna must clarify her relationship with her father, even though it raises questions about potential favoritism.[18]

Beyond proximity to the subject, Anna's statement that she is the daughter of the emperor and the empress, born in the porphyry chamber of the palace, is authorizing within the context of her culture, because nobility was sometimes seen as a factor that might enable women to transcend their nature. When, in the mid-eleventh century, Michael Psellos wrote a speech for the Empress Theodora to make before her court, he has her explicitly transcend her female nature by virtue of her royal birth and long study of divine Scriptures.[19] Theodora's noble birth became one of the factors that allowed her to speak like a man. Anna's nobility may have similarly been seen as predisposing her toward masculine levels of self-control and sound judgment.

Anna further claims that her history is authoritative because her narrative is without favoritism. Anna displays her understanding of the central task of history as being an unbiased, truthful appraisal of human character:

> For when one takes up the moral character of history, it is necessary to forget good will and hatred. One must frequently deck enemies with the greatest praise, when their deeds demand this, but also frequently castigate blood relatives, when the failings of the pursuits indicate. Therefore one must neither shrink to upbraid friends nor to praise enemies.[20]

She will not be partial to Alexios and write an encomium, nor will she let her natural respect for her father prevent her from criticizing him when he deserves it.[21] Her claim to impartiality fits within the Byzantine historical tradition of claiming to display only the truth without regard to favor.

Anna maintains that the validity of her history will be acknowledged because her narrative can be checked against the memories of people still living. She calls as witnesses to her veracity "both those seeing the events and those participating in the events. For the fathers and grandfathers of some men now living were witnesses to these events."[22] These witnesses, Anna trusts, will defend her history against accusations that she writes prejudicially in favor of her father.

Anna thus makes several strongly authorizing claims in her prologue. She explicitly and implicitly claims great education; she presents herself as an authority on her subject; she presents herself as participating in a tradition with the greatest Greek historians; and, by demonstrating her participation in the male discourse of history, she shows that she can write like a man. Since one of the traditional functions of a historical prologue was to establish the credentials of the author, this was the place where her statement of skills was most necessary and least offensive. These claims are necessary for her audience to accept her as a reliable historian.

Anna's authorizing statements, which justify her claims to be able to write history, immediately provoke disclaimers and expressions of humility. Interwoven with the authorizing discourses throughout the prologue are both implicit and explicit humbling gestures, discourses that relieve Anna of authorial agency, moderate the aggrandizement of her authorship, and create herself as an object of pity. While some aspects of her self-presentation in the prologue model Anna on male historical authors, others draw on ideal models of female behavior, casting her as a devoted daughter and loving wife.

The most straightforward strategy Anna used to combat the self-aggrandizement of historical authorship was to state openly that she was not boasting or writing to glorify herself. Even within her opening statement of her educational credentials, Anna pauses to defend herself against accusations of boasting: "For it is necessary to betray these things, and this is not bragging, how much nature and the zeal for learning gave and God above granted and the opportunity supplied."[23] Since she must describe her education to prove her ability to write history, doing so is not boasting. Anna does not take credit for her learning, but rather attributes her education to the agency of nature, zeal for learning, God, and opportunity. This presents her educated state as something that happened to her, largely due to forces outside of her control.

Anna also responded to the need to humble herself by variously effacing her authorship. Historical activity is not something Anna has chosen to take up to gratify her own creativity. Rather she is compelled by significant external factors.[24] The decaying effects of time provide the primary motivation. Anna creates an external impulse for the need to write history by emphasizing the dangers of oblivion. She forcefully describes the destructive power of time to erase memory, and extols the ability of history to oppose it:

> The art of history is the strongest bulwark against the stream of time and, to some extent, it stays time's irresistible stream. . ... It secures and embraces whatever it takes up and does not allow those things to slip away into the depth of oblivion.[25]

The dramatization of the risk time presents to memory provides a strong compulsion for Anna to commemorate the memory of Alexios. Anna takes up history because it can rescue memory: "I Anna . . . wish . . . to tell in writing the deeds of my father not worthy to be passed over in silence nor carried away in the stream of time into a sea of forgetfulness."[26] Immediately after stating this motivation, Anna clarifies precisely that her history is not intended to display her rhetorical skill, but to rescue her father's memory from oblivion:

> In saying these things, I come not making some display of rhetorical exercise, but so that a matter so great may not be left without witness for those coming later, since even the greatest of the deeds, if not immediately guarded by words and passed down in memory, are extinguished in the dark of silence.[27]

The necessity of preserving her father's memory from oblivion compels her to write, not a desire to show off her learning and authorial power.

Anna provides a second external motivation for her historical activity in describing it as a continuation of her husband's work. She describes her husband, the Caesar Nikephoros Bryennios, in glowing terms, and relates that he was working on a history of Alexios in between accompanying emperor John (1118–1143) on military campaigns. Nikephoros had taken up task of writing a history of Alexios at the request of Anna's mother, the Empress Eirene. Anna explains that Nikephoros wrote a history about Alexios's early years, but was unable to complete the work before his death. Nikephoros's inability to complete his writing was harmful, Anna says, to both the history he was trying to preserve and his readers. It is for this reason that Anna took up the task of writing about her father's deeds: so that they would not be ignored by future generations.[28] Presenting one's history as a continuation of another's was a normal technique for enhancing a historian's authority.[29] In addition, in this presentation neither Anna nor Nikephoros desired to become historians but were pushed into it. For Anna, the need to complete the work left unfinished by her beloved husband provides a strong moral obligation for her historical efforts.

The story that Anna was carrying on the work of her late husband serves to efface Anna's agency in taking up the task. Just as a widow can acceptably manage the affairs of her late husband, Anna could be the executor of her husband's history. She does not credit herself with the act of choosing to write a history, but rather casts her authorial intentions as an act of devotion to her husband and to her father's memory. By presenting herself as acting in fulfillment of her role as a dutiful wife and daughter, Anna softens the force of her authorial agency.

Anna thus creates a strong set of motivations for writing history that tactfully effaces her agency in choosing to write. By writing, Anna is rather responding to the needs of others. Anna's self-presentation as writing only in response to the need to fight time, preserve the memory of her father's deeds, and complete the work left to her by her husband, implicitly denies her agency in taking up the task of history. In this Anna is creating a particularly forceful instance of a fairly common rhetorical stance among Byzantine authors. Historians often speak of the pressing need to rescue the memory of great deeds from time, and sometimes severely criticized the work of previous historians. Both stances provide external motivations pushing the author to write history.[30]

While in many respects Anna includes the standard elements for a twelfth-century historical prologue, she also includes elements that are jarring and inappropriate for history. Whereas the voice of the historian is dispassionate and detached, Anna expresses profound emotion when she describes her husband and her mourning at his passing. She then turns attention to herself and constructs herself as an object of extreme pity through claims to have suffered grievously.

The shift of focus from Anna's historical work to her own person, and more particularly to her emotional suffering, constitutes a serious disruption of the historical genre she has just established for her text. In the final paragraphs of her prologue, Anna adopts a tragic voice and begins to spin a tale of woe, moving from praise of her deceased husband to her own life:

> At these thoughts my soul becomes filled with vertigo and I wet my eyes with streams of tears. Oh! What a councilor is lost to the Romans. His accurate understanding of affairs that he garnered through experience! His knowledge of words! His varieties of wisdom, indeed both from abroad and from our own garden![31] Grace spread throughout his limbs and his appearance was not only worthy of royalty, as they say, but better and even divine. For my part, I have been conversant with terrible things since my birth in the purple as they say, and I have been assailed by ill fortunes, if one could reckon it not good and smiling fortune for me to be so born and a child of emperors and produced in the purple room. The rest full of waves! Full of turmoil! Orpheus moved stones and wood and even inanimate nature simply with his singing; Timotheos the flutist once playing the martial tune to Alexander and immediately moved the Macedonian to weapons and the sword. The narratives about me are not the subject for movement to weapons and battle, but would stir the hearer to tears, and not only a sensitive one, but would even force emotional suffering from inanimate nature.[32]

The tale of woe is a strategy for talking about oneself while being less obnoxious to Greek taste.[33] Anna adopts it to a slightly different function. Anna's presentation as an object of pity that could force emotion from a stone, asks for an entirely different emotional response from the audience than her initial claim to be a worthy historian. While her statement of credentials inspires respect, admiration, and quite possibly also jealousy and resentment, her presentation as a sufferer elicits pity, compassion, and condescension from the audience who are now rhetorically placed above the miserable Anna. Anna elaborates, not on the specifics of the injuries she says she has suffered, but on her widowed state and her mourning for her husband:

The suffering about the Caesar and his unexpected death reached to
my soul and wrought the depth of pain. I hold all the misfortunes coming before this terrible misfortune as but a drop of rain compared to
the whole of the Atlantic or the waves of the Adriatic. Rather it seems
they were the prelude, and the smoke from the furnace of this fire overwhelmed me, both this scorching heat of that unspeakable burning and
the continuous flames of the unutterable funeral pyre. Oh! Fire that
turns to ash without matter! Fire burning secretly! Burning, but yet
not consuming! Parching the heart, yet appearing that we are not also
burned; even though we receive fire-wounds until the division of bones
and marrow from the soul.[34]

Here Anna becomes a poor and miserable widow left alone with memories.
She aligns her behavior with an archetypal female object of pity and compassion. The proper social response to a widow is to offer care and sympathy.
Anna's presentation as pitiable widow is a play to shift the emotional response
her historical work creates in her audience. In lamenting her misery, Anna is
trying to elicit condescending sympathy from her audience.

The pity is necessary to offset the great imposition she has placed on her
audience by asking them to listen to her narrate history. Within the few pages
of her prologue, Anna makes her presentation as a miserable widow far more
elaborate, explicit, and gripping than her presentation as an authoritative
writer capable of participating in male traditions of political and historical
discourse. As a woman able to write fine Attic Greek, Anna was a woman
of education and wealth. Education and wealth were both signs and conse-
quences of power within Byzantine society. In a simple sense, Anna could
only be a powerful woman. In choosing to write history in the tradition of
male Greek historiography, Anna was acting with power and authority. To
make this authoritative action socially acceptable within her society, Anna
needed to humble herself before her audience. She tried to do this by presenting herself as utterly miserable, pitiable, and bereft of husband, father, and
family.

Anna does not narrate the entire *Alexiad* through the voice of the piteous
widow. Expressions of emotional suffering that were typical parts of the presentation of widowhood have no place within the impersonal and emotionally disengaged discourse of history. At the end of the prologue she makes an
explicit switch back to historical discourse:

But I perceive that my feelings have carried me away from what is
needed. The Caesar stood by me and the mourning for him instilled
great mourning for me. Now drying the tears from my eyes and recov-
ering from my emotional suffering I will have double share of tears,
according to the Tragedian, with misfortune recalling misfortune.…
For to recall [Alexios] and bring his reign to the public is subject of

lamentation to me, and reminds others of their loss. Now one must begin the history of my father, where it is better to begin. Henceforth the narrative will be better, more clear and more historical.[35]

In promising that she has recovered from her sadness and will make her narrative "more historical," Anna is clearly signaling that she is putting aside her emotional, female persona in order to write history. At this point we need to remember how tight the connection between expression of emotion and gender was in Anna's culture. When Anna presented herself as overcome by sorrow, she was acting like a woman. When she presented herself as able to dispassionately write history, unaffected by her emotions, she was claiming the ability to master herself and act like a man.

Anna's expressions of misery serve two functions in her prologue. First, they humble her before her audience and mitigate the self-aggrandizement inherent in her claim to be able to write history. Second, they present her as possessed of a normal female range of emotion, and hence a normal female nature. Anna seems eager to work within her culture's construction of proper gender roles and avoid, if possible, being seen as an unnatural disruption to the social order. By showing that she is subject to normal female emotions, and by claiming the ability to control those emotions in order to write "more historically," Anna casts herself as one of those extraordinary women who are able to occasionally transcend the weaknesses in their female nature in order to exercise masculine self-control.

In the prologue Anna shows her natural female emotion, but also her fine ability to exercise reason and her education. She places herself among philosophers and historians as people able to control emotion and exercise judgment. Through her tactful humility she presents herself as a good woman. She thus establishes herself as possessed of the skills, training, knowledge, and moral character necessary to be a reliable historian.

{ 3 }

Unbiased Historian and Devoted Daughter

One of the greatest obstacles Anna faced in writing a history of her father was the conflict in her culture between a historian's imperative to be impartial and a daughter's imperative to be supportive and devoted to her parents. If Anna showed partiality to her father or spared him criticism, she would be a bad historian. If, however, she criticized her father, she would be a bad daughter. Anna's discussions of both her historical impartiality and her filial affection betray a keen awareness of this fundamental problematic for her history. Readers can agree that the *Alexiad* presents a glowing, laudatory image of Alexios. Yet the text is also a key source for his losses, mistakes, and problems. Impartiality and devotion are held in tension throughout the work as Anna works strenuously to be convincing as an impartial historian and devoted daughter.

Ancient and medieval historians writing in Greek agreed that freedom from bias or favoritism was an essential criterion for good history.[1] Byzantine historians showed a great concern to present themselves as impartial and free from constraints of patronage or any other debts to the people who form the subjects of the histories. Historians who engage in flattery or needless criticism are roundly condemned. The natural tendency to take sides was perceived as "the consistent danger in writing history."[2] In Anna's own prologue, she says that "when one takes up the moral character of history, it is necessary to forget good will and hatred" and "one must neither shrink to upbraid friends nor to praise enemies."[3]

Anna was well aware of her need to substantiate her impartiality in writing about her father. Anna expects her audience to assume that she would lie to flatter her family and frequently insists that she does not. Anna says she will tell the whole story of Alexios's reign "in however many ways he succeeded or failed in ruling."[4] She claims the ability to write fairly about her father:

> For, if it should prove to me that one of the things done by him was not good, I would not spare as a father, nor will we pass over his virtuous actions on account of the suspicion of fawning because it is my father about whom I am writing. In both cases I would do injustice to the truth.[5]

A similar sentiment occurs much later in her work:

> By the dangers of the emperor for the good of the Romans, by the contests and sufferings he endured for the Christians, I swear I do not favor my own father in the things I say and write! Rather when I see that he fell, I straightaway transgress the natural law and cling to the truth; holding him with love, but having greater love for truth.[6]

Presenting herself as able to overcome natural affection to write honestly is necessary to establish Anna as a reliable and trustworthy historian.

Yet Anna cannot simply maintain a straightforward stance of dispassion toward her family because that would implicate her in dishonorable behavior as a daughter. In her prologue she expresses fears that her work will be dismissed as an encomium for her father and that she praises her father to flatter herself.[7] But she also expresses fears about readers who would think that she did not praise her father *enough*. If she speaks well of her father, she risks being dismissed as a flatterer, but if she does *not* praise him, she will also be in trouble:

> On the other hand, if things happened or he did anything that would force me to censure him (not on account of him, but on account of the nature of the events) I again fear the scoffers who will consider me like Ham the son of Noah, since they are all eyeing everything jealously and not discerning what is right, out of jealousy and envy, and as Homer said, they blame the blameless.[8]

The story of Ham and Noah represents a lack of respect for the father on the part of the child. In Genesis, Noah sets a horrible curse on his son Ham because Ham had seen him drunk and naked.[9] Byzantine tradition held that Ham was punished so severely because he had gossiped or laughed about his father's faults publicly.[10] A sermon attributed to Basil of Caesarea summarized the story: "Noah was mocked, Ham was cursed."[11] Anna seems to be referring to this tradition of blaming Ham, not only for seeing his father naked, but for making public his father's private faults. Anna implies that, if she points out her father's faults, some readers would think she shared Ham's sin of failing to honor his father.

Fear that any mention of Alexios's failings would be taken as sinful disrespect toward a parent greatly complicates Anna's performance of historical impartiality. She is naturally called to respect and honor her father. Her culture held that devotion to one's parents was a key virtue. The historian's need to treat the subject without favor or prejudice is at odds with a daughter's need to give honor to her father.[12]

The interest of ancient and medieval historians in impartiality is fairly easy for us to perceive, because it has some similarities with modern historians' concerns with historical objectivity.[13] The need for Anna to treat her father's memory with respect and devotion is less obviously imperative to many modern readers. Those readers who disparage Anna's doting stance in the *Alexiad* do not seem to consider that it would have been thought sinful for her *not* to dote on her father. It seems that within Anna's culture, a good daughter was required to treat her father with extreme honor.

Anna expects that she will be condemned for criticizing her family. When she criticizes the policy of her kinsman, emperor Michael VII, she appeals to the need for historical impartiality to exculpate her actions:

> Let no one feel resentment if I may upbraid one related to me by blood (since that blood flows also in me from my mother's side), for I have elected to write the truth above all things, and, as for him, I have restrained the universal criticism of him.[14]

Anna uses her comments on Michael as an opportunity to claim historical impartiality, but she also clarifies that, by restraining the "universal criticism," she castigates Michael less than most people. She is not calling out resentment because, on the one hand, she is devoted to telling the truth, and on the other, she is less critical of Michael's disastrous reign than most commentators. So, even though she appeals to the accepted rule that historians ought to be impartial, she still apologizes for her negative comments by saying she moderated the blame that was commonly heaped upon her kinsman.

The strength of the Byzantine cultural value that daughters ought to support their parents is illustrated by a passage in the funeral oration for written for Anna by George Tornikes. In this complex text, which we will explore further in chapter seven, Tornikes strongly emphasizes Anna's own devotion to her parents.[15] At one point he also explicitly disassociates Anna from women of antiquity who transgressed gender boundaries. In his efforts to carve out a meritorious cultural space for Anna's intellectual activities, he exclaims that Anna was nothing like those women. He says Anna had nothing in common with:

> the father-loving Electra and the mother-hating Cassandra and Polyxena, the daughters captive with Hecuba, not able to evade capture! … Among the Greeks there were some remarkable and famous

characters, manly women and womanish men, base mannishness and womanishness, Teiresias and Penthesilea, and Artemis, an archer among the gods, and Athena, the warlike despoiler god.[16]

These women of antiquity are taken by Tornikes as grand examples of women who transgressed their nature. Teiresias changed into a woman after he killed one of the pair of snakes having sex. Later the same thing happened again, and he turned back into a man. Penthesilea was the queen of the Amazons, killed by Achilles. Tornikes mixes these mortal women with goddesses like Artemis and Athena who had masculine characteristics.

That Electra, Cassandra, and Polyxena are also mentioned in this context tells us something about Byzantine conceptions of the gendered nature of female virtue. Before Tornikes's list of women who clearly crossed gender boundaries, they form a list of women who transgressed female virtues. The transgression of the father-loving Electra and the mother-hating Cassandra and Polyxena seems to be that they showed lack of devotion to their parents. Electra was a father-lover because she desired the death of her mother, Clytemnestra, who had murdered her husband, Agamemnon, Electra's father. Cassandra and Polyxena are described as hating their mother, Hecuba, the queen of Troy, presumably on the basis of their relationships with her enemies. After the fall of Troy, when Hecuba and her daughters were captured by the Achaeans, Cassandra became the concubine of Agamemnon and Polyxena was claimed by Achilles's ghost and sacrificed on his tomb. To modern sensibilities it is surprising to see these women, who were denied freedom of action, reckoned as having betrayed their mother. That Cassandra and Polyxena have the status as "mother-hating" seems to elide them into Tornikes's category of transgressive women. Devotion and loyalty to parents was apparently an aspect of female virtue. By not displaying devotion to their parents, Polyxena and Cassandra were not enacting proper femininity. They were not "good girls," both in not being good and in not being fully girls. The lack of filial devotion is hence an ethical lapse as well as a gender transgression.

Anna's own last testament also attests to the value of filial devotion for daughters. Anna forcefully presents herself as a dutiful daughter in the prologue to her will where she emphasizes her love for her parents and her innate obedience to them:

> During my entire time of my life that I spent together with my parents, I never disobeyed them nor did I do anything else against their wish and will. . . . Never did I have any wish, which was not also their wish, nor did I not want what they also wanted; neither in serious pursuits, nor in playful ones, neither as a little child, nor as an adolescent, nor when I became a woman and a mother of many good children. At every age, from my birth until now, I carried out their wishes and—as that centurion in the gospels says—when they ordered me, I was present,

when they so wished, I went away; I was like a shadow that follows the bodies closely.[17]

This relationship entails having a deep respect for her parents and a natural, willing, obedience to their wishes. The presentation of this theme in the testament lets us know that Anna wanted to highlight her daughterly devotion as a prized aspect of her character.

Devotion to parents therefore seems to have been an aspect of proper femininity in Anna's culture. Respect for parents was undoubtedly an important virtue for men as well.[18] Yet it was a particularly significant virtue for women, perhaps because of the centrality of caring for family among women's responsibilities. Whereas men were expected to succeed in various endeavors, a woman's main goal in life was to support her family, showing devotion first to her parents and later to her husband. Also, since female virtue was expressed by upholding masculine authority, a woman's respectful obedience to her father marked her as a good woman. Although honoring parents is not considered an activity with particularly gendered implications in most Western cultures, apparently it was an important virtue for Byzantine women especially. This cultural norm would lead Anna to feel compelled to speak well of her father.

How then does Anna square the circle of maintaining her filial devotion while laying bare her father's failings? Anna does make good on her claim that she will not omit negative information about Alexios. Anna is our key source for a number of Alexios's significant mistakes and failures. We know more about Alexios's problems than most other emperors. Yet she manages to present this negative information in such a way that readers always know she doted on her father. She has several strategies for sugarcoating her descriptions of her father's failings as well as expressing her filial devotion.

One of Anna's most frequent methods for revealing her father's faults is to present a base story that exposes the truth of his failure, while rhetorically elaborating that story in a highly flattering manner. Anna does provide important historical information about Alexios's losses; she did not take the sycophantic step of leaving his losses and defeats out of her history. She is careful, however, to efface the negativity of these descriptions by rhetorically presenting the story so that Alexios looks good even as he is losing. Anna describes an ill-fated military campaign where Alexios was forced to hide the Virgin Mary's veil in the bushes as he fled the battle, which he lost despite carrying such a holy relic.[19] She says that Alexios had to hide the veil because he lost the strength to carry it.[20] Alexios's abandonment of this precious relic highlights both his military loss and the abscense of the divine help that such holy objects were hoped to confer. Carrying holy relics and icons into battle was supposed to enlist divine aid, which was not forthcoming in this case.[21] Not only was Alexios badly defeated, but in fleeing he was too weak to carry a reliquary. This battle is one of several that Alexios is described as losing in the *Alexiad*.

Anna peppers this highly unflattering story of Alexios's flight with details about mighty blows that Alexios delivered to individual Scythians and other brilliant martial exploits by those in his entourage. She describes Alexios as ready to stay and fight to the death only to be persuaded to flee by his brother-in-law Michael Doukas, who argued that his death would put everyone in danger.[22] Then she describes how Alexios personally fought off several Scythians and effectively warned one of his companions of an imminent blow to his back.[23] These and other details help her construct a story in which Alexios flees the battlefield bravely and heroically.

Anna's descriptions of Alexios bravely running away have not succeeded in making her seem like an impartial historian to many of her modern readers. Part of her overall compulsion to portray Alexios positively, however, should perhaps be attributed to the gendered virtue of filial devotion. She was an honest historian in that she included a story about how her father lost a battle and hid one of Christendom's most holy relics in a bush. We would never know that he had lost the veil, or the battle, if Anna had not told us. Yet in so far as she tried to make him look good in the midst of this damaging narrative, she was a devoted and virtuous daughter.

Another technique offsets Alexios's moral errors with descriptions of his penance and redemption. This is most clearly seen in the case of her description of Alexios's bloody coup. Anna provides a frank description of the destructive behavior of Alexios's troops plundering Constantinople during his usurpation.[24] She relates that Alexios's troops, many of them foreign mercenaries, attacked the city on Holy Thursday, thus combining violence with sacrilege. Elsewhere she denigrates the Crusaders for daring to attack Constantinople in Holy Week.[25] While she does not similarly castigate her father for doing the same, she easily could have omitted the reference to the liturgical year when giving the date.[26] Later she explains that the Komnenoi were left highly vulnerable because of the ill-discipline of Alexios's army. Anna returns to the topic of the sacking of the city in an extended discussion of Alexios's penance. She describes how he and all the members of his family undertook extravagant, but essentially personal and private, penitential activity.[27] This can easily be seen as an attempt to redeem Alexios's reputation in the aftermath of a violent start to his reign. The attempt would not be necessary, however, if Anna had taken the truly flattering tactic of omitting the stories of violence in the first place.

Beyond trying to make Alexios's failings look good, Anna uses several other strategies for proving her filial devotion while maintaining her historical objectivity. Anna presents her obedience to her parents as beginning even before her own birth. She relates the story that Alexios had not yet returned from campaigning when her mother felt the first labor pains. Eirene made the sign of the cross over her belly and said, "Little one, wait a while for your father's arrival." Anna obeyed her mother's command and was born two days later, after Alexios had arrived home.[28] So Anna obeyed her parents even in the womb.

Anna proves her devotion by slipping flattering descriptions of her parents into her history. She does praise Alexios, from time to time, in a manner that would be fitting for a speech in his honor.[29] She also praises her mother, Eirene, as well as her grandmother, Anna Dalassene.[30] Anna does not let the praising speech slip out thoughtlessly because she just cannot help herself. Rather the existence of encomiastic speech, amidst her disclaimers that she will not speak encomiastically, serves to show her true devotion to her parents. She acknowledges that such praise speech causes her to break out of her historical discourse, but does it anyway.[31] She is not willing to completely sacrifice her cultural obligation to act as a loving and devoted daughter in her pursuit of history.

Another strategy Anna uses to prove her loyalty to her father is to claim that she has suffered for him. After the story of how she obeyed her parents even in the womb, Anna explains,

> I was wholeheartedly at one and the same time mother-lover and father-lover. I have many people as witnesses to this aspect of my character, indeed all those who know about me, and further testifying are my many struggles and toils and dangers on my parents' behalf, into which I threw myself out of love for them, not sparing honor, money nor life itself: for my love for them so inflamed me that I often gave up my very soul for them.[32]

Anna then says that it is not yet time to talk of these things and turns the narrative back to the events surrounding her birth. She does not later offer explanations of any specific toils or struggles she endured for her parents. Her protestation that she has endured much on her parents' behalf seems to be a statement of loyalty and devotion appropriate for a good daughter. She claims for herself innate obedience to parental wishes and complete willingness to support her parents.

Another case of Anna claiming to have suffered for her father occurs in the context of seeking to defuse suspicion that she is working to flatter Alexios rather than to give an unbiased account of what happened. After a digression in which she praises Alexios's willingness to fight by stratagem and wit as well as with straightforward bravery, Anna pauses to say,

> Again I ask here not to be blamed that I am convicted of talking about myself; since often I have apologized that the goodwill for the father does not lead the story, but the nature of the material. For what prevents, save for the truth itself, to be in this regard both lover of father

and lover of the truth? For I have chosen to write the truth about a good man. But if he happens to be also the father of the writer, then the name of the father must be added there as an appendage; yet history writing by nature must depend on truth. I have shown my good will to my father in other ways and on account of this, I have whet spears and sharpened knives of enemies for myself, and they know, whoever are not ignorant about our matters.[33]

Anna here restates her firm principles of impartiality: that she will not spare her father if the truth requires she speak negatively of him. In this passage she argues for her lack of bias by claiming that she already had suffered for her father and so did not need to prove her devotion by writing about him favorably. In granting herself licensed to write without devotion because she had proved her loyalty already, she is substantiating both her proper loyalty and her historical impartiality. While the problem of impartiality is more easily recognizable to modern readers, the problem of expressing filial devotion was also significant for Anna.

In the standard reading of Anna's biography, in which she is seen as fighting vigorously against her brother John for political power, this allusion to her enemies is taken as referring to John, and as confirming her political losses. As we shall see in the second half of the present book, the narrative of the attempted coup is built on shaky foundations. While discussions of politics will wait, here we have to establish what her rhetorical motivations were for saying that she suffered for her father. The claim that she gathered enemies for herself out of devotion to her father has the rhetorical function of excusing her lack of partiality toward him. She is asking the audience to trust that she is telling the truth, because, since she has already proven her devotion, she has no reason to lie about her father. She is simply telling the true story of a truly good man.

Yet another strategy Anna uses to appear simultaneously devoted and impartial to her parents is to say that she has omitted even more flattering details from her narrative. At several points Anna admits that she has erred on the side of plainness in her descriptions. After describing Alexios's efforts to care for reformed heretics, Anna breaks off, saying,

Nothing more must be said about these things; yet more has been omitted. And let no one cast blame on the history that the writing is corrupt. For there are now living many witnesses of the matters narrated, and I am not condemned for lying.[34]

Anna has just praised her father resoundingly. Yet by saying she could have honestly gone much further, she makes a rhetorical ploy for being seen as impartial, which she backs up with an appeal to contemporary witnesses. Similarly, after a glowing description of her mother's charity, Anna explains that

I would have many more things to say about this empress, if the daughter
were not held in suspicion of lies, and that we are pleasing our mother.
For those who have suspicions, I will present deeds that confirm the
words.[35]

Anna has plenty more good things to say about her mother, but claims that
if she said them her audience would think she was lying. Anna uses the suspicion of flattery as an excuse not to be more flattering. This makes an overt
display of her lack of bias while simultaneously laying claim to even greater
unstated virtues for her mother.

Anna's efforts to appear devoted and loyal extend beyond her father
and mother to include her husband as well. Anna takes great care to present herself as ardently supportive of her husband, Nikephoros Bryennios.
Anna expresses affection for Nikephoros and awe at his skills at almost every
moment he appears in her text. She says that Nikephoros surpassed his contemporaries, as much as Achilles had surpassed the Achaeans.[36] Memories
of Nikephoros immediately fill Anna's soul with mourning and sorrow.[37] He
excelled in military matters in letters, and in the writing of history.[38] When
narrating how Nikephoros commanded a troop of archers on the wall of
Constantinople during the contentious passage of the armies of the First
Crusade, she describes his skill in archery in glorious terms. First she says that
the other archers in his contingent were as good as Teucer, but Nikephoros
had the bow of Apollo.[39] Then she says he did not shoot in the manner of
the Homeric Greeks, but rather was like Heracles, shooting immortal arrows,
and missing only on purpose. Then she says that he in fact surpassed Teucer
and the Ajaxes of the *Iliad*.[40] She describes his actions in the engagement
glowingly with a number of Homeric allusions that burnish the heroic portrait she draws of her husband. In a history filled with good men who fought
well, Nikephoros appears as an epic hero far surpassing all contemporaries.
She expresses an admiration and affection that makes a strong case for her
devotion and love for her husband.

Anna may have been particularly interested in looking like a devoted wife
because comparing her history with that of her husband reveals strong disagreements between Anna and Nikephoros. The overarching argument of
his work runs contrary to that of the *Alexiad*. Nikephoros's history criticizes
Alexios's character and strongly suggests that Nikephoros's grandfather (who
was defeated by Alexios) would have made a better emperor.[41] In her efforts
to exonerate and valorize her father's memory, Anna wrote a refutation of her
husband's history.[42] In making a strong and sustained case that her husband
was wrong, at least about her father's character, Anna's historical work does
not show the deference to her husband's opinion that her culture's construc-
tions of proper wifely behavior would lead us to expect. Anna's expressions of
admiration for Nikephoros, and the intensity of her mourning for him, may

be in part a response to the potential charge that she did not respect his work, or his memory. Anna would have her audience believe that while she may have disagreed with her husband about history, she had loved him deeply and her devotion should not be doubted.

While her devotion to her husband, her father, and her mother is important for demonstrating Anna's good character, it is highly problematic from the point of view of presenting herself as an impartial historian. She needs to prove her devotion so that she is not accused of being a disrespectful daughter and wife. Yet obviously any expressions of devotion impugn her impartiality.

The necessity of proving her filial devotion also causes a different set of problems for Anna, in that any praise for her family could be taken as Anna flattering herself. As was discussed in chapter 1, self-praise, or even self-description, was considered distasteful and obnoxious in Greek culture of both antiquity and the middle ages. Positive speech about relatives ran the risk of being construed as Anna boasting about *herself*. Anna says that in writing about Alexios she was afraid that her audience might think she was "writing about the deeds of my father to praise myself."[43] She opened herself up to accusations of self-praise whenever her history brings her to speak well of her father.

While self-praise was a known problematic for male rhetoricians of Anna's era, it may have presented an even greater problem for Anna because of the conflict between boasting and appropriate feminine modesty. In general boasting is intrinsically bad. It is an activity Anna ascribes to murderous conspirators, unstable Franks, and heretics.[44] More particularly for Anna, boasting is an aspect of immodesty and hence the exact opposite of the modesty that was one of the central virtues for a Byzantine woman.

Beyond its simple distastefulness, arrogance calls out wrath and jealousy. Envy, *phthonos*, was thought to have the power to cause great harm to those whose good fortune provoked it.[45] Boasting may have been made more problematic for women in Byzantine society because of long-standing associations between envy and the death of infants. Baby-killing demons were associated with jealousy, and infants were considered particularly vulnerable to *phthonos*.[46] Especially in that the death of children was seen to be a punishment visited upon women who excited daemonic jealousy, women would have been careful not to boast. While we do not know the stance the philosophical Anna would have taken toward the notion of baby-snatching demons, fear of malignant forces provoked by envy was a part of her culture. In her reading of classical mythology, Anna would have received similar messages about the danger of arousing the jealousy of the gods. The stories of Cassiopeia boasting of her daughter Andromeda's beauty, and Niobe boasting of her many children provided stark warnings about the dangers of self-aggrandizement: both Cassiopeia and Niobe called out the righteous anger of the gods and suffered the deaths of their children as a result. Regardless of whether it was based on a

real fear of demons, the need to avoid exciting jealousy was a cultural imperative for Greek women in Anna's era. We can be sure Anna did not want to be
seen as boastful.

The maintenance of Anna's appropriate feminine modesty in the midst of
history writing was thus one of the key problematics of her historical writing.
As Alexios's daughter, she could not describe his glory without being accused
of glorifying herself and basking in his reflected radiance. When Anna had
occasion to speak positively about her father's care for the communities he
governed in the midst of his illness, she interrupted her story to say, "In no
way blame me for talking about myself because I admire my own; nor suspect I am lying about the emperor; since I am telling the truth."[47] When she
first introduces Constantine, the son of Michael VII, to whom she had been
betrothed, she says, "And let there be no righteous anger, if I should praise
my own when constrained by the nature of the matter."[48] Anna here appeals
to the truthfulness of her statements as a protection against wrath that is a
natural consequence of jealousy. In describing her studies of astronomy as an
aspect of the flourishing of science under Alexios, she explicitly disavows that
she speaks in order to "glorify myself."[49] By addressing the problem directly, it
seems Anna tries to defuse accusations of self-aggrandizement.

Occasionally Anna appeals to her feminine modesty as guiding her
authorial choices. Anna's modesty forbade her from narrating the whole of
a salacious story about papal politics she found in one of her sources. Anna
declares that "I would say the outrage, if my feminine and royal shame did
not stop me."[50] Near the end of her history, Anna again says that her feminine modesty prevents her from telling the whole of the story. In this case
she is discussing Alexios's efforts to combat the Bogomil heresy. She refers
readers wanting to understand the heresy more fully to a book on dogma
commissioned by her father.[51] Anna tells us that it would defile her tongue
for her to describe the heresy. She quotes Sappho as saying "shame prevents
me" and reminds her readers that "I am an historian, and also a woman and
the most honored firstborn of Alexios, born in the purple." As such, it is better for her to pass over gossip in silence.[52] Anna's status as a woman and an
aristocrat compelled her not to speak about common rumors. The theories
of the Bogomils fall into this class of discourse too inappropriate for Anna
to describe.

Anna's descriptions of her mother also show great concern for demonstrating her modesty. Anna becomes particularly apologetic when mentioning her
mother's actions in accompanying Alexios on campaign. She describes Eirene
as naturally possessed of an extreme sense of modesty: while the philosopher
Theano did not want her elbow to be seen publically, Eirene did not want her
elbow or eyes to be seen, or even her voice to be heard by strangers, so great
was her modesty.[53] Eirene's "innate modesty" gave her an intense desire to stay
inside the palace, but her "devotion and burning love" for Alexios compelled

FIGURE 3.1 *Alexios Komnenos offering Christ a book of refutations of heresies. Vat.*
gr.666, f.2v.
© *Vatican Apostolic Library.*

her to accompany him so that she could tend to his illness and protect him
from conspiracies.[54] Anna justifies Eirene's actions in traveling with Alexios
by arguing that Eirene was the best possible person both to sooth the pains
in his legs and to vigilantly guard him from harm. For these reasons Eirene
"pushed aside her natural female modesty and braved the eyes of men."[55] Yet
even while doing so, she maintained her decorum and made herself mostly
"unknown" by controlling her gaze, by her silence, and, with the help of her
servants, by shielding her body from view.[56]

By laying great stress on Eirene's natural modesty and the compulsions of
wifely devotion, Anna works here to soften the impropriety of Eirene's fundamentally immodest act of leaving the home and participating in a military
campaign.[57] In reality, Eirene's behavior in traveling with the army may not
have been as unusual or transgressive as Anna's expressions of her mother's
deep desire for domestic seclusion imply.[58] But Anna's strong refrain of modesty is consonant with the rhetorical overtures to traditional female virtues
running throughout her history. Anna mentions in passing that she also
joined in Eirene's vigilant labors and accompanied Alexios, along with others

who loved the emperor.[59] She immediately apologizes for including this discussion of her mother and herself in the history on the grounds that

> these things are written for those whose tongues love scoffing and abusing. They bring accusations against the innocent (Homer's Muse knew this was a human way) and they disparage noble deeds and blame the blameless.[60]

Anna's disclaimer that she *needed* to describe her mother's actions provides her with cover against further accusations that she was boasting about her family and flattering her mother. Anna is not explicit about what kind of scoffing and accusations she was expecting, but the overwhelming emphasis in the passage on Eirene's modesty suggests that she was countering allegations that Eirene was overstepping the bounds of female propriety by potentially exposing herself to public view.[61]

Anna's truthfulness is her chief bulwark against the accusation that she flatters her subjects and boasts of herself. The need to verify and substantiate her ability to write a truthful history is therefore acute. Anna's claims of truthfulness form her key defense against the accusation that she is aggrandizing herself by talking about the achievements of her family. Yet it is extremely difficult for Anna to speak about her access to sources of information, her learning, or anything else that would help substantiate her ability to write a truthful history, because doing so would be self-aggrandizing. We will examine Anna's struggle to establish the reliability of her historical sources while maintaining her humility and feminine modesty further in chapter 5.

The issues of historical impartiality, familial devotion, and personal modesty are all entangled in a digression in book four about Anna's authorial proclivities. This passage has so many internal contradictions that at first it can seem almost nonsensical. Yet when viewed in light of the cultural forces at play in Anna's authorial enterprise, her aims in the passage become clearer. The remainder of this chapter walks through this statement of Anna's methods trying to clarify how she wished her audience to respond to this moment of self-revelation.

The digression comes at the end of a story about Alexios's miraculous escape at the end of the first battle of Dyrrachion, which he lost badly to Norman invaders under Robert Guiscard. Contextually, Anna has just concluded perhaps the most hyperbolic description of Alexios's personal heroism in the *Alexiad*. When cornered alone by Robert's men, in the aftermath of this disastrous loss, Alexios was saved from capture by the marvelous dexterity of his horse, which leapt onto a high rock as if he had been raised on wings like Pegasus.[62] With several other deeds of extreme daring, Alexios was able to escape capture.[63]

In this story we see Anna use the same technique that she did when describing how Alexios abandoned the Virgin Mary's veil. She provides an account of events that go extremely badly for Alexios, but sugarcoats the story with lots of laudatory details. Even in the midst of telling a fundamentally unflattering story, she focuses on Alexios's personal good conduct and luck. This embroidery of bad events helps Anna honor her father while narrating his losses. Alexios's flying horse and personal fighting strength are details that depict him gloriously in the midst of a stunning loss. Then Anna pauses in her story to say,

> But for my part, in the midst of these words, on the one hand because of the nature of the history, and on the other because of the extremity of the deeds, I let escape me that I am writing about the successes of my father. For not wanting the history to be viewed with suspicion, frequently I run over the matters of my father neither increasing nor attaching emotion. For if I were free of paternal feeling for him and independent, so that as if taking a whorish tongue to the copious material, I would make plain how much affinity [my tongue] has for matters of great deeds. Natural affection shields my enthusiasm; by no means do I wish to seem to feed people's suspicion that I am telling marvels about my family because I want to. For, while often remembering paternal successes, yet I distil away the soul in writing and narrating how many ills befell him, and I could not pass the place without monodies and lamentation. But since elaborate rhetoric has no place in this part of the history, like an unfeeling and unbreakable stone I summarize the sufferings of my father, which require even me to utter an oath just as that Homeric young man. For I am not worse than he who said "By Zeus, Agelaus, and by my father's sufferings" in consequence of which he was a father-lover, and was so called. But the paternal suffering must be left to me alone to honor and lament, while the history must continue.[64]

In this short paragraph Anna tries several different strategies for substantiating her impartiality while maintaining her filial devotion.

The heroism of Alexios's escape plays a clear rhetorical role in distracting the audience from the magnitude of the defeat he has just suffered. Coming just when he barely had taken control of the empire himself, this loss of Dyrrachion to a foreign invader was politically and militarily disastrous for Alexios. Anna's stories of Alexios's physical heroics and military glory carve a positive story out of the dire reality that the new emperor had lost control of a key strategic city and had been very nearly captured by the Normans. While Anna's heroic narrative may be stirring, it is an obvious band-aid on a wounding episode.

It is perhaps the conspicuousness of her efforts to clean Alexios's record at this point that prompted her to claim emotional distance from her subject. As if expecting that this passage would make readers think she was casting an artificially heroic glow around her father, Anna pauses to say that she had forgotten that she was writing about her father:

> But for my part, in the midst of these words, on the one hand because of the nature of the history, and on the other because of the extremity of the deeds, I let escape me that I am writing about the successes of my father.

Here Anna first says that it had slipped her mind that the subject was her father because of the excitement of the story and the nature of the history. History writing, Anna claims, made her lose sight of her relation to the subject, perhaps because it made her so dispassionate and blind to familial affection. In the next sentence, however, Anna pivots, saying that she habitually tries not to exaggerate or write extravagantly about Alexios's deeds: "For not wanting the history to be viewed with suspicion, frequently I run over the matters of my father neither increasing nor attaching emotion." The second claim, that she took care not to magnify her father's deeds, implies not that she had forgotten that she was writing about her father, but that she took particular care whenever she did write about him, in order to avoid suspicion. The conjunction of these two fairly contradictory rationales for avoiding aggrandization lets us know that this was a significant problem.

Clearly Anna does not want readers to see her as exaggerating her father's greatness, but the disavowal of affection was not straightforward. Anna does not want to appear lacking in filial devotion or affection for her father, or unable to write in an extravagant style. She continues, "For if I were free of paternal feeling for him and independent, so that, as if taking a whorish tongue to the copious material, I would make plain how much affinity it has for matters of great deeds." As a counterfactual statement, this claims that Anna *did* have affection for her father and was not independent. Her actions are grounded in her status as a devoted daughter. If she did not care about her father, she would be able to write in a truly extravagant fashion, because her tongue is comfortable talking about great deeds. But since she does care about him, she must write in a restrained fashion. Anna claims to be restraining her natural ability for elaborate rhetoric.

When Anna speaks about the kind of tongue she would have, if she were not a devoted daughter, she chooses a term fraught with sexual imagery.[65] Anna says that if she were free and independent of affection for her father, she would be able to "take an insolent tongue to the copious material," that she could make plain how good it was at describing great deeds. In medieval Greek, the term she uses to describe her hypothetically liberated tongue, *sobada*, means "rushing, swaggering, fearless," but also refers to whores who chased after customers.[66] The expressive, enthusiastic tongue is thus closely associated very strikingly with sexual impropriety. Such a speaker was immodest in all senses. Modesty of speech and self-depiction seems to have been intricately linked with sexual modesty. One of the things Anna is telling us in this passage is that in reality she does not have an insolent tongue. She is making a claim for her own personal modesty.

Anna explains that what prevents her from giving license to an insolent tongue is her affection for her father: "Natural affection shields my enthusiasm; by no means do I wish to seem to feed people's suspicion that I am telling marvels about my family because I want to." Her natural affection for her father hinders her eagerness for writing about him because, if she did write in a way that expressed her devotion to her father, people would think she was just telling stories out of desire for praise or glory. Any honest reflection of her enthusiasm for her father's deeds would lead to the suspicion that she was lying to boast about herself. Therefore Anna shows true filial devotion precisely in *not* glorifying the deeds of the father. The plain language she uses to describe her father's deeds is the result of the affection she has for him. True respect for her father requires that she not be seen as self-aggrandizing. Since she is not self-aggrandizing, she is telling the plain truth.

It is not enough, however, to claim she is writing about her father's successes in a plain manner. Anna next undercuts Alexios's success by emphasizing that he was also beset by tragedies. The true filial response, Anna claims, would be for her to lament her father's history:

> For, while often remembering paternal successes, yet I distil away the soul in writing and narrating how many ills befell him, and I could not pass the place without monodies and lamentation.

This turn constitutes yet another reason why Anna was not exaggerating her father's deeds: if she were to really, truly, assess his deeds, she would need to be lamenting. The substance of his deeds was not glory, but tragedy. This claim about Alexios's lack of success is not maintained throughout the work. Anna is not making a serious argument that Alexios was a tragic figure. Rather, the claim that she needed to be lamenting somehow helps her make her case in this passage.

The need for lamentation appears to be a response to the obnoxiousness of talking about oneself and one's family. Anna here fends off criticism that describing her father's successes is fundamentally boastful. The authorial strategy of rendering stories about oneself acceptable by cloaking them in a tale of woe explains why Anna suddenly claims that Alexios's story is one of tragedy.[67] If she is lamenting Alexios's losses, she cannot be convicted of exulting in his triumphs. In this way the appeal to lamentation helps her in both diffusing the accusation of boastfulness and in strengthening her claim to impartiality. She is not telling great stories about him because she wants to boast about her family, but because it is the plain historical truth.

Even though Anna says the right response to her father's story is lamentation, she cannot engage in singing monodies, because that would not be good history writing. Anna does not continue with lamentation for the ills that befell Alexios, but rather turns away to return to history writing:

> But since elaborate rhetoric has no place in this part of the history, like an unfeeling and unbreakable stone I summarize the sufferings of my father, which require even me to utter an oath just as that Homeric young man. For I am not worse than he who said "By Zeus, Agelaus, and by my father's sufferings" in consequence of which he was a father-lover, and was so called. But the paternal suffering must be left to me alone to honor and lament, while the history must continue.

Anna restrains her rhetoric in recognition that it was out of place in history writing. Because historians should be dispassionate, she prevents herself from lamenting. Yet she is as good a child as Telemachos who took an oath by his father's sufferings.[68] Through this allusion, Anna claims that she has proper affection for her father and should also be known as a father-lover. These sentences highlight both Anna's affection for her father and her ability to prevent that affection from pulling her away from good, dispassionate history writing. The tension between the two ideas emphasizes her emotional self-control.

Anna's claims of a modest tongue and insensitivity to her subject must be taken in their context, following on a lavishly extravagant description of Alexios's heroism. Anna's claim to plain speaking is a rhetorical fiction, clearly belied by the lush descriptions she has just given her audience. On one level then, the passage implicitly makes authorizing claims for Anna's rhetorical abilities. After the extravagant rhetoric, Anna says that she has kept herself in check. In prompting her audience to wonder what she could do if she were not holding back, Anna makes a case for her own rhetorical brilliance. Anna's strategies of self-effacement do not go so far as to place her skills as a writer in doubt.

The strongest goal of this passage is to establish Anna's impartiality. The overarching claim is that she is not biased as a historian because she is writing about her father. Yet the passage also betrays a serious anxiety about boastfulness. Anna does not want anyone to think she is telling fabulous stories about her father to glorify herself. While Anna exults in her willingness to transgress the law of nature in order to cleave to the truth, she also strives to present herself in the positive role of a dutiful daughter, maintaining a proper, natural relationship with her father and mother. She wants her readers to see her as loving her father deeply. Through her Homeric allusion she is assimilating herself to Telemachos, who represented filial devotion.[69] The whole passage highlights the tension between impartiality and familial affection.

Anna was not willing to be a bad daughter. Or rather, while she would not spare her father in selecting information to include in her history, she would simultaneously strive to maintain her proper relationship with him as much as possible. These two ideas are in conflict, but they are both important parts of Anna's self-presentation. Anna's desire to be seen as a dutiful daughter must have been strong enough to motivate her to include it throughout her history, consistently, even though it risked undermining her authority as an impartial historical witness.

Anna does not resolve the fundamental tension in her exercise of impartiality. She appears subject to contradictory impulses, not because she was wishy-washy, but because she was trying to do two conflicting things at once. We easily see the discussion of impartiality, but we do not perceive or appreciate the expressions of daughterly loyalty and modesty so clearly. We are not satisfied by Anna's response to the problem of impartiality because we do not perceive her as also responding to the problem of filial devotion. Her writing expresses strong methodological conflicts, but holds them in deliberate, balanced tension. When we understand better the causes of these conflicts in her writing, we may be able to see them more sympathetically as responses to complex, competing cultural imperatives, rather than as signs of disjointed thinking or ineptitude.

Crying like a Woman and Writing like a Man

By participating in discussions of politics and warfare, not to mention writing a history, Anna was engaging in what were considered masculine activities in her culture. By participating in the Greek tradition of historiography, she performed a masculine rhetorical discourse—she wrote like a man. Yet it seems that Anna did not want to speak consistently as a man throughout her history. Writing pseudonymously would have allowed her to compose her history in a uniformly masculine narrative voice. Anna rejected this option in favor of trying to be both "woman and historian."[1] Sporadically throughout the *Alexiad*, Anna breaks with historical practice to speak with a voice her culture recognized as female. Anna's feminine rhetorical voice is generally that of a mourning woman, which was designed to spark pity and sympathy among her audience.

In Byzantine culture, people most often expressed their character by aligning their behavior with ideal types or models. Individuality was displayed and created by clarifying not how one was different, but whom one was like. Emotions were expressed by bringing to mind the kinds of people who had been characterized by those feelings.[2] To express herself textually as a good woman, Anna therefore needed to draw on positive models of female speech. Speaking with a virtuous female voice was not straightforward because silence and reticence were highly prized characteristics of Byzantine women. Anna's attempts elsewhere to align herself with the idealized behaviors of a modest woman or devoted daughter are rendered problematic by the essential silence of those roles. Modest women were supposed to be silent, and the filial devotion of daughters was shown through caring deeds, not words. Positive models for forceful female self-expression were rare. The role of the lamenting woman was an exception that allowed Anna to act like a good woman according to the rules of her culture.

When male writers modeled their action on ideal types, they had many patterns to choose from. In addition to the many male characters on which to model their behavior, male rhetors could also perform female characters. The mournful Niobe and Hecuba were typical subjects of rhetorical exercises.[3] Male preachers also enacted female biblical characters, particularly the widow of Nain and the Virgin.[4] Male writers were able to play female roles because it was believed that their masculine nature allowed them to control emotion so that they could fake it when necessary, without becoming subject to it. Since perceptions of female nature created the expectation that women were subject to emotion, it would be far more difficult for them to portray characters exhibiting masculine self-control. Our few examples of female Byzantine writers suggest that they may not have had the latitude to perform both female and male characters. Aside of Anna, the female writers in Byzantine culture were hymnographers, who often wrote in praise of female saints or enacted female characters such as Eve, Mary, or Miriam.[5] In the most widely known Byzantine liturgical poem written by a woman, Kassia speaks in the voice of the sinful woman who anointed Jesus.[6] It may have been easier for the female hymnographers to have their work accepted when they portrayed female voices.

Anna naturally needed to avoid aligning her behavior with a negative type of female character. Some Byzantine histories include scenes in which women make striking speeches. Empress Theodora stirs Justinian to suppress a rebellion in Procopius's history, emperor Isaac Komnenos's wife Katherine urges him not to abdicate in Psellos's history, and Anna Dalassene pushes her husband John to make a bid for power when his brother Isaac abdicates in Nikephoros Bryennios's history. At first glance it may seem that Byzantine women of the ruling class could acceptably make speeches of political counsel. Yet in each of these histories the advice of the women was either disastrous or unwelcome. Theodora's speech sparked a ruthless and bloody slaughter of civilian protesters. Both John and Isaac Komnenos display their strength of character by resolutely ignoring their wives' advice.[7] The woman who gave her powerful husband advice about politics does seem to be a familiar type in Anna's culture, but it was a negative type. On the contrary, the ideal woman did not speak in public or give advice.[8] Anna needed to look elsewhere to find a positive model of female speech.

Women crying out in lamentation and mourning formed a standard model of behavior in which female speech was appropriate. Using the voice of a mourning woman was one of the ways Anna presents herself in a positive female role. Also, since lamentation was appropriate for women in positions of misery and weakness, it helped Anna construct herself as an object of pity and hence deprecated her authorial persona, mitigating the arrogance of female authorship. By aligning her behavior with the type of the mourning woman, Anna both participated in normal, appropriate female behavior and attempted to elicit pity in her audience, thereby balancing the inherent aggrandizement of her choice to write history.

In the course of her history, Anna punctuates her story with bursts of anguish at the mention of the deaths of her husband, Nikephoros Bryennios, her betrothed, Constantine Doukas, her brother Andronikos, her mother, and her father. Although Anna's expressions of personal emotion take up only an extremely small portion of her total text, they dominate both the beginning and ending of her story. The voice and role of the lamenting woman is one of the most easily identified of Anna's voices, because in this case she was participating in one of the most clearly defined, long-standing modes of female speech in Greek culture.

Women wailing with grief and making ritualized gestures of irrationality have been a recognized cultural pattern of behavior in the Mediterranean from the archaic period through the twentieth century.[9] In Anna's reading of Homer and Attic tragedy, this is what she saw good women doing.[10] Mortal women in the classical literary tradition spend a great deal of their time lamenting.[11] While men cry in both ancient and medieval Greek culture— and the tears of men were necessary in certain situations—their tears were one of numerous options for their personal expression. Positive female characters, in contrast, spoke almost exclusively through laments.[12] When Anna surveyed classical literature for positive role models for female speech, she would have found women primarily speaking in lamentation.

The ancient models of women speaking in lamentation were well known and influential in Anna's twelfth-century culture. Anna's contemporaries could have accessed classical traditions of female lamentation in a number of ways: rhetorical training, liturgical poems and sermons based on classical models, and direct reading. Medieval rhetorical training exercises called on students to compose character sketches using classical characters, such as Niobe, as models.[13] Gregory of Nyssa's sermon on the widow of Nain, whose grief moved Jesus to bring her son back to life, follows second-century rhetorical handbooks for writing monody.[14] This sermon, in which Gregory performs the role of the grieving and lamenting widow, was much admired in the medieval period, and frequently repeated and quoted by preachers of the twelfth-century.[15] The audiences for the sermons modeled on Gregory of Nyssa's would have been moved by the images of the mourning widow, regardless of how much they were aware of the ancient roots of that model.

Medieval liturgical poems depicting the lamentations of the Virgin, performed during memorable church services on Good Friday, also drew heavily on the imagery and form of the classical and Second Sophistic tradition of lamentation.[16] Images of female saints painted in burial contexts in Byzantine churches provided a visual confirmation of the continued association between women and mourning.[17] When Anna turned to reading the original lamenta-tions in the ancient tragedians and Homer, such scenes would already have been familiar from the tradition of Christian lamentations. She may not have acknowledged much of any distinction between her culture and that of clas-sical antiquity.

When Anna's lamentations take the form of descriptions of her dead kinsmen, she adheres closely to the recommended practices for speeches of mourning, which were designed to provoke sorrow in the audience. The rhe-torical training manual of Menander, widely used in Anna's era, taught how to compose a speech that would elicit the proper feelings of sadness among an audience of mourners. Menander advised the writer of a monody on a young person to lament the deceased's age and talk about his good quali-ties.[18] Menander recommended drawing on contrasts between past and pres-ent and describing the former appearance of the youth in life, saying for example: "What beauty he has lost—the bloom of his cheeks—the tongue now silent! The soft beard wilted! The locks of hair no longer to be gazed at!"[19] Anna follows this advice closely. Anna's initial lament for her husband, Nikephoros Bryennios, dwells on his positive qualities and former beauty:

> Oh! What a councilor is lost to the Romans. His accurate understand-ing of affairs that he garnered through experience! His knowledge of words! His varieties of wisdom, indeed both from abroad and from our own garden! Grace spread throughout his limbs and his appearance was not only worthy of royalty, as they say, but better and even divine.[20]

In her monody for her betrothed, Constantine Doukas, who died before Anna was old enough to marry, Anna brings up his youthful beauty to heighten the contrast with his early death:

> This youth was a work of art of nature and, so to speak, the pride of God's hands. If one only looked at him one would say he flowed from the golden race the Greeks described in their myths, so extraordinary was his beauty.[21]

In the description of the former beauty and greatness of the deceased, Anna's descriptions set up this contrast between former happiness and cur-rent mourning. Anna's lament for her younger brother Andronikos, who died in battle at a relatively young age, also draws attention to his youthful graciousness:

> He was coming into the most gracious age of life; daring yet wise, and in war he had both physical skills and excellent judgment. Before his time he departed and, without any expectation, he left us and, as the sun, went down. Oh! Youth, and Flower of Body! How did you then plummet down from nimble leaps on horses?[22]

The lament over Andronikos displays a number of characteristics common in both classical and more modern lamentation traditions: contrast of past and present, imagery of light, and antithetical imagery of high and low.[23] In the lament for Andronikos, Anna also voices regret at the unexpectedness of death and employs a direct second-person address to the dead—a characteristic of ancient and modern laments that emphasizes the contrast between the mourner and the dead.[24]

In these descriptions of her youthful betrothed, her brother, and her husband, Anna takes on the role of the orator who prods an audience into feeling sorrow for others. Yet Anna often goes beyond this to make herself the chief object of pity. She effectively turns the focus onto her own mourning and misery, prompting the audience's sympathy. She does not speak from a position of emotional control endeavoring to elicit mourning from her audience so much as to present herself as subject to sorrow and suffering. The intended effect is to elicit compassion and pity from the audience more than grief. In describing her own heartache, Anna imitates more closely the emotional patterns and extremes of classical texts.

To present herself as an object of pity, Anna drew closely on classical models of mourning women. In her prologue, when she turns from a description of her husband to an expression of how his death made her feel, Anna alludes to Euripides's *Hecuba*, in saying she too had a "double share of tears, as the Tragedian says."[25] At the death of her brother, she expresses a longing for the ancient days when grief could turn one into a stone, bird, or tree, alluding to the stories of Niobe, Philomela, Prokne, and Daphne.[26] A phrase Sophocles' *Antigone* used to describe her brother's grieving is applied to Anna's mother near the death of Alexios.[27] At the very end of the history, when grieving for her parents and husband, Anna wonders how she did not die of grief, and quotes Electra's words at the opening of Euripides's *Orestes* that there is "no suffering or God-sent affliction" that she cannot bear.[28] Contemplating the deaths of her parents and husband, Anna again wishes that she could turn to stone like Niobe.[29] Anna also characterizes her emotionalism overtly with the terminology of mourning. Remembering Alexios is a lamentation, a *threnos*.[30] She sings a monody for Andronikos.[31] At the point of Alexios's death, Anna describes herself, her mother, and her sisters as keening, wailing, and tearing at themselves, unambiguously setting their response within ancient traditions of Greek female lamentation.[32]

The tendency to talk about herself and her miserable state further align Anna's expressions of grieving with the classical traditions of female lamentation.[33] Sophocles's Electra turns attention to her own grief in her first line, "Ah me, wretched me!"[34] Andromache bewails how Hector has left her a widow.[35] Anna describes distant memories of her loved ones as driving her to weeping and intense grief in the present moment. At the memory of her husband, Anna says, "I become filled in my soul with vertigo and I wet my eyes with streams of tears."[36] Regarding her betrothed, she says, "At the memory of this youth I am suffering in soul and my reasoning becomes confused. . ... And I am filled with tears remembering this youth after so many years."[37] At the end of the monody for Andronikos, Anna turns the attention from Andronikos to herself:

> But it is to marvel how one does not become a stone or bird or tree or something else without a soul, just as they say happened of old, changing nature in these ways in response to great evils (whether it is a myth or some true story). And perhaps it would be better to transform my nature into something without feeling rather than feel so much evil. For if this were so, then quickly these horrible things would render me a stone.[38]

The focus of pity shifts from her brother, cut down in his prime, to Anna, living on in grief. Anna centralized her own emotional state in a way that conforms to traditions of female lamentation in which the woman focuses on her own pain.[39]

Anna also expresses negative wishes for herself, participating in a tradition in which the mourner wishes she had not been born or had died earlier.[40] At the end of her story, Anna regrets being still alive: "I am displeased only that my soul remains in my body. And if I may not, as it seems, be something adamantine or some other wondrous form and be estranged from myself, may I be destroyed immediately."[41] The imagery of Niobe returns after describing the death of her parents:

> From some we hear the wondrous story of Niobe, changed into a stone by grief for her children, but then even after the transformation to soulless stone, insensible by nature, suffering accompanied her immortal being. It appears that I am yet more wretched than she, since even after these greatest and last calamities, I have remained thus having feeling. It would have been better for me, it seems, to have been changed into a soulless stone streaming rivers of tears. But still I remain, not insensate to misfortunes. I must endure so many horrors and now men may stir up yet other unbearable things that are more unfortunate than even the ills of Niobe. For her terrible suffering had an end after it came to this point.[42]

Anna follows the extreme cases in which the mourner claims to be more unfortunate than the deceased: "Living I have died a thousand deaths."[43] Anna wonders why she is still alive after describing the death of Alexios:

> How has he perished from the living and I am still reckoned and numbered among them? How did I not give up my soul too, or expire, with him expiring, or die unfeeling? If this did not happen to me, why did

I not jump violently from some high mountain or hurl myself into the waves of the sea? My life is enclosed by the greatest misfortunes. As the tragedian says, "there is no suffering or god-sent affliction" which I have not borne. Thus God has made me the dwelling place of great troubles. I have lost the light of the world, the great Alexios, and yet my miserable soul guards my body.[44]

Anna even denies that the death of Alexios took place and wonders if it was all a bad dream.[45]

These negative wishes for herself focus the audience's attention on the piteous state of the woman left in mourning. The dead are mourned, but the mourner is pitied. At the very end of her story, Anna pivots the focus from Alexios, and all those mourning his death, to herself and her own misery:

The death of my Caesar and both of the rulers and the grief over these events was enough for the destruction of my soul and body. Now just as some rivers rushing down from high mountains roar, so the streams of misfortunes overwhelm the single riverbed in my house. The story must have the end, lest writing about such painful things I may become more bitter.[46]

The bitterness that overwhelms Anna is that of grief. Anna's description of Alexios's death seems intended to make the audience feel sorrow for the departed emperor, but also deep pity for Anna herself.

One explanation for Anna's lamentations is that they allow her to express herself in a form that conformed to gender ideals for a good woman, wife, and daughter. Anna's discourse of lamentation serves to express her natural femininity. In singing a dirge she was behaving properly. When caught in the act of the male gendered activity of history writing, Anna's enactment of female lamentation shows that indeed she was a woman, and a normal woman. As Euripides's Medea said, "Women by nature are given to weeping."[47] In weeping Anna did natural womanly things and fulfilled cultural expectations for her gender. The models provided by Homer, Attic tragedy, and the liturgical laments of the Virgin were certainly sufficient to impress on Anna that lamentation was the form of speech most appropriate to women. For both Mary and Hecuba, lamentation was a characteristically female activity and the most appropriate discourse for a woman. Readers who see the objectivity of Anna's history as mared by histrionic emotionalism miss how her expressive lamentations were the moments in which she was properly playing her gender.

That women were most acceptably heard when participating in funeral lamentations may have contributed to Anna's choice to open and close her history with lamentations for Alexios. Women did not give speeches at funerals, but their presence as loud mourners was expected. Anna frames her history with funeral lamentation by beginning and ending the *Alexiad* with her own tears for her father. Encapsulating her history in an appropriate expression of female mourning may have given her greater license to speak forcefully. In so far as she was able to set the *Alexiad* within a funeral lament, she had greater warrant for speaking in public.

Since all of Anna's authorial models were men, her literary examples of women in mourning were images of women's voices as portrayed by male writers. In modeling her behavior on that of Hecuba or the Widow of Nain, Anna was constrained to imitate them as they had been portrayed by Euripides, Gregory of Nyssa, and the other male writers. In the absence of alternatives, these remained Anna's models for describing female behavior. We have no indications that she conceived of her literary models of female grieving as somehow inauthentic because they had been written by men. Rather, the examples of these male writers rhetorically performing female voices, and to some extent thus enacting femininity, may have helped Anna conceive of writing as an activity in which it was possible to cross gender boundaries. Michael Psellos constructed a rhetorical gender for himself that drew on concepts of femininity.[48] In a letter describing his reaction to the birth of his grandson, he calls himself female by nature.[49] Anna knew Psellos's work well and may have read the letter in which Psellos presents himself as female, which had been written to her maternal great-grandfather and preserved as an example of fine writing. Psellos's ability to play with the rhetorical construction of gender may have provided a model for Anna's own artfully constructed self-presentation.

A second function of Anna's lamentations is that, by making her an object of pity, they counteract the boldness and presumption of her historical authorship. Anna's efforts to elicit pity and condescension from her audience mitigate the presumed effrontery of a woman judging and narrating the deeds of men. If an audience feels sorry for a poor old widow, they cannot easily be simultaneously offended by the arrogance of a woman who thinks she would have the ability to write history. Anna's use of tragic self-narration to create a kindly and sympathetic emotional response among her audience draws on a long-standing rhetorical tradition of expressing self-disclosure through a tale of woe. In classical texts, the tale of woe was an effective strategy for rendering talking about oneself before strangers less offensive.[50] Telling tragic stories about oneself made it difficult for the audience to feel annoyed. In Anna's era, the concern not to appear boastful or to excite resentment among the audience continued to make the tale of woe one of the preferred forms of self-disclosure.[51]

Anna presents herself as a tragic, suffering narrator when she is prompted to talk about herself in her history. For example, when an explanation of politics causes her to mention Constantine Doukas (to whom she was betrothed as a child) Anna's own life story enters the history. She makes her self-description tragic by promising to "bewail my own misfortunes" and lament Constantine.[52] Anna's calls for pity correspond to her moments of potentially burdensome self-description. As we shall see in the following chapter, when Anna needs to speak about her own process of historical research, the focus on herself prompts her to engage in tragic self-presentation.

Yet for Anna, the tale of woe serves not only as strategy for inoffensive self-disclosure, but more generally to humble herself before her audience by making her an object of pity and condescension. Presenting her life as a tragic story seems intended to lessen the burden placed on the audience by Anna's authorial enterprise. At the beginning and end of the work, and in places where she talks about her research methods, Anna presents herself as miserable and beset by countless troubles. Her statements about what specifically those misfortunes entailed are quite vague:

> For my part, I have been conversant with terrible things since my birth "in the purple" as they say, and I have been assailed by misfortunes, if one could reckon it not good and smiling fortune for me to be so born and a child of emperors and produced in the purple room; the rest full of waves! Full of turmoil![53]

The juxtaposition of the unnamed misfortunes with the obviously good fortune of having been born in the palace makes this a jarring statement. Anna's question of whether one could count being a princess as bad fortune, acknowledges that her claim to a sorrowful life was at least dubious, if not unbelievable. Anna continues immediately, however, with highly wrought assertions of personal misery and sorrow.[54] While such passages have prompted many readers to wonder what horrible things must have happened to Anna, they function as a form of self-abasement before her audience. Anna's adoption of a posture of extreme piteousness may be a strategy for rendering more palatable the writing of a woman of extreme privilege. Anna adapts the rhetorical tactic of telling a tale of woe at points where she could expect her audience to be particularly bothered by her authorial boldness.

Anna makes another kind of play for the good will of her audience when she asks for pity because of the difficulty of the task she has taken up. When challenged by difficult material, Anna makes an overt request for her audience's sympathy. Bothered by inelegant transitions in her writing, Anna asks her audience to feel sorry for her because she is working so hard. She begs indulgence:

> As I write these words, it is nearly time to light the lamps; my pen moves slowly over the paper and I feel myself almost too drowsy to write as the words escape me. Since, by necessity, I am required to use barbaric names and narrate successively changing subjects, the connections in the body of the history and continuity of the narrative seem disjointed.

Let this be "no cause for anger"[55] among those who are well-disposed
toward the text.[56]

An emphasis on the laborious nature of the task of history was a common way
of enhancing the authority of the historian. Descriptions of the effort the historian lavished on his work seem to have been intended to reassure audiences
that the work has been done with care.[57] Here, by trying to get the audience to
sympathize with how hard she is working, Anna attempted to elicit good will
and create an audience that is well disposed toward her history.

In addition to humbling herself before her audience and allowing her
to perform femininity appropriately, Anna's lamentation and piteous self-
presentation have the further function of displaying her exceptional self-
control over her emotions and, hence, her ability to write dispassionate history.
Each departure from normal historical discourse gives her the opportunity
to show how she can regain her composure and return to a logical narrative.
Whenever Anna steps into the role of mournful widow, she steps out of the
role of historian. Each moment of feminine emotionalism provides an occasion to then exhibit masculine self-control.

Anna's breaks from the conventions of the historical genre can be striking. Anna's bursts of heightened grief can intrude jarringly on descriptions
of politics and battles. Ancient and medieval Greek historians were expected
to keep emotional distance from their subjects. Thucydides's and Xenophon's
manner of writing about their own actions in a detached third-person established a tradition of emotional dispassion, even when an author's loyalties
were clear. The distancing narrative voice of the historian is one of the key
characteristics that distinguishes history from tragedy.[58] Ancient historians
may appear in their histories to comment on the direction of the argument;
they may indicate their opinions regarding the course of events and the lessons to be drawn from history, but they rarely emote, let alone weep.[59] Readers
who have internalized the standard practices of the Greek historiographical
tradition would naturally feel a sense of disjuncture or impropriety at Anna's
outbursts. In that modern history also has aimed at dispassionate objectivity, we may be taken aback when Anna's weeping intrudes on the historical
narrative.

Anna carefully marks the points where she deviates from standard historical writing, overtly displaying her self-consciousness in leaving or returning to proper historical discourse. Anna lets us know every time she moves
away from historical discourse, displaying her knowledge of the form and
rules of historiography. In describing the death of her younger brother
Andronikos she says that "suffering forces me to sing a monody for him,
but the law of history pulls me back immediately."[60] At the mention of her
betrothed Constantine Doukas, she says, "I hold back the tear and store it up
'for the proper place,' lest mixing my monodies with historical narration, I

confuse the history."[61] In the passage discussed at length in chapter 3, about Alexios's narrow escape from capture after having been defeated by Robert Guiscard, Anna explains that weeping is inappropriate in history.[62] In each of these cases, Anna both begins a lament and then protests that she must stop lamenting in order proceed with writing history. Thus she calls attention precisely to how lamentation transgresses the rules of history.[63] By making her departures from historical writing so clear, she points out that she uses a standard historical voice most of the time.

Anna was fully cognizant that history has "laws" and that those laws forbade the expression of emotion. She advertises her view that history was not the place for speeches of praise or mourning.[64] Anna also marks her expressions of moral judgment and commentary as departures from true history. After expressing disapproval of the general Monomachos's betrayal, prior to the first battle of Dyrrachion, Anna says, "The horse of history got off the highway; I brought him back to the previous road, since he got out of hand."[65] When, in the course of discussing the teaching of Michael Italikos, Anna pauses to tell a story about her mother's study of theology, she opens the digression by remarking that the "laws" of rhetoric allow for an anecdote, and closes it by saying that she is pulled back from these reminiscences by the "law" of history.[66]

Anna also carefully marks her encomiastic speech as inappropriate for history. Anna nearly always tells us that she is breaking her own rules when she indulges in highly flattering descriptions. Anna generally claims not be do encomiastic speech at precisely those moments when she is caught lavishly praising her father, mother, and grandmother. Anna points out several situations where, in her view, she stops short of being encomiastic. In the opening of her description of Anna Dalassene, Anna says that if she were writing an encomium she would describe her grandmother's illustrious ancestors, but that she declines to do so because her subject is history. She explains that history does not characterize people by their ancestors or blood, but by their character and their virtue.[67] This is one of three instances where Anna reminds readers that she is not writing an encomium of her grandmother.[68] Anna asks her readers who know the great virtues of her grandmother Anna Dalassene to not blame her for giving only a shabby account of her grandmother's character. She excuses herself on the grounds that history is no place for an encomium.[69] Anna's account of Anna Dalassene here is in fact deeply flattering, to the extent of following some of the major features of an imperial panegyric. Her overt claims not to be speaking encomiastically do not hide her extravagant praise, but rather serve to bear witness that Anna knew she was her transgressing the normal rules of history.

Anna strongly affirms the connections made in her culture between rational dispassion and historical discourse, and between irrational emotionalism and feminine discourse. Anna presents her grief as a natural, reflexive response to death, but history as matter of intellectual deliberation. In the image of the undying fire of her mourning for Nikephoros, Anna uses vocabulary that emphasizes that grief and rational spoken discourse are incompatible. The funeral pyre of her grief is an "unspeakable burning" and an "unutterable pyre."[70] Later, at the memory of her betrothed Constantine, Anna's "reasoning is confused."[71] Grief is again a marker of irrationality at the death of Alexios, as Anna recalls that in her anguish she became disdainful of reason and philosophy.[72] She says she had become mad.[73] In these cases Anna's historical discourse is interrupted by lamentation that cannot be expressed through words. It cannot be part of a rational historical discourse because it is unspeakable, unutterable, inexpressible, and destructive of reason.

While Anna associates grief with irrationality, she considers history a discourse requiring reason. With the exception of the final pages of the *Alexiad*, every time Anna engages in lamentation she makes an explicit statement of her need or ability to stop lamenting in order to return to history. After the opening image of the funeral pyre of Anna's grief for her husband, she makes an explicit turn away from lamentation. Anna promises to pursue a "clearer and more historical discourse" henceforth.[74] Having acknowledged her particular grief, Anna asserts that she will dry her eyes to take up her task.[75] This act of drying her eyes and controlling her emotions to return to clear history is repeated in her laments for Constantine and Andronikos. Regarding Constantine, Anna both mourns and elaborates on her ability to curtail her mourning:

> I hold back the narrative about him, guarding everything for a fitting place. This only I cannot refrain from saying, even if I speak out of turn, this youth was a work of art.... And I am filled with tears remembering this youth after so many years. However I hold back the tear and store it up "for the proper place," lest mixing my monodies with historical narration, I confuse the history.[76]

Again Anna is forced by her pain to sing a monody for her brother but is pulled back by the "law of history."[77] Here she explicitly balances her need to express mourning with the need to write historically.

Anna thus indicates that the heightened emotionalism of a classical lamentation is something she can both start and stop. The explicit drying of eyes should be seen as standing testament to Anna's control over her own emotions. When Anna holds back her tears, she exercises strength and self-control—both paradigmatically masculine virtues. In presenting history as requiring a rational and dispassionate voice, Anna implicitly argues that history requires a masculine voice. In repeatedly emphasizing her ability to dry her eyes and put her natural emotions aside, Anna makes the case for her own ability to write in a masculine fashion. When saying that she will hold back her tears for Constantine "for the appropriate time," she uses a line from Demosthenes about doing everything in due course.[78] Demosthenes's line may have been proverbial by the twelfth century, but it may yet be significant that after the monody, Anna associates her actions with those of a male public actor. Anna's self-description, as drying her eyes to take on the straight road of history, calls attention to her ability to write dispassionate historical narration.

Just as by weeping Anna displays her proper performance of femininity, by overtly and explicitly stopping her lamentations, Anna performs masculine self-control, dispassion, and rationality. By doing so, Anna is claiming the ability to transcend her female nature. It was a common idea in Byzantine culture that individual women, through the exercise of emotional restraint, could transcend the limitations of their female nature to become more like men.[79] Anna's repeated practice of breaking out of the proper boundaries of history, breaking out of a masculinized historian's voice, to speak and participate in the discourses her culture marked as feminized, only to point out and apologize for her transgression, focuses attention both on her essentially female nature, and her ability to transcend that nature. She speaks as a woman who possessed the ability to control her natural emotionalism in order to write dispassionate history. She transgresses the law of history in order to highlight how much she maintains it. Once Anna's lamentations and expressions of devotion to her parents and husband are understood as the times when she was enacting proper female behavior, the masculinity of her discourse in other places becomes clearer.

The one scene where Anna does not pull herself back from lamentation is the final chapter of the *Alexiad* dealing with Alexios's death. She opens the chapter by remarking that henceforth, since she needs to write about the death of the emperor, she has a new "double task: to do history and tragedy at the same time."[80] She must "on the one hand . . . tell a history of his agony, on the other . . . sing a monody on what has wrung the heart."[81] Anna continues to say that her father often told her not to write a history of his deeds but to sing threnodies.[82] Alexios, she reveals at the end of her long history, never wanted a history about himself, but rather a song of lamentation. In the pages that follow, history and tragedy are mixed unapologetically. She goes "outside the bounds of history" again to talk in detail about Alexios's medical condition, using precise and detailed medical vocabulary that shows she can write like a doctor as well as a historian.[83] As the final chapter progresses, Anna, her two sisters, and her mother become increasingly hysterical as Alexios reaches his end, and the history becomes a description of lamenting women. Here Anna does not restrain lamentation to stay on the historical path, but allows history to give way to grief. The final paragraphs are pure tragedy, as Anna sings her father the threnody he asked for. Like the *Iliad*, the *Alexiad* ends in lamentation.

The text of these final paragraphs of the *Alexiad* is fragmentary because they were rarely copied and exist only in damaged manuscripts. A number of our medieval manuscripts stop short of Anna's ending.[84] Presumably the mournful song on the death of Alexios was seen as less central to the history by some of Anna's medieval readers. In a sense, the copyists who left the ending of the *Alexiad* out, because they did not see it as part of the history, were right. The history ended when Anna took her final turn to tragedy.

In portraying herself as a writer for whom lamentation was a natural, but controllable, impulse, Anna asserted a particularly female historical voice. As a woman—a natural, good, and proper woman—Anna grieved acutely and participated in long-standing traditions of female lamentation. Yet as a capable woman historian, she displayed her ability to recognize the irrationality of grief and control it. Anna marks the boundaries between the two discourses so carefully in order to show us that she was in control of her emotions. We can trust her when she writes historically because we witness her drying her eyes to take up the masculine task of history writing. The final, fully tragic paragraphs of the *Alexiad* naturally come across to us as self-pitying, yet the intention was to sing a proper funeral lament.

{ 5 }

Gathering Research without Leaving the House

Great historians of the ancient and medieval Greek world learned about events by being near the action. Whenever the historian could say, "I saw," his account was considered more reliable. If he could not be present, he ought to find people who had been and interview them, making up for his lack of direct familiarity with extensive research. Readers could trust his interpretations of his research because—even if he had not been at that particular battle or debate—he had experience with similar situations, and so understood them.[1] The good moral character of the historian convinced readers that he would not distort information, but rather provide an accurate appraisal of events.

So how was Anna supposed to convince her audience that her history was reliable, while simultaneously acting like a good woman who stayed at home and did not talk to men outside her family? Any claim Anna could make for traditional source gathering would involve her in potentially damaging participation in the public sphere or inappropriate conversations with men. If she did research, she would not have good moral character. Without good moral character, her audience could not be expected to trust her narrative, especially since her reliability was already challenged by her status as the daughter of her subject. She wrote under the constant suspicion of being a mere encomiast, which made it all the more important for her to substantiate the quality of the research. The accuracy of her research would uphold her history as reliable.

Anna needed to speak simultaneously with humility and authority when discussing her sources. She had to convince her audience that she had a robust and trustworthy basis of information underpinning her narrative, without which she could too easily be dismissed as her father's flatterer. On the other hand, she needed to maintain her feminine modesty and defend her moral reputation in light of undertaking the culturally transgressive activities involved in conducting research. This chapter explores Anna's attempts to deal with this conflict, first through her quotation of documents, and then in her description of her methods in book 14, where we see her most explicit effort to substantiate her historical research, as well as some of her most extreme self-abasement.

Anna's practice of document quotation may have been a way of modestly insisting on the accuracy of her material. While medieval Greek historians would commonly rework or copy passages from each other's histories, without attribution, Anna also engaged in a different kind of explicit, attributed quotation of whole documents, complete with their framing. Anna quotes a chrysobull Alexios wrote giving authority to his mother, Anna Dalassene, a letter Alexios wrote to Henry IV of Germany, and the text of the Treaty of Devol following Bohemond's defeat at the second battle of Dyrrachion in 1108.[2] These sections of the *Alexiad* are presented as texts written by others that she is quoting, and indeed differ enough from her style that they have been accepted as copies of real texts and have received treatment as independent sources.[3] Anna's practice of telling the audience that she was quoting a text, and presenting it as having been written by someone else, was not common among her contemporary Byzantine historians.[4]

The quotation of documents removes Anna's authorship from key moments in her history. Quotation can be a form of authorial self-effacement. Authors of hagiography can use quotation to shift the teaching of virtue from themselves onto their saintly subjects. By recording words attributed to another, they enact humility while engaging in moral instruction. Authority is ascribed, not to the author, but to the subject of the hagiography, whose words are quoted.[5] Similarly, Anna displaced these sections of her story onto other authors. Anna's quotations may be motivated by the desire to mitigate the potential arrogance of authorship. While she is quoting a text, Anna ceases to be the author and has no responsibility for the content of those texts.

Anna seems to quote documents at points where she had cause to write with particular authority. Especially in the cases of her grandmother's imperial power and Alexios's victory over Bohemond, Anna quoted documents when she may have wanted to be certain that her audience believed her. These were both situations where she may have reasonably thought that the audience would need extra convincing. The quotations of official documents function powerfully as an appeal to an external, unbiased authority.

For instance, Anna faced challenges in writing about the political and administrative activities of her grandmother, Anna Dalassene. After seizing the throne in 1081, Alexios entrusted all of the administration of the empire to his mother while he served as a field general. Anna Dalassene remained in power until sometime in the early twelfth century.[6] Given the political situation at the beginning of Alexios's reign, in which his hold on power was tenuous, his rivals many, and foreign enemies aggressive, it made a great deal of sense for him to leave the capital in the hands of a person he knew he could trust, his mother, while he devoted his time fully to military matters. The practical brilliance of this arrangement did not, however, make the political empowerment of a woman less problematic from the point of view of Byzantine conceptions of ideal gender roles. Dalassene's administration was harshly criticized, and Alexios was seen as weak because of his deference to his mother.[7]

Anna had reason therefore to describe her grandmother's power with great care. In presenting Anna Dalassene's authority over the administration, Anna quotes verbatim Alexios's chrysobull in which he gave his mother full control over domestic administration of the empire.[8] By including a direct quotation of imperial document, Anna attributes the authorship explicitly to her father. The male emperor is the person who describes the extraordinary authority given to a woman, not the female author. Anna's own descriptions of Anna Dalassene present her as humble, devoid of power lust, and practicing monastic simplicity.[9] It is not Anna, but her father's chrysobull that reveals the extent of Anna Dalassene's administrative and political authority.

The unprecedented divestment of power from an adult male emperor to his mother was such an unexpected move that people in later years could easily doubt that it had really happened. Anna relieves herself of the task of convincing her audience that she is telling the truth by having Alexios's chrysobull speak for her. The quotation of the document powerfully substantiates the validity of Anna's narrative.

Alexios's letter to Henry IV, in which he seeks to fortify an alliance against Robert Guiscard, reveals Alexios's conciliatory and flattering attitude toward a Western ruler as well as his own need to ask for help. The letter describes the arrangement negotiated between Alexios and Henry's envoys by which Alexios gives vast sums of money to Henry in return for his support. Alexios sent 144,000 pieces of gold and other precious gifts with the letter and promised another 216,000 after Henry had taken the oath. Alexios also suggested a possible marriage alliance through his nephew.[10] Anna does not comment on the content of the letter at all, but presents it as one of several steps Alexios took to combat the dangers besetting the empire at the moment he took power. The letter is striking in its display of money as a tool of Byzantine diplomacy. Alexios seems to dictate terms to Henry, and the description of the payment fundamentally casts Henry as Alexios's servant or mercenary. Anna may be holding up the letter as an example of how emperors ought to treat Western kings. On the other hand, if this arrangement was remembered as having been overly generous to Henry, without getting as much benefit as perhaps Alexios had hoped, quoting the text of the letter of absolved Anna of any need to critically describe her father's behavior. She does not need to comment on whether the treaty with Henry was a brilliant diplomatic move, or a tactical mistake, because readers are able to judge the matter for themselves.

The Treaty of Devol is quoted at another instance where Anna may have wished for her writing to be particularly strong. This treaty, which established the humiliation of Bohemond and the final victory of Alexios Komnenos over the Norman threat after the second battle of Dyrrachion in 1108, is a highpoint in the structure of Anna's narrative. It is her response to Alexios's great failure at the first battle of Dyrrachion in 1081. These two clashes are set up in her text as defining moments in Alexios's reign: in the first he is brought to the brink of ruin, but in the second he is completely victorious. Anna elides the characters of Robert Guiscard and his son Bohemond so that they serve as a single grand nemesis to Alexios throughout the *Alexiad*.[11] Alexios's first loss against Robert is more than redeemed in his victory over Bohemond.

Anna's direct quotation of the treaty strikingly establishes the depth of this victory. For this victory to have the rhetorical effect she desires in the overall structure of the *Alexiad*, Anna needs her readers to appreciate its implications in a forceful manner. Quoting the text of the treaty allows all of its details to be known without asking readers to trust Anna's representation. The text of the treaty substantiates Alexios's victory in a more authoritative way than any claim Anna could have made.

The quotation of documents from the imperial archives also proves that Anna had privileged access to information about her subject, and hence possessed one of the qualifications necessary to be a reliable historian. Anna's presentation of these documents exhibits her ability to access sound information. Her inquiry is based on substantive material. This access to imperial documents makes a rich display of Anna's position within the imperial court and, with it, her own power and authority. While the quotation of documents removes Anna's agency as author, it thus simultaneously presents her narrative as authoritative. In a strong way, the presentation of primary sources substantiates Anna's status as a good historian.

In addition to establishing her authority, Anna's quotation of documents helps elicit trust in her portrayal while avoiding making aggrandizing claims. Since Anna claims no authorship over the contents and serves as a mere copyist, no glory is reflected on her by either her father's victories or her grandmother's power. The audience did not need to take Anna's word for the extraordinary extent of Dalassene's authority or Alexios's victory because they could see the evidence for themselves.

Anna takes up the issue of her sources and research practices explicitly in a passage in book 14 that has long been considered her statement on methods.[12] This discussion of methodology is not at the opening of the history, where it would be more expected, but near the end. It occurs after Anna has veered into an encomiastic summary of her father's virtues that prompts her to turn yet again to the problematic of impartiality and thence to a description of her sources for writing history. Anna reveals that she did in fact rely on the traditional historical methods of speaking with old veterans and collecting written narratives to gather information for her history. Yet she intersperses her descriptions of her sources and assertions that she has conducted research with overwrought outbursts of her feminized discourse of piteousness, claiming solitude and personal tragedy.

Anna's explanation of her methods is thus deliberately contradictory. Since the discussion of historical method is fundamentally aggrandizing and masculinizing, Anna splices it together with self-deprecating and feminizing statements. While the discussion of sources substantiates her claim to be a good historian, and fundamentally participates in male historical discourse, her mournful asides humble her and place her in the female role of piteous widow. Here we see Anna's attempt to build an authorial persona that, on the one hand, was strong, impartial, intellectual, accurate, driven by research, trustworthy, and authoritative, and on the other, female, modest, devoted, and humble.

Anna is prompted to discuss her historical sources because she indulges in one of the most straightforwardly encomiastic descriptions of Alexios in her history. Anna explains how after a victory over the Turks, Constantinople was full of the news of his successes. She then claims that Alexios dealt with a greater number of difficulties and enemies than any previous Roman emperor. She describes how the empire during Alexios's reign was attacked on all sides, and how, in contrast to previous emperors, he did not deal with one difficulty at a time, but rather was forced to deal continuously with multiple invasions and disasters.[13] Anna makes the case that therefore Alexios should be considered the greatest Roman emperor ever.

This clear, exuberant praise for Alexios's virtues and skills as a ruler raises the specter of partiality and the accusation that Anna was writing a panegyric rather than a history. Anna therefore turns from praise for her father to a discussion of her historical methods. She begins by addressing directly the charge that she flatters her father:

> But perhaps someone coming to this point in the history would say that my tongue had been corrupted by nature in the composition. By the dangers of the emperor for the good of the Romans, by the contests and sufferings he endured for the Christians, I swear I do not favor my own father in the things I say and write! Rather when I see that he fell, I straightaway transgress the natural law and cling to the truth; holding him with love, but having greater love for truth. For when two things are dear to us, as some philosopher said, we should prefer truth more. Rather I speak and write following the events themselves, neither adding anything of my own nor plucking out events.[14]

Anna acknowledges that by nature she ought to support her father and only speak about him favorably, and she proclaims her enduring love for him. Yet Anna willingly transgresses the "natural law," according to which she would whitewash her father's history, in order to follow Aristotle's dictum and uphold the truth.[15]

While her willingness to subvert traditional female behavior of devotion to family is the key to substantiating her claim to impartiality, it creates an additional problem for her efforts to construct a positive female authorial persona. As we saw in chapter 3, devotion and affection to parents was a key moral virtue for women, and one that is central to her self-presentation in the preface to her will, and in several passages in the *Alexiad*. To counter the negative effects of the dispassionate, detached, unnaturally cold aspects of her authorial persona, Anna takes great pains to establish an additional authorial stance in which she is a deeply affectionate and devoted daughter.

Although Anna takes an oath here, swearing that she does not favor her father, she seems to recognize that this proclamation of her impartiality is insufficient to win the trust of her audience. Consequently, she then turns to a discussion of how she established the truth of her narrative. The discussion of her sources serves to substantiate the validity of her history and to fend off the accusation of authorial bias.

Anna begins the discussion of her sources by pointing out the relative proximity of the events she describes. Since she is writing nearly contemporary history, it is still possible to find people living who could witness to the events of Alexios's reign:

> And the refutation is at hand: because I do not take up writing about things that happened 10,000 years ago. Rather there are some people around today who both had known my father and tell me things about him; from them not a small part of the history here was contributed, one narrating and remembering one thing and another something else of what happened to each of them, with everyone concurring.[16]

This claim to have gathered information from living witnesses strongly authorizes Anna's history. On a simple level it substantiates Anna's claim to have good information. Since the interrogation of participants was a standard element of traditional historical methodology, it also serves to place her firmly in the Greek historiographical tradition.[17]

Anna next makes a claim for the direct experience that was the single most important way for historians to craft their authority. Historians have the greatest authority to narrate events in which they themselves have participated. Anna tries to give herself just this sort of authority when she claims to have accompanied her father and mother on their travels: "For the most part we were with and we accompanied our father and mother. For it was not our lot to be raised close to home, in the shade, with delicacy."[18] Anna here reveals that she did not live a cloistered life in the palace, but traveled with her parents, on what presumably were military campaigns. This repeats an earlier fleeting assertion that she had accompanied her father on campaigns.[19]

This claim to have learned about Alexios's activities from her own experience, and to have written history on the basis of personal observation is strongly authorizing. These two claims—that she talked to living witnesses, and that she left her home to go on campaign—are powerful in substantiating her ability to write history, but also transgressive for a woman. Both actions are fundamentally immodest and do not conform to the norms for appropriate behavior for upper-class medieval Greek women. Presumably, Anna did not stress her personal experience on campaign more strongly, because traveling outside the home was considered inappropriate behavior for a woman of her stature.

Anna was deeply apologetic when discussing her mother's habit of accompanying Alexios while he went on campaign. Her treatment of this issue shows how immodest some of her contemporaries thought it was for Eirene to leave the palace.[20] Anna excuses her mother's behavior on the grounds that she needed to care for her husband as his health declined.[21] She also insists that Eirene was overcome with modesty every time she needed to appear in public ceremony, far preferring to stay at home reading hagiography and practicing charity.[22] By presenting her mother's deeds as acts of devotion, Anna seems to offer excuses for behavior that some thought broke with the ideal seclusion of women. Anna's attempts to explain, and even valorize, her mother's behavior testify to the prevailing cultural stance that it was not appropriate for women to venture outside of their domestic sphere.

Given this prevailing attitude, Anna's revelation that she herself left the palace to accompany her father and mother creates a serious problem for Anna's self-presentation as a respectable woman, even as it helps her to solve the problem of historical authorization. Not surprisingly, Anna immediately backs away from her masculinizing, transgressive discourse and makes a play for the pity and indulgence of her audience. The moment after she utters the claim to write on the authority of personal observation and the interrogation of witnesses, she pivots to humble herself before her audience. To do this she turns again to the strategy of telling a tale of woe:

> But from my swaddling clothes, I swear by God and his mother, I have received continual pains and afflictions and misfortunes, some from outside the home, and some from within. Those I have had from my body, I wish not to describe; let the people in the women's chambers talk repeatedly about them. Those from outside, how many befell me not yet at my eighth year, and how many enemies the malice of men raised up against me, would need the Siren of Isocrates to tell, or the grandiloquence of Pindar, the rushing of Polemon, the Kaliope of Homer, the

lyre of Sappho, or some other power beyond these. For there is nothing terrible, either small or large, or near or far, that did not fall heavily immediately against me. Aye, the wave rose above undoubtedly, and from then until now and until where I write these words, the sea of sorrows has howled at me and still wave overtakes wave. But I forgot, swept away in my own troubles. Now then, coming to my senses I will swim again upstream, as it were, and I return to the first topic.[23]

Anna here, caught up in her troubles, makes a plea for her audience to pity her as one who has suffered great misfortunes. The intended effect of gaining sympathy and pity is designed, I believe, to mitigate the effrontery of Anna's claim to write history from the standpoint of questioning witnesses and personal observation.

Anna declines to say what any of these misfortunes were. The matters of her body she leaves for people in the women's quarters to gossip about. This could plausibly be an allusion to the deaths of at least three of her children, but Anna provides no hints to guide speculation. She is more expansive about how bad the problems from outside the home were, claiming that their description would be beyond the power of the greatest rhetoricians, but again she leaves the audience wondering what they were.

Scholars have connected Anna's statement that she had suffered a disaster before her eighth birthday to Zonaras's statement that her betrothed Constantine Doukas was deprived of his purple shoes and removed from the succession. The misfortune she mentions here is seen as the removal of her future husband from the line of succession, and Anna's eighth birthday is used to date Constantine's demotion.[24] This is a reasonable supposition if one approaches the matter looking for a single event that could explain Anna's self-presentation as suffering in this passage. Yet when Anna's expressions of tragedy are seen as aiming to defuse accusations of self-aggrandizement, the connection with Constantine's demotion seems far less likely.

Anna's literal claim is that it would take superhuman rhetorical skill to describe how many misfortunes befell her, and how many enemies rose against her, even *before* her eighth year, starting when she was a baby. So finding one traumatic event that took place in her eighth year would not be sufficient to give her lament a specific literal interpretation. Rather it seems that Anna was referring to the close of a distinct phase of early childhood in Byzantine culture. The passage from early childhood to pre-adolescence, reckoned as taking place at age seven, was considered a major transition with educational and legal implications.[25] Anna laments the torrent of troubles that befell her even while she was a young child, starting in the cradle and even before she left childhood, and continuing throughout her life.

Anna's expression of personal tragedy has a clear and important rhetorical function in that it humbles Anna before her audience and attempts to elicit pity. It is an effort to render her masculinizing claims to historical observation and interrogation of witnesses less obnoxious to her contemporaries. The rhetorical function, and indeed the rhetorical necessity, of her expression of tragedy is sufficient to explain why it is there. It is possible that Anna had Constantine's demotion in mind when she wrote about the afflictions that constantly beset her life, but at no point in the *Alexiad* does she even allude to that event. Her claim was that she had experienced continual misfortunes from the time of her birth. If we are to look for a real event that Anna was thinking of in saying that she experienced troubles before her eighth year, are we also to look for real events that caused Anna trouble when she was in her swaddling clothes? Anna needed to present herself as having suffered horrible things regardless of whether she actually had a miserable childhood or not.

After the outburst of personal lamentation that constructs Anna as an object of pity, she quickly returns to the topic at hand: her historical sources. The rapidity with which she moves from the discussion of sources to personal tragedy and back again, fuels the impression that her recitation of personal tragedies was an aside, a necessary declaration of piteousness in the midst of an authorizing and masculinizing discussion of historical sources:

> Some (material) then, as was said, I have from myself, and other material from the fellow-soldiers of the emperor, learning frequently from them and from some messengers bringing news of the things that were happening in the wars to us, but more often I heard the emperor and George Palaiologos describing them in person.[26]

Here Anna reiterates her claim to have learned from personal observation and from witnesses, and reveals other sources of her information. The couriers she describes as bringing material about the wars presumably brought either oral or written messages to the palace. If they were written documents, Anna may still have had access to them as she wrote decades later. Anna further asserts that she heard stories directly from her father and her uncle, George Palaiologos.

To these sources of information that were contemporaneous with Alexios's reign, Anna adds a second set of sources she gathered long after Alexios's death. Anna emphasizes her own role in gathering this information:

> In this way I collected much of my material, and best of all in the reign of the third emperor after my father, when all flattery and lies about his grandfather had faded away, everyone flattering the one sitting on the throne, no one exhibiting flattery toward the departed, the events were laid bare and told just as they had happened.[27]

The accent on Anna's own role in collecting the information highlights the effort she put into getting the story right. Claims that the historian has gone to considerable trouble to collect accurate information are normal in the Greek historiographical tradition.[28] Anna's emphasis that she conducted most of her research during the reign of Manuel (1143–1180) works to insulate her history from accusations of flattery and bias. Since she gathered information in the era when everyone was trying to flatter Manuel, and no longer cared about Alexios, she was able to get the pure, true story about her father's reign.

Anna thus claims to have gotten information both through her personal observations and memories of conversations she experienced when her father was alive, and to have searched for information later, nearer the time of composition. This gathering of information implies active research on Anna's part; and with it conversations with men who would have been able to provide it. The natural implication that Anna spent considerable time talking and interacting with men to whom she was not related prompts her to make counterclaims about her own isolation. At just the moment when the audience could be imagined as wondering how she conducted the interviews and interacted with men in gathering stories, Anna turns the audience's attention back to her own piteousness and the isolation of her widowhood:

> But I, lamenting bitterly my own misfortunes, mourning for all time three emperors, the father and autocrator, and my lady, mother and empress and, ah me!, my husband the Caesar, I stay secluded mostly and I am devoted to books and God, and not even will it be allowed for the more obscure among men and those of my father's familiars to visit us so that we are not able to learn what they have heard from others.[29]

Here Anna makes strong claims for her own isolation and proper seclusion from the public sphere and worldly matters. Anna asserts that she stays secluded and devotes herself to books and God because of her mourning for her parents and her husband.

Anna's statement that she mourns three emperors, namely her father, her mother, and her husband, has been given a political reading. Anna's choices of whom to include in this list have been seen as an effort to exclude John from Alexios's legacy.[30] This reading interprets the purpose of the list as a statement of political succession. If Anna were naming the emperors who followed Alexios, then the inclusion of her mother and husband needs as much explanation as the exclusion of her brother. Rather the list serves to allow Anna to project a certain emotional state, and hence define who she is. Alexios, Eirene, and Nikephoros are chosen, of all the people Anna may have mourned, in part because her relationship with them defined her as daughter and wife. Her mourning of her parents and husband casts her in the praiseworthy women's roles of devoted daughter and loving wife. In that it aligns her with expectations for good female behavior, this expression of devotion helps reassert Anna's virtue and modesty. While her claims to active research pull her out of the domestic sphere, her protestations of devotion to her primary role as daughter and wife shore up her self-construction as a virtuous woman.

Her second reason for isolation is that her father's familiars, and "the more obscure men among men," are not allowed to visit her. This claim that Anna lives a life of seclusion, even forced seclusion, contradicts the implication that her research involved her in conversations with strangers. Her self-presentation as a pious, mourning widow—who is not able to talk to even very obscure people—is logically inconsistent with her claims to have conducted research. Yet she is not making a logical argument so much as trying to use her own story of piteous isolation to drown out the thought that she was engaged in inappropriate conversations. While the identities of the hidden men are unclear, Anna next elaborates on her isolation from her father's men:

> For in thirty years, I swear on the soul of the blessed autocrator, I have not seen, I have not looked at, have not spoken with my father's people, as on the one hand many have passed away, while on the other many have been confined by fear. For those in power condemned us to obscurity for these aberrations, but we are hated by the majority.[31]

The condemnation in the last line is usually taken as referring to Anna personally, but Anna switches suddenly here to masculine plural grammar, suggesting that the condemnation applies to Anna and an unspecified group of men. Anna's prose is obscure here, and I see the ambiguity as motivated by a desire to claim greater isolation than she in fact experienced. Throughout the *Alexiad* Anna does not switch randomly from talking about herself as a feminine "I" to a masculine "we." She uses a plural for herself as a guide to the historical narration, in phrases such as "we shall see," or "let us return," and a singular for her normal voice of self-expression. Only very rarely, in a large work, does she use masculine grammar for herself.[32] In this passage her feminine singular voice mingles with the masculine plural "us." People cannot visit "us," "we are hated," but "I lament," "I mourn." She is vaguely associating herself here with some other group that may include her companions in prayer, or the whole group of Alexios's old supporters, or everyone out of favor at the current court. I see the emphasis falling on isolation from the halls of power, fitting with her argument that her history is unbiased because nobody cares about Alexios anymore.

This claim of isolation serves both Anna's construction of herself as an object of pity and the substantiation of her sources' purity. Since she has not been talking with her father's close supporters, her information is not swayed by their loyalty for Alexios, nor can she be she deceived by their courtly rhetoric. Anna's insistence on her isolation from Alexios's supporters corroborates her next point: that her information came from simple soldiers and the eyewitness testimony of ordinary men.

Anna's claims to isolation are revealed as limited, if not entirely rhetorical fiction, by the following sentence in which she is back to talking with lots of male strangers for the sake of historical research. Unlike her father's men, these men were simple and artless:

> By God, by his transcendent mother and my mistress, that which I have collected for the history, I collected from some entirely unfitting and un-learned compositions and from some old men who served in the army at the time my father held the scepters of the Romans, who, having been assailed by misfortunes, then changed from worldly tumult to the peaceful state of monks. For the writings falling into my hands were simple and artless in expression and keeping to truth and they displayed no cleverness nor slurred rhetorical barbs.[33]

The lack of rhetorical skill among these soldiers, who had become monks, helps Anna substantiate that she got her information from reliable sources. By emphasizing the simplicity and artlessness of the texts she collected, Anna denies the influence of encomia, laudatory histories, and other high court rhetoric that would have presented Alexios's actions in glowing terms. The oral testimony of the old men is declared to be similarly plain, and hence truthful. Anna emphasizes the simplicity of the sources she received in order to demonstrate that they were free of bias in the first place. That the men she spoke with were monks perhaps enhances the trustworthiness of their stories, and lessens the impropriety of Anna's conversations with them.

Anna ends this discussion of her sources by summarizing how she ascertained the truth about Alexios's deeds through a process of comparing and crosschecking the written and oral sources she collected, with what she had learned directly from her father and her uncles:

> The detailed narrations of the old men were the same as the writings in word and meaning; and I judged the truth of the history from them, collecting and comparing the things I had learned myself with those things they told me, and the things they told me with what I had from frequently listening to my father and from my uncles on my mother and father's side. From all these things the body of the truth was woven together.[34]

This final summary statement places Anna's methodology firmly within the best practices of Greek historiography.[35] She has gathered information both from her own experience, through discussions with men who had been on Alexios's campaigns, and through the collection of other written accounts. She has avoided gathering the testimony of people who would be naturally biased, yet she draws on sources that are well placed to understand Alexios's reign.[36]

On the whole, Anna's description of her sources and methodology makes a strong case for her authority as a historian, the validity of her history, and her ability to participate in the masculine tradition of Greek historiography. It is the very strength and audacity of these claims, I believe, that prompts Anna to play simultaneously the piteous, lonely widow. She certainly jumps back and forth between the roles of miserable widow and authorized historian with remarkable speed and agility. The main topic is clearly her various methods for gathering valid historical data. Her bursts of lamentation, self-pity, and claims of isolation unexpectedly disrupt that methodological discussion. Whenever the audience might be tempted to see Anna as intellectually arrogant, immodest in her behavior, or flouting traditional norms of womanly conduct, she pauses to abase herself before the audience by becoming a subject of pity, or to claim a more appropriate level of social seclusion. These interjections seem designed to shift the emotional effect of this discussion on Anna's audience.

Within Anna's text, this discussion serves to explain her sources and substantiate her ability to write an accurate, factual history. Yet this passage has been used as a key text for establishing Anna's biography. The statement that she was isolated for thirty years and was condemned to this isolation by those in authority has been taken as evidence that John had sentenced her to an internal exile of monastic confinement following the failure of her attempt to seize imperial power in 1118. In fact, as we shall see in chapter 8, the whole story of Anna's forced monastic retirement hinges on this statement. The claim of isolation however, falls between two statements about how she gathered her information, both of which imply contact with men. Anna's ambiguous use of the masculine plural makes it difficult to see the condemnation as referring only to Anna.

Anna's description of her isolation from her father's old friends functions in her text to support her impartiality: she did not get her information from biased sources or courtiers, but from simple old monks. Further, the condemnation to obscurity separates Anna and her companions from the seat of power, and hence the major source of bias and flattery. By thus presenting herself as removed from power, Anna makes clear that she could be an impartial historian. Through this description she asserts that she did not get information from those who would flatter her father; they are all disregarded by those in power and disdained by the masses. Her claims of isolation also help efface the social transgression of her conversations with men to whom she was not related. As explained above, Anna's point is that she lives a secluded life and is a proper, morally upstanding woman.

The humbling, feminizing, and isolating interjections Anna splices into her description of her historical methods cause internal inconsistencies, and do not always make much sense in themselves. The claim that she has constantly been beset by waves of misfortunes since her infancy can hardly receive a rational, factual explanation. Anna's statements about her degree of isolation are not consistent with her stated methodology for gathering sources. The coherence of these statements, however, seems to be less important than how they make Anna's audience feel about her. Understanding how the various statements fit within the overarching rhetorical goals of Anna's history can help us see why she made such extraordinary and contradictory statements. We do not need to look for real events in her life to explain them.

In Anna's detailed discussion of her sources in book 14, and her choice to occasionally quote her source texts directly, we can see her responding to some of the challenges of female historical authorship identified in chapter 1. Anna was fully capable of examining written narratives and interviewing veterans to compare with her own experiences and memories in order to create a reliable historical narrative. Some of those activities, however, required her to step outside of the culturally expected seclusion of Greek aristocratic women in the domestic sphere. However real or illusory that seclusion was in Anna's society, its maintenance was seen as an important aspect of a good woman's behavior. While the reality of Anna's life may have been that she accompanied her father on campaign, and interviewed retired soldiers about their experiences, she did not want to be seen as having exercised such a degree of license in her personal interactions. Anna thus weaves exclamations of piteousness and claims of modest seclusion into the description of her historical method. Yet the antagonisms inherent in these stances are not resolved because, while she may have wished her audience to think that she was truly cloistered, she simultaneously needed to assure the audience that she used proper historical method. The tragic self-presentation humbles her before her audience, while her claims to proper research methods authorize her history.

PART II

A Power-Hungry Conspirator?

Deathbed Dramas

If the last five chapters were convincing, you might be surprised that Anna comes across in Byzantine scholarship as an ambitious and arrogant woman who desperately wanted to rule the empire. Clearly her self-presentation as modest, demure, and sympathetic has not stuck. Rather her life is seen as consumed by her efforts to rule in place of her brother John. Anna is considered the mastermind behind an abortive coup against her brother at the moment of their father's death in 1118, and then a conspiracy to have her husband, Nikephoros, murder John, which failed at the last minute because Nikephoros did not participate. After this failure she is thought to have been forced to retire to a monastery where she languished, continually nursing her grudge against her brother, until her death decades later.

This story is precisely what Anna was trying to avoid—it makes her look like she had a great desire for personal power, born of vanity and self-aggrandizement, as well as lack of natural familial affection, and a transgressive lack of deference to John's male authority. The modern story about Anna is the *exact* opposite of how she wanted to be seen. She worked to avoid being considered arrogant, ambitious, and unnaturally cold to her family. So we have to ask whether there are connections between her negative portrayal in scholarship and the cultural challenges Anna faced in trying to write history. Did her efforts to counteract the transgressive, masculinizing self-aggrandizement of a woman writing history work? Or, more pointedly, how much of the modern narrative has arisen because her efforts to be perceived as a virtuous woman in the *Alexiad* failed?

Now it is possible that while she tried to *appear* humble and modest in her writing, in *reality* she was ready to murder her brother to rule the empire. If we had strong contemporary evidence for Anna's ambition and desire for authority, this would be a reasonable conclusion. As it happens, the only medieval source that speaks to Anna's ambition was written about forty years after her death by Niketas Choniates, who most likely had read the *Alexiad*. What if her efforts to be modest did not work and Choniates thought she was arrogant and power-hungry because she had written a history? Beyond the medieval sources, if modern scholars reading the *Alexiad* did not perceive her techniques for appearing humble and demure (and they mostly did not), they would naturally read the evidence already thinking that Anna was the kind of woman who would want to rule—that it was just the sort of thing a woman like that would do.

With fragmentary and complex medieval evidence, it is easy and natural for your prior assumptions to shape what you think you are looking at. So we have to ask how much of the standard narrative about Anna is based on firm evidence, and how much is due to looking at that evidence with the assumption that Anna was arrogant, unfeminine, and unnaturally concerned with things outside of the female sphere. The core of the modern narrative about Anna first took shape in the eighteenth century, based on a small fraction of the evidence now available. Substantial advances in our understanding of Byzantine culture and history allow for markedly different readings of the medieval evidence than were possible 240 years ago. The story that Anna led a revolt is so old that it has become a "fact" that all Byzantinists know without giving it much thought.

In the next few chapters we will look at depictions of Anna's character and evidence about the politics surrounding John's succession in 1118. We do not have enough information about Byzantine politics to know absolutely who did what during the tense transition of power from Alexios to John. As we shall see, the most contemporaneous source, that of John Zonaras, gives us the most ambiguous account. Scholars differ in how much they trust medieval texts. Some are happy to dismiss stories in medieval histories as most probably completely made up, whereas others steadfastly uphold the idea that, however elaborate the rhetoric, a grain of truth stands behind the tale. Ultimately your judgment about what happened is the only one that should matter to you. The presentation of evidence in the following chapters should help you draw your own conclusions.

The question of what happened on August 15, 1118 is, however, secondary to our goal of understanding whether perceptions of Anna have been shaped by the cultural challenges she faced in writing history as a woman. We are hence looking to see how Anna's character is depicted in medieval texts and how much the modern narrative of Anna is grounded in accurate assessments of medieval evidence. We will begin with the medieval narratives that give our clearest picture of imperial politics.

One of the major sources used to reconstruct Anna's life is the history of the jurist and author John Zonaras, written around the middle of the twelfth century.[1] Zonaras criticizes Alexios's reign, but also sometimes presents him as a good and effective leader. Anna appears briefly, and positively, in Zonaras's history. She is present primarily as an intellectual rather than as an aspirant to political power or as an author.

Zonaras explains that as Alexios's health declined, he gave authority to his wife, Eirene, sparking a rivalry between Eirene and their son John, who had been crowned co-emperor years earlier. Tension grew as John was sidelined because Eirene was managing imperial administration herself. Zonaras says that Eirene was so powerful that "even her son and Emperor was subordinate to her."[2] Zonaras explains that this subservience to his mother was "intolerable" for John because he was already a grown man who had a wife and children.[3] Independence from maternal authority was a key aspect of male adulthood. He came to fear for his rule, and his life, because he saw his mother "displaying great affection for her oldest daughter and son-in-law Bryennios."[4] John called on his supporters to renew the oaths they had made that they would accept no one else as emperor after his father's death.[5] This angered Eirene, who had John followed by spies and attempted to forbid contact with him.[6] While most of his relatives supported John, his younger brother Andronikos opposed him.[7]

Later Zonaras describes Eirene as having a strong preference for Anna's husband, Nikephoros Bryennios:

> The empress was extremely powerful. Much power also belonged to her son-in-law Caesar Bryennios, and the whole palace administration was decreed through him. For this reason everyone was attached to him. The giving of justice was entrusted to him, and he was governing imperially.[8]

Zonaras's description of Eirene's preference for Nikephoros also includes his only mention of Anna:

> The man was inclined to learning and his wife no less, if not more than he, for she clung to education in words and had a tongue that atticised accurately and a mind most sharp for higher theory. She added to her natural intelligence through study. She was engrossed by books and learned men, and spoke with them not superficially.[9]

This is hardly a negative assessment of Anna. Zonaras may have included these positive statements about the extent and seriousness of Anna's intellectual endeavors because he thought they were worthy of historical record. Embedded as they are in the discussion of Nikephoros's influence, they may serve to explain Nikephoros's popularity.[10] The admiration for Nikephoros is presented as a problem for John equal to that of his mother's opinions.[11] Zonaras does not provide any hints about what Alexios may have thought of all this.

Zonaras interrupts the story of familial tension for a digression on storm-damage to Constantinople and a narrative about Alexios personally returning to the field to defeat a Turkish incursion.[12] This story, in which Alexios is victorious mostly because of the fear he inspired in his enemies, presents him in a highly favorable light. Zonaras creates a provident, caring, and thoroughly imperial characterization of Alexios working to settle refugees displaced by the Turkish invasion. The effect is to highlight the contrast with the stories of invidious familial infighting. Alexios appears at his most regal in these accounts of his campaigns that interpose Zonaras's stories of familial tension.

As his narrative returns to the palace, Zonaras's focus returns to the story of tension between Eirene and John: "The empress reigned, and she was expected to usurp the autarchy. Yet her son and emperor did not acquiesce, but struggled in all sorts of ways against his mother's apparent attempt."[13] Zonaras thus presents Eirene as attempting to seize control for herself, rather than on behalf of Nikephoros or her daughter. Zonaras then describes the course of Alexios's illness and the various methods his doctors attempted, including cauterizing his throat with a burning iron and moving him from the Great Palace to the Mangana Palace, which was thought to have better air.

Zonaras creates a pathetic portrait of Alexios as a dying man. Although his doctors had acknowledged that their efforts were fruitless, some monks were said to have deceived Alexios into thinking that he would not die before he saw Jerusalem, thus leaving Alexios unprepared for his end. Alexios spent his last day laboring to breathe while surrounded by his grieving wife and daughters. Zonaras's detailed description of the late afternoon position of the sun at the moment when John came to his father on the day of Alexios's death serves to point out John's absence from his father's bedside throughout the difficult day Alexios spent struggling to breathe.[14] Zonaras continues more critically to say that John did not come to mourn his father's passing, but merely to verify that he was dying. John left immediately, followed by many of the people who had been attending Alexios. Upon leaving the Mangana Palace, John met and was immediately acclaimed by a delegation from Abasgia who were bringing into Constantinople the girl betrothed to Nikephoros and Anna's older son.[15]

Zonaras then begins a series of vignettes he presents as competing versions of what happened by Alexios's deathbed. The first report is this:

> They say the empress excitedly told the dying emperor about the departure of his son, but he uttered nothing about it; either not wanting to, or unable, but raised his hands high; I do not know whether was to pray for his son or to curse him.[16]

Here Eirene is presented as wanting to incite her husband against her son, but Alexios's response was highly ambiguous. The emperor's gesture of raising his hands could be equally a blessing or a curse, and Zonaras does not attempt to guess which. The next story is a variation of the first:

But others say the dying one did not raise his hands, since he was unable and already failing. But as the empress was continually crying, "Your son goes off taking the empire while you are still living," he was smiling briefly and faintly, or laughing at the idea that he would think to worry about the empire when breathing his last and already departing from earthly matters, or preparing the final disposition of his soul.[17]

This version also presents Eirene as rebuking John, but has Alexios too weak to move and past caring about temporal power. It is more favorable to Alexios, showing him as focused on spiritual matters. Like the first story, it leaves readers wondering whether Alexios approved or disapproved of John's actions. The third story is presented as having been circulated by John:

> For note, it was said by others, and by the *porphyrogennetos* emperor [John] himself, that he did not prepare for himself the passage to the empire without a paternal approval, but he was enjoined by his father to the procession and to take his father's ring from him as a token; but this happened when the empress was not present and not knowing that they had done it.[18]

This third story would need to be placed at a different time from the others, if Zonaras intends his audience to believe his first statement that Eirene and her daughters constantly attended Alexios during his last day. Zonaras presents all three versions as stories some people tell, refusing to endorse the factuality of any of them. Together the stories present a wide range of possibilities, from Alexios cursing his son, to privately giving John a token of succession. They present the question of whether Alexios approved of his son's succession as a matter of ongoing gossip and rumor.

Zonaras next tells how John gathered supporters as he moved across town, but was blocked from entering the Great Palace by the Varangian guards. In response John sent someone to ask the guards what they wanted and sent another person to the Great Church, bringing the message that the emperor had died. John was quickly acclaimed by the clergy, but the Varangians said that they would not yield the palace while the emperor lived. The messenger affirmed to the Varangians that the emperor had died, and then at their insistence, swore an oath to that effect. This double narrative, with messengers interacting with two different key constituencies, has the effect of telling the story of John's perjury twice. John then enters the palace where he is said to take council about what he ought to do in regard to his mother, siblings, and especially his brother-in-law: "Since he had been afraid of them and fearing them perhaps to start a revolution, they were in held in suspicion."[19] Nothing is said about what he decided to do about them however. After the description of John worrying in the palace, Zonaras turns to Alexios's death, not to return to John and his relationship with Eirene and Nikephoros.

Alexios died around evening. Zonaras says that he completed his reign successfully, but not so his death, because he was abandoned by nearly all of his servants, so that there was hardly anyone to give his body a final bath or adorn it in a manner befitting an emperor. Zonaras says that Alexios also did not succeed in managing a smooth transfer of power, even though he was succeeded by his own son, whom he had honored as an emperor.[20] Zonaras takes this as a reminder that nothing in human life is steadfast or stable, and turns to a final evaluation of Alexios's reign and the conclusion of his history.

While neither Eirene nor John looks particularly good in this account, Zonaras does not treat one more harshly than the other. John is portrayed as the victim of his mother's plotting, but his own character does not receive favorable treatment in Zonaras's hands. He nowhere appears in the stories of Alexios's campaigns. Zonaras usually refers to John as emperor in his narrative of Alexios's reign, but he offers no explanation for why Alexios did not enlist his son's help with governing when his health failed. Alexios seems to have had opportunities to promote John's cause that he did not take. In allowing Eirene to manage imperial administration during his illness, Alexios did not give that same power to his son. Zonaras provides no explicit condemnation of Eirene's preference for Nikephoros. It is possible to read Zonaras's narrative and wonder if Alexios himself did not trust his son.

Both Anna and her husband, Nikephoros, are remarkably absent from Zonaras's history. Nikephoros appears as a competent and popular figure put into position of administrative authority by Eirene. After Alexios's final campaign, Eirene is said to have been suspected of trying to usurp rule. The common interpretation that she intended the usurpation for her daughter has been added by modern historians. The detail that John was first acclaimed by the entourage of Nikephoros's future daughter-in-law undercuts any idea of Nikephoros actively working to effect an usurpation. This group would have been highly incentivized to see Nikephoros succeed to the throne, because the girl in their charge would then be the daughter-in-law of the emperor rather than a member of the extended imperial family. Whatever Nikephoros was doing on Alexios's final day, he was not canvassing for supporters among his natural allies, according to Zonaras.

Anna is only mentioned tangentially as Nikephoros's wife. While she was presumably included among the daughters gathered around Alexios on his final day, she plays no individuated role. John is described as fearing his mother because she was showing off Anna and Nikephoros.[21] The idea that Anna was the chief conspirator clearly does not originate in Zonaras's history. His history is ambiguous, casting a negative gaze on John, as well as on Eirene and Alexios. His multiple stories of Alexios's deathbed present the succession as a matter of ongoing rumor. None of the rumors Zonaras reports, however, implicates Anna in any bid for power. Rather her appearance in this text is as a remarkable intellectual, admired for the rigor and depth of her learning.

If Zonaras had read the *Alexiad*, it did not lead him to think badly of Anna. If he had not read it, his positive portrayal of Anna as a great intellectual may reflect the reputation she had at the time he wrote, or how she looked in other sources at his disposal. It is possible that he read the *Alexiad* and was persuaded by Anna's text to consider her as an intellectual woman who deserved neither blame nor censure.

Doubts about John's succession may find their echo in a text most likely composed on Mt. Athos. Known as the *Diegesis Merike*, this text is composed of letters interspersed with bits of narrative and tells a story of misconduct by monks of Mt. Athos.[22] The story mostly revolves around the efforts of some monks to get the Patriarch Nicholas Grammatikos (1084–1111) to rescind an injunction he had issued against unacceptable behaviors that some of the monks thought was overly harsh. Alexios is depicted as resenting being bothered by the complaining monks, and the Patriarch as denying he had ever issued the injunction. After a search of the patriarchal register found no trace of it, Alexios and Nicholas were reconciled.[23] Eventually a monk confessed to the Patriarch that he had forged the injunction.[24] After Alexios's death, John started a new search for the injunction when he came to power, effectively nullifying the agreement made between his father and the Patriarch, and causing so much trouble that demons roamed over heaven and earth.[25] The story cannot be described as favorable toward either John or Alexios (who threatens to cut the noses off the monks because of their whining).[26] While sections of this narrative are ostensibly letters written by people alive in the early twelfth century, including Alexios and Nicholas, other parts of the story deal with the reign of John and, in one of the two manuscripts, the story ends with document written by a late twelfth-century patriarch.

This narrative may bear on our discussion because of a brief scene in which the Patriarch Nicholas predicts that John would become emperor. After Alexios had been satisfied that Nicholas had not written the injunction, he returned to the palace, but John stayed behind for a moment. John then asked the Patriarch if things will turn out as he trusts. The Patriarch told John to remind his father of his agreements and declared that John would succeed his father.[27] The inclusion of the anecdote predicting John's accession would seem to indicate that some people had thought the succession was uncertain. This narrative implies that rumors doubting John's succession would have reached beyond Constantinople and perhaps were remembered for a long time.[28]

The succession of John Komnenos in 1118 was also described in the history written by Michael Glykas, sometime in the second half of the twelfth century. His text is similar to Zonaras's for the reign of Alexios, but he condenses Zonaras's story about Eirene's dislike of John into one terse treatment of familial problems.[29] Glykas omits all of the palatial tension surrounding the death of Alexios. His description of Alexios's death does not mention Eirene,

FIGURE 6.1 *This marble roundel, about three feet high, is in the collection of the Dumbarton Oaks museum. A matching roundel is set into a wall of a courtyard in Venice, the Campiello de Ca' Angaran. Since the type of imperial regalia is well attested for the early twelfth century, it is likely that the two represent Alexios I and John II, perhaps from their period as co-emperors. [BZ.1937.23.A2010.S1985.1].*

© *Dumbarton Oaks, Byzantine Collection, Washington, DC.*

John, or Anna. Rather he moves seamlessly from Alexios's death to the state-ment that Alexios was succeeded by John, which ends his history.

Glykas's choice to include the negative stories about Eirene, but to omit the stories about palace tension at the death of Alexios Komnenos, suggests that Glykas actively decided that those stories were either untrue or unimportant. We have no evidence to suggest that he knew Anna, but he may have known her, or admired people who had. His history opens with a long description of the first six days of creation discussing the natural philosophies of Aristotle, Plato, John Philoponos, and Basil of Caesarea. This was exactly the sort of Christian antiquarian intellectual material Anna is described as enjoy-ing.[30] The numbers of people engaged in this kind of intellectual activity in Constantinople in the middle of the twelfth century were not so vast as to ren-der unreasonable the supposition that Glykas was acquainted with Anna or people who knew her. It is possible, then, that he omitted stories about John's succession out of respect for her intellect or deference to a possible patron. Whatever Glykas's motivation, it is significant that the succession disputes had not become a consistent part of historical memory about Alexios's death in the second half of the twelfth century.

Another story about Alexios's death is told in the funeral oration written for Anna by George Tornikes in around 1155.[31] This oration was most likely commissioned by Anna's daughter Eirene to honor her mother's memory. George Tornikes certainly knew Anna, and probably quite well. He was born sometime in the second decade of the twelfth century and became a prominent teacher in Constantinople in the 1040s and 1050s.[32]

Regarding the role of imperial politics in Anna's life, Tornikes depicts Anna as expressly lacking in political ambition, although he presents her as having assisted her mother with her imperial duties, and he refutes the rumor that she was her brother's rival. She behaved dutifully toward her parents, and so helped them, but was mostly interested in learning throughout her life. Her intellectual endeavors were the activities that she strove for consistently.

Anna's lack of political ambition is pointed out first in Tornikes's description of her betrothal to Constantine Doukas. He describes God as intervening in her parents' well-laid plans because God understood that Anna wanted a partner in a life of contemplation rather than the distractions of politics. God's intervention was the death of Constantine Doukas. God foreknew that Anna "did not cherish love for ruling so much as grasping for wisdom." So God "removed from among men what would have been an impediment for her toward this end—since he did not cultivate love for learning—and recommended another whose external splendor was just a little bit lower, but whose virtues in spirit and also body rose by nature above the common measure."[33] Constantine had more "external splendor" than Nikephoros because Constantine's father had been emperor, but since Anna cared about learning rather than ruling, Nikephoros was a better match for her.

Rather than presenting Anna as deeply mourning Constantine—the stance she adopts in the *Alexiad*—she is shown as blessed by the removal of a potentially unsupportive husband. That Constantine's death could be seen as a gift of divine providence strongly confirms that we are right to think that Anna's expressions of grief in the *Alexiad* are designed to elicit a particular emotional reaction from the audience, rather than revealing what she "really" felt. If the memory of Constantine drove Anna to tears, Tornikes's presentation of his death as a godsend would have been mocking and inappropriate.

Tornikes does describe Anna and Nikephoros as helping Eirene and Alexios with the internal management of the empire: "As the Caesar was with the Emperor, so his wife was with the Empress: he took a share in caring for external matters and she helped in maintaining the internal matters."[34] Tornikes provides a double-frame for this description, however. The paragraph opens with a statement about Anna's modesty: Anna was so modest that she always behaved as a bride with her husband. Because of her ability to withstand pleasure, she was able to discern the right governance of body and soul. Tornikes here aligns Anna with the cultural idea that spiritual strength leads to emotional control. This led her to love her parents tremendously and reflect their virtue.[35] From here Tornikes describes Anna's activities in support of her mother:

> There was no one who did not approach the empress through her: for some she gained goodwill, for others she dispersed ill-will, for some she dissolved anger, for others she released public debt, and for others she obtained gifts. There was nothing gladdening that was not gained through her; there was nothing painful that was not relieved by her; only consolation of the afflicted, only abundance for the needy, only encouragement for the good and refutation for the wicked.[36]

As the empress did her work, Anna was with her, helping to do whatever there was to do.[37] This passage provides another opportunity for Tornikes to discuss Anna's virtues, but it also presents Anna and Nikephoros as having been significant people at the imperial court while Alexios was alive.

Tornikes's story is not that Eirene favored Nikephoros over John, but rather that Nikephoros and Anna behaved like Alexios and Eirene because children are like their parents. John is entirely absent from the discussion. Without Zonaras's story about how Eirene handed the administration to Nikephoros, it is doubtful that this passage in Tornikes would be seen as evidence that Anna participated in the administration. It may well be merely another form of flattery that would have been given to any imperial child. Yet it equally may memorialize a time in which Anna was able to erase debts and provide imperial largess.

When it comes to Tornikes's description of Alexios's death, everyone was behaving properly and doing what was most important. Tornikes describes Anna as working bravely with the doctors in their efforts to save Alexios, directing them with masculine courage and authority.[38] She boldly told the angels that she would exchange her soul for her father's.[39] At the moment of Alexios's death, "the story refutes the crowd."[40] Where Zonaras told several competing stories of discord, Tornikes has only appropriate behavior:

> On the one hand, her father, the emperor, who not unwillingly gave his soul into the hands of attending angels, ascended to the heavenly palaces. . . .. On the other hand, his son, also emperor, while his father was still alive, embarked on his sole rule and went to the palace. And indeed it was necessary, because in such circumstances time is short; and the many suddenly plotting against the heirs would have been roused, if they had shown the slightest hesitation.[41]

John tended to the matters of transfer of power, not because anyone in his family was opposing him, but because such precautions are always necessary. Anna was wholly absorbed in grieving:

> But she, called the rival of her brother the emperor by those who say anything lightly, understanding fully that her father shortly would be departing, forgetting the name of empire with her children and her husband, they mourned with their empress and mother, kneeling bareheaded on the ground around the emperor; then they alone stood guard, instead of chamberlains, instead of companies of those many worthy spear-carriers, because both relatives and subjects had left with the new emperor.[42]

This version of Alexios's deathbed scene is ostensibly supportive of John, but draws sympathy to Anna and those remaining with the dead emperor.

Clearly Tornikes expected that some of the people in his audience would have heard that Anna had been her brother's "rival." The stories Zonaras says circulated about family contention at the point of Alexios's death presumably were known to Tornikes's audience as well. While Tornikes's version of the story remembers all of the participants behaving well, it also provides testimony that Anna was considered by some to have been John's competitor. By Tornikes's testimony, Anna made no efforts to thwart John, and only idle gossip suggests otherwise. Tornikes does not spend much time on this defense of Anna's political actions, however, but moves on from Alexios's death to a discussion of how Anna's personal grief led her to study philosophy. Altogether, these sections of the oration that can be considered as bearing on Anna's political life are relatively minor, greatly overshadowed by the discussion of her education and intellectual endeavors.

The chief source used to argue that Anna was a woman lusting for power is the history of Niketas Choniates. In the opening book of Choniates's history, Anna appears as desiring an unnatural inversion of female nature. Anna, however, is not the only member of her family who receives highly negative treatment at Choniates's hands. His lurid depiction of Anna needs to be assessed in light of his rhetorical and historical goals for this section of his history.

Niketas Choniates was born in Chonai, in western Asia Minor, in the middle of the twelfth century, and had a successful career as a high-level imperial administrator, flourishing in the reigns of Isaac Angelos (1185–1195) and Alexios III Angelos (1195–1203). He was dismissed from office by Alexios V Doukas, who ruled from February to April of 1204, just before the empire fell to the Crusaders. Choniates and his family fled Constantinople during the sack of the city. They eventually settled in Nicaea, but he was not able to secure a position in the nascent government-in-exile there and died in poverty in 1217.[43]

Choniates wrote one version of his history during the reign of Alexios III Angelos, whose regime he served. He revised it thoroughly around a decade after the sack of Constantinople in 1204.[44] Writing in exile in Nicaea, Choniates made the final version of his history a lachrymose and elegiac accounting of the horrors of the sack of Constantinople, and an exposition of the failures that led to the decline of the empire. Criticism of imperial immorality and mismanagement becomes far more acute in the revised version.[45] Yet while the first version is more polite, it is also unmistakably a story of decline fueled by the failures of the Komnenos family.[46]

In his layered use of classical and biblical allusions, playful and obscure word choice, and grammatical structures that play with the audience's perceptions, Choniates's prose is extremely complex, artful, and polysemic—so much so that even near contemporaries found it difficult to comprehend.[47] Each detail comments on another: "Both in terms of plot and wording, everything in the *History* may verge on something else, expected or unexpected, and admit a projection to the past as well as to the future."[48] No details are random: all aspects of the text work to create overlapping nested boxes of meaning. Choniates does not indulge in obscurity for its own sake. Rather, reading his history is work because the audience is continually forced to think, and then reconsider, how all the parts fit together, and how personal morality and human choices affect the lives of others.

To understand the stories about Anna in his history, we therefore need to consider what role those stories play in the overall structure of his history. After a particularly complex preface, Choniates opens his history with a brief book on the reign of John Komnenos, which starts before Alexios's death with stories about familial dissension. He explains in the preface that he will treat the reign of John in much less detail than later events because he does not have first-hand information about it and will rely on things he has heard. Why did Choniates both include a book on the reign of John, and tell his audience that his sources for it were not good? He alludes to the traditional need to pick up where a previous history left off as a reason to start with the death of Alexios, but he certainly knew that other historians had written about John.

The first book of Choniates's history functions as an artful setup for the main body of his history. It has been considered his "archaeology." Just as Thucydides wrote an "archaeology" that provided the moral backstory to his history of the Peloponnesian war, the discussion of Alexios's household at the opening of Choniates history serves as an "excursus into the past and a 'silent' investigation into the source of evil."[49] The problems animating the later, far more detailed sections of his history have their origins in the dysfunction within Alexios's household:

As the root of this evil he considers the rivalries which arose and developed between the prominent members of the reigning dynasty, the

Komnenoi, and which led to progressive weakening of the empire's stability.[50]

Choniates's treatment of Alexios's reign is an abbreviated family drama, a prelude to the history that starts more properly with John's reign but gains detail and depth with the reign of Manuel. Choniates uses the story of the succession dispute to create an image of an unharmonious and unnatural imperial family in which all the familial and gender roles are inverted. His warning that his history of the reign of John would rely on second-hand information perhaps should be taken as disclaiming responsibility for the facticity of those stories.

The book on John opens with an enumeration of Alexios's children and the statement that Alexios favored John while Eirene favored Anna. In casting the dissension as between two children of Alexios and Eirene, Choniates fundamentally alters Zonaras's basic narrative. Where Zonaras described Eirene as preferring Nikephoros, Choniates establishes the essential conflict as between John and Anna, each championed by one parent. Choniates's opening lines bring to mind the first words of Xenophon's *Anabasis*, which describe a division among brothers that ultimately underpins the civil war that animates that history.[51] Recalling Xenophon here is a way of signaling that sibling rivalries in royal families can cause large-scale destruction. Choniates may use this allusion to signal that dissentions in this family are the root of later problems.

In the ensuing discussion of Alexios's household, an undercurrent of immorality runs through the text. Choniates vividly describes Eirene slandering her son to Alexios. Choniates's exquisite use of double-entendre allows him to have Eirene complain simultaneously about John's physical weaknesses of "diarrhea, feebleness from recurring twisting of his bowels and general ill-health" and his moral weaknesses of "rashness, luxurious lying about and lack of virtue."[52] It is difficult to determine which of these is the overt meaning, and which the subtext. John's alleged gastrointestinal weakness would seem to bear less moral culpability, and thus perhaps should be taken as the surface meaning. Yet scatological references are highly discourteous. Additionally, a mother's ongoing interest in her son's bowels is infantilizing, and hence these physical complaints undercut John's adulthood. Most likely, then, the moral weaknesses should be considered the main text and the bodily ones the subtext. Either way, Choniates has given Eirene a remarkably unsavory set of complaints about her son.

Eirene added extravagant praises of Bryennios's virtue and capabilities to her complaints about John, saying that Bryennios was skillful with both words and deeds, and well-prepared for the exercise of power.[53] Alexios, who, according to Choniates, "understood the affection of a mother," sometimes pretended that he had not heard what she had said because he was preoccupied. At other times he acted as if he were considering the proposal; and, finally, sometimes he would answer vehemently.[54] The statement that Alexios understood "the affection of a mother" has been taken as a reference to Eirene's affection for Anna.[55] However, coming as it does after Eirene's degradation of her own son and exultation of her son-in-law, it may equally serve as a somewhat ironic comment on the unnatural state of Eirene's affections: instead of the natural affection of a mother for her son, Eirene has a mother's affection for her son-in-law. Choniates is pointing out how unnatural Eirene was in her lack of motherly love for John.

Next, Alexios is put on display as a conniving, deceptive, and illegitimate usurper with a bad temper. Choniates achieves this in the course of a speech in which Alexios angrily denounces his wife's efforts to persuade him to alter the succession. Choniates says that Alexios normally ignored Eirene, but when he could no longer take it he would say something like:

> Oh woman, sharer of my bed and empire, will you not stop admonishing me on behalf of your daughter, undertaking to destroy praiseworthy harmony and order as if you had been struck mad? Put it down to good fortune. Or rather let's now study and observe together who of all of those taking up the scepters of Rome until now, who had a son appropriate for rule, overlooked him and selected instead his son-in-law? Even if this did happen at some point, oh woman, we should not follow the rarity as law. The whole of Rome would laugh out loud at me and conclude that I had lost my senses if I, who seized the empire, not in a praiseworthy manner, but with the blood of compatriots and ways departing from Christian laws, when I need to find an heir for it, would banish the one from my loins and welcome in the one from Macedonia.[56]

Choniates has Alexios make the argument that supporting Anna against John would destroy the natural order and contravene historical precedent.[57] Choniates also has Alexios remind the audience that he and his dynasty came to power in 1081 through a bloody and unlawful coup in which Alexios's disorderly troops looted Constantinople. After having made the speech, Alexios returned to his practice of pretending to consider the matter. Choniates explains that Alexios "was a secretive man, more than any other, who was always considering the crafty thing wise, never meaningfully revealing to many people what he was doing."[58]

After this assessment of Alexios's character, Choniates turns to the description of Alexios's death. In place of Zonaras's competing rumors, Choniates tells one story that most closely resembles the version of events Zonaras said was preferred by John:

> [Seeing] his father nearing his last days, and his mother seemingly loving him no more, and the empire courted by his sister, John consulted with those of his relatives who favored him, of which the best

was his brother Isaac, about what was to be done. Escaping the notice of his mother, he entered his father's bedroom and falling down as if in mourning he secretly purloined the sealing ring from his hand.[59]

Choniates's version of this story differs significantly from Zonaras's in that it suggests that John stole the ring without his father's approval.[60] Choniates continues, "There are some who say he did this with the approval of his father, an impression they get from the things to be said soon."[61] Those who believe that Alexios did approve are led to that opinion by the rest of the story. Yet nothing in Choniates's subsequent story confirms or suggests that Alexios had given John his approval; the palace guards are not persuaded by the ring. This is a case of Choniates playing with his audience's expectations. Perhaps Choniates signals that it was John's success in taking control of the empire that made some people believe that his father approved of him. Nothing succeeds like success. The suggestion that people believed John had his father's approval because he was successful implicitly proposes that if he had not succeeded, people would say he had not had his father's approval. Choniates's writing often points out the contingency and instability of human affairs.[62]

Once he had the ring, John took up arms, gathered his supporters, and set out toward the Great Palace. On the way, he was acclaimed emperor by supporters and citizens who were gathering together at the news of the events.[63] After describing John's aggressive efforts to seize power while his father was alive, Choniates turns to Eirene's responses:

> Eirene, the empress and mother of John, astonished at what was happening, sent to her son exhorting him to abstain from the undertaking. When John was entirely committed to action and in no manner corrected by his mother, she encouraged Bryennios to make an attempt on the empire with her help. Then seeing nothing proceeding according to her plan, she approached the bed where her husband was lying and indicating by short breaths that he was living, and throwing herself on his body cried out vigorously against her son, 'flowing as a spring of dark tears,'[64] decrying how while Alexios was still enrolled among the living John acted to plunder the empire.[65]

Choniates's story differs from Zonaras's in suggesting that Eirene tried to get Nikephoros Bryennios to attempt to gain the throne himself. This exposes the hypocrisy of Eirene's fury with her son for trying to seize power while his father was alive: if she genuinely wanted Alexios to remain in control until he died, she would not be pushing another candidate for the throne forward.

Choniates follows Zonaras in describing the ambiguity of Alexios's response to his wife's anger:

> He gave no response to what she said to him, considering, as it seemed, matters of mortality—judging the life he was leaving, his passing on

in a short time—and inclining his eyes to those angels who conduct souls. With the empress insisting more urgently and not able to bear her child's actions, Alexios, making a small indication and forcing a smile, raised his hands to heaven, perhaps relaxed by this news and offering thanks to God about these things, or to taunt the woman and smiling at seeing her exercised with talk about power when he was reaching the separation of his body from his soul, or propitiating the divine for those times when he had gone astray from what was right.[66]

Whereas Zonaras did not guess at how Eirene reacted to Alexios's ambiguous gesture, Choniates presents Eirene as certain that Alexios was mocking her. Eirene does not believe that her husband was piously contemplating his end but rather glad that John had been acclaimed. Choniates describes her bitter response:

> The woman, thinking it was indisputable that the man rejoiced on account of what he had heard from her, so that she was now entirely cheated of her earlier hopes and disappointed by promises, in deep groaning she said: "O man, living you distinguished yourself with all sorts of falsehoods, the tongue answering with a wealth of designs, and now departing from life unchanging, you continue unfailingly in your old ways.[67]

Eirene here voices a strong denunciation of Alexios's craftiness. Choniates has Eirene second his critique of Alexios as a mendacious trickster. Eirene is here doubly lacking in proper wifely devotion: on the one hand she openly denigrates her husband's character, and on the other she is talking about politics when she should be doting and tending to her husband's physical needs in his final moments.

Choniates adds a new story about John's entrance into the Great Palace. He says that some of the guards were not satisfied with being shown the ring, but demanded further proof that Alexios wanted John to enter the palace. According to Choniates, John's followers pulled the palace gates off their hinges, allowing him to enter freely. Along with John's supporters, some of the common crowd also entered the palace and began to plunder whatever they could find. Choniates's version does not directly accuse John's supporters of perjury, as does Zonaras's, but it is a highly disordered and violent image of imperial succession. In doing damage to the palace, and allowing it to be plundered by the common rabble, Choniates denigrates John's ability to create proper imperial order: "Closing the gates again immediately, those outside were prevented from going in and those inside were not allowed to go out; for some days they lived there in the palace. In this way then passed the 15th of August.[68] The fifteenth of August is a major feast of the Orthodox liturgical year in which the Dormition of the Mother of God is celebrated.

On this day in particular it would be important for he city to be at peace. In Anna's history, the death of her father on August 15 serves to heighten the solemnity of his passing, if not to associate his passing with that of the Virgin. In Choniates's history, the proximity of the date to the description of the rabble camping in the palace shows John's inability to maintain appropriate order in the city.

The negative portrayal of John continues as the next morning he refused his mother's injunction that he ought to come to accompany the procession of his father's body from the palace to the monastery Alexios had built in honor of Christ Philanthropos.[69] John refused to come,

> neither spurning paternal honor nor neglecting the rites for his mother, but because he guarded his newly found power and had feared his adversaries still hot with conceiving lust for the empire. For which reason he clung to the palace as an octopus to the rocks, but he disbanded most of his relatives to his father's funeral procession.[70]

By expressly explaining that John clung to the palace not because he spurned his father's honor, Choniates points out precisely that John *did* dishonor of his father and neglect the rites due his widowed mother. One who thought John had shown the proper respect for his parents would have glossed over the issue or omitted the story of the funeral. The description of John as clinging to the palace like an octopus is similarly unflattering.

Choniates then begins to contrast the perverse discord of Alexios's family with the nobility of one of John's servants, his grand domestic, John Axuch. Axuch is described by Choniates as "a Persian by race" who is given to Alexios after the Western armies had captured Nicaea on their way to Palestine. Axuch was the same age as John and became his playmate and most beloved servant. John Axuch's "liberality and nobility of mind much overshadowed his lack of noble family and made John desired by everyone."[71] The virtues and loyalty of John Axuch, the man with no kindred, are contrasted with the lack of loyalty among John's own family. The lack of true support or loyalty within families becomes a running theme through the rest of Choniates's history.[72]

After introducing the character of John Axuch, Choniates describes a plot against John created by his relatives:

> But when his reign had not yet run a full year, a plot was stitched up against him by some of his relatives, exceedingly wrathful against him and casting the evil eye, by what manner it is not possible to say. And indeed an evil scheming band, giving faith to each other, adhered to Bryennios and would yield sovereignty to him since he was extremely well-educated in letters and showed a form worthy of rule and was from an exceedingly royal family; indeed, as we have said, he had been

married to the Caesarina Anna, the sister of the emperor, who displayed care in the practice of philosophy in all sciences and had been educated in all learning.[73]

Choniates describes the actual attempt as a hypothetical situation:

> Perhaps by night they would have struck with murderous weapons when the emperor was camping not far from the gates at the Philopation riding grounds, having corrupted with fat bribes the guard at the entrance to the city, had not his sluggish and flaccid custom stopped Bryennios from taking in hand the attempt on the empire and compelled him to remain in place, forgetting his compacts, and extinguishing the hot desire of the conspirators.[74]

The vocabulary in the second half of this sentence is highly sexualized. Nikephoros is held back by his "sluggish and flaccid custom." The term translated here as "flaccid" literally means "slack" or "loose," and seems to have a sexual connotation of physical limpness.[75] Choniates pairs this term with sluggishness or sloth that implies a simple inability to wake up. In saying Nikephoros was sleepy and limp, Choniates makes it easy to see the sexual double-entendre that he was not excited and hard. Nikephoros's lack of aggressive passion doused the flames of "hot desire" among his conspirators. Choniates thus describes Nikephoros's failure to murder John with an extended metaphor of failed orgasm.

This already sexually charged narration then turns to Anna's response:

> It is said that the Caesarina Anna was so disgusted with her husband's frivolity that she considered herself as suffering something terrible and blamed nature most of all.[76]

The term here translated as "frivolity" also refers to passive anal penetration. Nikephoros's failure to violently pursue power leads him to be cast by Choniates in the passive sexual role of the penetrated partner. Anna's desire for political power puts her in the position of desiring a masculine role. The "nature" Anna blamed can be a euphemism for female genitals, implying as great a dissatisfaction with her own body as with the political situation.[77] Choniates elaborates on Anna's desire for gender inversion:

> Nature was placed under a grave indictment on the grounds that Anna's genitals were spread wide and hollowed whereas Bryennios had the long member and balls.[78]

Here the sexual innuendos that have been simmering just under the surface of Choniates's text come to the open in a way that cannot be missed. There is no doubt that Choniates's presentation of Anna's desire to be a man was intended to be deeply derogatory. The bald statement that Anna wished to have a man's body is but the culmination of the theme of gender transgression that Choniates has woven throughout his history to this point.

From the vulgar description of Anna's frustration, Choniates's narrative turns to John's great clemency, which Choniates attributes to the influence of John Axuch. The morning after the plot was discovered, the conspirators were not harmed or tortured, but deprived of their property. This confiscation was brief, however, and soon John restored most of their property. John's clemency "began with the chief-instigator of the plot, the Caesarissa Anna."[79] Choniates describes John as standing before the confiscated property that had belonged to his sister and lamenting dramatically about how the natural order had been reversed, so that his relatives had become his enemies and strangers his friends. John gave all of the goods to John Axuch, who, after thanking John and asking permission to speak freely, urged John to forgive Anna as his sister and allow her to recover his affection, displaying his own virtue through clemency. Axuch's stirring call to forgiveness and familial affection "persuaded, or more truthfully, shamed" John, and he restored all of Anna's property to her.[80]

John Axuch's reminder of the deep virtue of forgiveness and the importance of bonds of love between siblings rhetorically heightens the contrast between this ideal and the behavior of the Komnenos family. Anna becomes the focus of discussion, and the "chief instigator," in the story of her reconciliation with John, because Choniates has turned this episode into a referendum on proper familial behavior. Choniates's description of the rest of John's reign is increasingly positive, and he eulogizes John as one of Rome's great emperors. In this story, however, John gains moral superiority over his sister by taking to heart the advice of a foreign servant, captured in childhood, who somehow knows how families are supposed to work. The story of John's forgiveness of Anna plays a role in further highlighting the lack of familial cooperation and virtuous character in Alexios's household.

Choniates says that Eirene did not participate in the attempt on John's life and attributes an aphorism to her that "it is necessary to find an emperor when there is no successor, but the present one should not be removed."[81] She also said that the pains she would experience upon the murder of her son would be far worse than her birth pains and would bring her unending sorrow.

Choniates's history differs from Zonaras's in implicating Anna in the bid to alter the succession. He includes "a sister courting the throne" in his catalog of John's worries. At the opening of his story about John's clemency, Anna is called the "chief instigator" of the plot. The description of John's adversaries on the day after his takeover as "still hot with conceiving lust for the empire" metaphorically casts them as women acting on sexual impulses.[82] Eirene and Anna could both be implied. Yet Choniates's focus shifts among the characters, following the purposes and proclivities of his rhetorical presentation. When he is describing how Eirene and Alexios squabbled, Eirene was John's chief antagonist. The story of how Nikephoros could not pull off the murder focuses on his limitations, and Anna appears only as his foil, the mannish woman for his womanish man. When the focus turns to how the foreign slave schooled John in how families ought to behave, Anna comes to the spotlight.

Choniates's description of Anna's desire for gender inversion need not be taken as related to the reality of Anna's emotional life. Whatever he may have known about the efforts to make Nikephoros emperor, Niketas Choniates was not privy to the private complaints Anna may have had about her husband's shortcomings. We are justified in asking why he would include such a story, and what role it played in his text. As we have seen, his description of Nikephoros's failed attempt to murder John is more a story about twisted familial and gender relations than about politics. Similarly, his descriptions of the relationships between Alexios, Eirene, John, and Anna form a catalog of inversions of proper domestic order: the wife does not support and defer to the husband; the siblings do not love each other; the mother does not love her son; the son does not honor the father or mother. In not waiting for his father to die before seizing power, and refusing to go to his father's funeral, John is depicted as significantly lacking in filial devotion. All the proper relations are reversed. The domestic drama of the Komnenos family grounds the opening of Choniates's history in a locus of deeply unnatural, perverse, and foul behavior. As later books become a detailed meditation on the political failures of Choniates's era, they are more attentive to political realities, but continue to trace and elucidate moral corruption among the ruling house. This discourse of corrupt and unstable foundations of the dynasty goes some way to explaining why Choniates would also depict Anna as unnatural and morally corrupt.

Choniates appears to have personally upheld his culture's belief in the virtue of female deference to male authority. Although his work defies generalization, the strong women in his history are usually negative characters. Choniates's own wife was described by his brother as "reared by a good mother and kept at home."[83] As an apparently affirming participant in a culture that valorized female seclusion and deference, he may have found Anna's decision to write a history distasteful or even offensive. We do not know if Choniates had read the *Alexiad*, but it is likely, and he was certainly at least aware of Anna's authorial activities.[84] It is possible that Anna's efforts to appear humble and polite in the *Alexiad* were ineffective in getting Choniates to think well of her. Choniates's choice to depict Anna as lusting unnaturally after power may have been motivated, at least partially, by his response to the idea of a female historian. She appears in his history as grasping at the imperial throne and deeply frustrated with her own gender. Choniates was a sufficiently creative writer that he may have come up with this portrait on his own, and we have seen how it serves his larger purposes well. Yet, given how authorship was linked in Byzantine culture with self-aggrandizement and the assertion of power, it may be that Anna's assertion of herself as a writer was enough to suggest Choniates that she lusted after political power as well.

Another story about John's difficulties seizing control of the empire was recorded in a brief paragraph of a Syriac chronicle written in Edessa in about 1240. In this version, the guards closed the palace against John when his father died, at the instigation of his mother and brother-in-law. John then told his soldiers that it was time to demonstrate that they were brave warriors and that all the contents of the palace would be their loot. The soldiers attacked the palace, opened the gates, and within an hour the palace was completely looted of gold, silver, jewels, and precious objects. John then proclaimed a general amnesty.[85] Anna is not mentioned in this story, which focuses on John's assault on the palace. The great wealth of the imperial palace in relics and material goods throughout the twelfth century makes the claim of the story that the palace was looted demonstrably false.

Anna's own narrative of her father's death gives her the opportunity to switch from history to lamentation and close her book in mourning, for reasons discussed in chapter 4. John appears briefly in Anna's deathbed scene, after the dying Alexios had been moved to a higher floor on the Mangana Palace. Anna next mentions that John had already left to go to his own apartment for the night when his father was dying. Then John hurried to the Great Palace.[86] She says that there was confusion in the city, but not complete disorder. Anna then describes her mother as crying out, "Let everything be cast down—diadem, empire, and privilege, all majesty, throne and authority!" and beginning to wail in lamentation. Thereafter Anna's story is entirely consumed with mourning.

How far do these stories support the idea that Anna was driven by her great ambition to dispute her brother's authority, even to the point of murder? Anna plays no role in Zonaras's history, which is primarily concerned with rumors about John's behavior during his father's final hours. Tornikes's and Anna's accounts mention John leaving to go to the Great Palace before his father died. Only Choniates's history implicates Anna in an effort to gain power, primarily in his second story of the conspiracy to kill John. I have explained a number of reasons to doubt that Choniates's story reflected any real events. The evidence of court oratory in the following chapter will provide more reasons to think that Choniates's picture does not correspond to reality. Given how precisely his picture of Anna as a woman unnaturally cold to her family, lusting after power, and wanting to be a man, parallels the problems Anna seems to have expected and attempted to counter in her self-presentation, it may be reasonable to think his portrait was fed by his response to Anna as an author of history.

Clearly the medieval evidence is not as uniformly of the opinion that Anna spearheaded a revolt as modern scholarship. Modern textbooks are certain that Anna was responsible for launching a revolt against her brother.[87]

The modern authors seem to know more about what really happened than Zonaras ever claimed. Most of the medieval texts indicate that the scandal at hand was that John did not wait for his father to die before going off to be acclaimed, a plotline that rarely makes it into modern scholarship. Readers can certainly draw different conclusions about what happened based on the ambiguous medieval evidence. But that Anna's role has been magnified by people who have read the *Alexiad* seems certain.

{7}

Celebrating an Odd Bird

Anna's family loved beautiful speeches. They celebrated major moments in their lives by hiring orators to perform speeches written for the occasion. From wedding toasts that would have taken a few minutes to funeral orations a few hours long, we have examples of delightful and moving compositions that reflect the flourishing intellectual culture of twelfth-century Constantinople. These texts open additional windows onto Anna's life and her relationships with her family.

We are fortunate to have George Tornikes's long funeral oration about Anna, commissioned by her daughter, in which he struggles to find ways of honoring Anna even though she fit so badly with the conventions of her era. Tornikes talks openly about how Anna's intellectual activities make it impossible for him to use any of the standard ways of praising a woman and how she also does not fit his categories for men. He ultimately gives up and calls her a phoenix. His difficulties in praising Anna closely parallel the gender problems I think Anna was dealing with in writing the *Alexiad*, and he and Anna used some of the same methods for diffusing tension.

Between the occasional speeches and Anna's funeral oration we can get a different picture of Anna than we saw in the political narratives. These texts provide information about Anna's position at court and relationships with her family after her father's death. They can also help us understand the court society and intellectual culture in which Anna wrote the *Alexiad*. We will start by looking at how the court rhetoricians depicted Anna and Nikephoros and then turn to Tornikes's funeral oration.

While some people may find Byzantine court rhetoric stilted, artificial, or overwrought, that is probably because of our culture's preference for expressing sincerity through originality and simplicity. Anna and her family did not share that cultural predilection. They would have hated Hemingway. They took great delight in the elaborate texts that playfully embroidered upon expected conventions of form and structure. The art lay in creating a particularly beautiful and appropriate expression of a rhetorical element everyone knew was coming. This stylized art form is what Anna's family listened to, paid for, and tried to write themselves. They commissioned orations to mark their important occasions because they felt such displays of rhetoric were appropriate and meaningful expressions of the emotions they felt. When we take court rhetoric on their terms, it becomes a significant source not only for details about their relationships, but for their emotional lives.

The professional orators may have had genuine affection for some of their aristocratic patrons, but they also were always looking for the next commission. Theirs is an inevitably rosy and flattering reflection on court life. They were constrained from mendacious flattery however by the need to speak appropriately to the context at hand. Given that the audience knew the reality of the situation, anything that was an outright lie would function to point out its opposite truth, and hence would not be flattering. The authors could endlessly elaborate or embroider to present a situation in the best possible light, but they would have a difficult time being counterfactual.

The court rhetoric that survives today seems to be an extremely small proportion of all that was written for Anna and her family. The surviving pieces were selected for inclusion in manuscripts that collected examples of fine writing. We tend to have manuscripts of several pieces by the same author, rather than collections based on content—so a collection of pieces by Michael Italikos, not a collection of all the marriage orations. The effect is of multiple pinhole windows into the lives of Anna's family. Each text strives to reflect an intense emotional moment, often leaving out basic information about circumstances that were known to the audience, but not to us.

The image of Anna that emerges from this corpus of court rhetoric is of a loving mother, a devoted wife, but overwhelmingly a remarkable intellectual. Her husband Nikephoros Bryennios is also portrayed as an outstanding intellectual and writer. Nothing suggests that Anna was suffering any sort of disfavor or internal exile during her brother's reign. On the contrary, Anna and her husband were both respected and prominent members of court society.

The clearest indication of a good relationship between Anna and her brother John is found in an oration Theodore Prodromos wrote to honor the marriages of Anna's sons, Alexios and John, who were married on the same day.[1] Alexios's wife was a daughter of King David II of Georgia.[2] Prodromos later wrote a funeral encomium for John's wife, in which we learn that her name was Theodora and that she came from a royal lineage.[3] In the marriage oration, Anna and Nikephoros appear to be well-regarded courtiers, whose sons' wedding was a grand affair attended by all the senate and court. Anna's brother John is described as having escorted the grooms in the marriage procession, and this is presented as one of Anna's great joys:

> And you [Anna], who I do not even know how to address properly, you most divine Porphyrogennete, rejoice, and with my lord, the learned Caesar, rejoice again. For behold, your wish is granted and your desire is realized. You saw your sons happily leading home brides, receiving crowns, being cheered by the senate, the people and the clergy, escorted to the wedding ceremony by their uncle and emperor who was yesterday escorted by songs of victory.[4]

Prodromos praises the nobility of the sons, the beauty of the brides, and exults in the general joyousness of the occasion. His writing reflects the festive happiness of the moment.

The dating of the oration is significant because it attests to a good relationship between Anna and her brother John. These marriages certainly took place after the death of Alexios. When, in praising the grandparents of the grooms, Prodromos evokes the memory of Alexios I, he urges his audience not to cry for the sake of the marriage celebration, indicating that they were expected to still be mourning the old emperor.[5] Some scholars date the oration close to Alexios's death, because they believe that Anna made an attempt on her brother's life and subsequently fell from favor.[6] On the other hand, John is described as recently having returned from a victory, which some scholars associate with the triumph over the Pechenegs that took place in 1122.[7]

The depiction of the court as still in mourning for Alexios may argue for an earlier date, but we do not know how long courtiers would have been expected to maintain a stance of mourning toward a revered emperor such as Alexios. In another text Prodromos presented the death of Alexios as a cause for Anna to mourn at the time of the death of her daughter-in-law almost twenty years later.[8] Similarly at the death of her son Andronikos, in 1130, Eirene was still expected to be lamenting the passing of Alexios.[9] Prodromos was obliged to mention Alexios in the marriage oration because the form of the text he was working with required describing the grandparents of the groom. It may have been impolite to suggest anything other than regret at Alexios's passing while his widow was still alive.

Another factor suggesting a later date is the tradition of having brides arrive in their new family's house several years before marriage. The mother-in-law was charged with caring for and training the young girl in preparation for her marriage. This tradition seems to have been followed in the case of John's bride, Theodora, who is described in her funeral encomium as having been raised by Anna and her mother, Eirene.[10] Zonaras mentioned that the bride for young Alexios arrived with her entourage in Constantinople on the day of the emperor Alexios's death on August 15, 1118.[11] If she had arrived a few years before adolescence, like her sister-in-law, the marriage would have had to wait for at least a few years after 1118. Tornikes's oration for Anna records that Alexios died just as Anna needed his help in embarking on the project of marrying her children, implying that these matters were hardly settled at the time of his death. On balance, it seems most likely that weddings took place in the early 1120s, well after Anna supposedly tried to murder her brother.

Other works indicate that Nikephoros continued to maintain a good relationship with John. Michael Italikos's lament for Anna's brother Andronikos mentions that Nikephoros brought Andronikos's body back to his mother from Asia, where they had been campaigning with John.[12] Italikos praises the letters he received from Nikephoros, at least one of which was written when Nikephoros was in the "east."[13] The Constantinopolitan rhetoricians betrayed no interest in what happened outside of the city, but presumably Nikephoros was working on a military campaigns, diplomatic missions, or provincial administration, any of which would require John to trust him to support his government.

Nothing indicates that Anna and Nikephoros were separated. Michael Italikos improvised an encomium for Eirene Doukaina, delivered sometime after Alexios's death, which indicates that Anna was present along with Nikephoros at the gathering. Italikos described Anna as the Siren of the Caesar.[14] This text also indicates the presence of Anna's sisters. Italikos creates an image of a harmonious family all enjoying Eirene's company. In Prodromos's lament on the death of Anna's brother Andronikos, Eirene is depicted as comforted by her daughters and by Nikephoros, with his sons.[15] Although Anna is not mentioned explicitly, it would be logical to think she was among the daughters mentioned in this context. In Italikos's lament for Andronikos, he likened Andronikos's mourning sisters to the Hiliades whose tears for their brother Phaëthon were changed into drops of amber.[16]

Perhaps the strongest evidence for Anna's affection for her husband is found in the funeral lament that Prodromos wrote for Anna's daughter-in-law Theodora, the wife of her son John.[17] Theodora died sometime after Nikephoros.[18] Prodromos follows the normal pattern of describing the origin and upbringing of the deceased. This brings him to describe the women who raised Theodora: Eirene and Anna. He begins to describe Anna, but can hardly bring himself to mention the name of her departed husband:

> [Theodora was entrusted to] the glory of the Doukai, the learned Anna, utter intellect, the home of the graces, the pink rose of the porphyry, even if now a black veil is on the ornament, the wife of my lord (stop myself river of tears), of my lord (do not break, my heart) of my lord (endure it wretched breast), of my lord the Caesar.[19]

Prodromos presents himself as almost uncontrollably overwhelmed with grief at the death of the Caesar at the time he is endeavoring to mourn Theodora. Anna may well have commissioned this oration. She certainly would have been in its audience. For the poem to be pleasing to her, it would need to reflect how Anna wished Nikephoros to be remembered. The extreme expressions of mourning for Nikephoros should be understood as something that Anna wanted to hear.

Other texts further indicate that Anna was a patron worth cultivating. Prodromos wrote a poem addressing Anna, in which he humorously explains that he wishes he had not taken his father's advice to study because he would have been better off as a craftsman.[20] He complains about an illness as well as his recent lack of success, and begs extravagantly for Anna's help. The poem is a playful and intricate piece of writing. In both the invocation of Anna at the opening of the poem and in the closing beseeching of her, Prodromos is highly flattering, but the focus is on the display of his own skills as a writer.[21] The help he was asking for was presumably a gift, a commission, or assistance in promoting his skills to others who could pay for them.

John Tzetzes wrote a letter to Anna, in which he tries to enlist Anna's help in a dispute he was having with another man.[22] Tzetzes's combatant had confronted him with the demand that he proclaim a third man, whose theology Tzetzes considered heretical, to be a saint. Tzetzes relates that they would have come to blows had he not been drawn up by his awe before Anna's "gate."[23] Tzetzes addresses Anna as his imperial mistress and humbles himself before her majesty in a way that emphasizes their disparity of rank. While the letter is clearly begging for help from a social superior, it has a humorous and familiar air. It does not appear to be a letter to a stranger, but rather to someone with whom Tzetzes has had other contact. The letter indicates that Anna was in a position to help him.

Anna is repeatedly characterized in the court rhetoric as a great intellectual. In his speech in praise of Eirene, Italikos professes that all his rhetorical skills are negligible compared to those of Anna; he offers mere streams, but she a great spring; he is lacking, as the Propontis must be filled from the Black Sea.[24] He praises everyone in Eirene's circle, including Anna's sisters and Nikephoros, as deeply philosophical.[25] Anna is "most wise" in Prodromos's begging poem.[26] In his marriage oration for Anna's sons, in the section praising the grooms' parents, Prodromos provides a laudatory description of Anna:

> What of their reverend parents? Certainly, let anyone not speaking in superlatives be mocked. I say this queen from the porphyry, whose eyes ... hint at great straining for intellect and for God, ... she who we may add as a fourth Grace, or a tenth Muse to the Muses, if perhaps the Hellenes spoke truth.[27]

Anna's intellectual achievements justify likening her to the ancient Graces and Muses, but her philosophical training was prompted by her desire for greater virtue:

> She initiated herself through the forces of virtue to the whole philosophy of character, whose end is not knowledge but action. Then, both more

nobly considering and more royally thinking that, just as the porphyry [is the] adornment of the royal body, so too the science of being [is the adornment] of the royal soul, she was initiated into knowledge and she hunted truth. She showed virtue to be a possession of deliberate choice, not family, and exceeding everyone in all goodness, she surpassed her own blessedness through marriage, sharing her bed with such a man, my lord and Caesar, such that no other may compare, either seen among us or recorded in the histories of the ancients.[28]

This is far from a generic description of a virtuous twelfth-century lady. Komnenian women were praised for their beauty, modesty, and loyalty.[29] Anna is presented as an intellectual with keen interests in philosophy. The idea that virtues are acquired by choice derives from Aristotle's *Nicomachean Ethics*.[30] Prodromos makes a tight connection between Anna's striving for learning and her fine moral qualities, which also becomes a major theme in Tornikes's funeral oration for Anna.

Nikephoros Bryennios is depicted as a suitable match for his wife's great intellectualism. When Prodromos turns to describe Nikephoros in the marriage oration, he emphasizes Nikephoros's engagement in poetry, rhetoric, and philosophy, as well as the more standard attributes of military and political acumen:

[Anna married] a man, my lord and Caesar, such that no other may compare, either seen among us or recorded in the histories of the ancients. For while various men of the Greeks and Romans happen to have been successful, for some were public leaders, and others were strategists, some were distinguished for speeches and others for some philosophy, or were carefully trained in poetry; but this same man leads armies and has charge of poetry and philosophizes, and elects by vote, and judges the rhetors, and regarding the perfection of everything does not fare badly, but in each thing surpassing . . . the experts in each. There could be none other than the Caesar.[31]

Nikephoros is considered incomparable because he succeeded in all arenas of activity. Prodromos depicts him as exceeding the achievements of the famous men of antiquity.

Other texts attest to Nikephoros's reputation as an intellectual. In the oration Prodromos wrote to commemorate the death of Anna's brother Andronikos, he describes Nikephoros as deep in mourning, unable to do philosophy because of his mourning for Andronikos, implying that philosophy was his normal mode.[32] Italikos wrote several letters to Nikephoros in which the latter's rhetorical and philosophical skills are highly praised.[33] Italikos laments that he is deprived of the Caesar's company: "For me there is only one great pain, the deprivation of your sweetness of language, marvelous character, moderation of thought, height of intelligence, hearth of the Muses, living library."[34] These letters are extravagantly flattering, but direct their flattery toward intellectual skills. Such extravagant praises would not have been gratifying if Nikephoros were not able to at least hold his own in intellectual conversations.

The image of Nikephoros and Anna as equally matched intellectuals and patrons of learning survived into their grandchildren's generation. In the late twelfth century, Constantine Manasses wrote a funeral oration for Nikephoros Komnenos, the grandchild of Nikephoros and Anna.[35] Manasses praises not only Nikephoros's parents, but also his grandparents, the "great-named Caesar" and his grandmother, "offspring of the porphyra."[36] Manasses emphasizes Anna and Nikephoros's intellectual activities, chiefly their interest in philosophy. He stresses the extreme harmony of their marriage. He makes the case that both men and women have been great thinkers, listing Pythagoras and Zeno for men, and Theano and Sappho for women.[37] He says that the Caesar surpassed eminent men, as in equal measure Anna surpassed women. He thought it was truly amazing how Nikephoros exceeded nearly all men, some by his extensive abilities and others by his wide education. It was nearly the case that Nikephoros's only equal was his wife.[38] Anna was as educated as Hypatia, and equal to Cleopatra in royalty and refinement.[39] Manasses's commemoration of Anna and Nikephoros, in the generation after their death, indicates that they succeeded in leaving a positive legacy as an intellectual couple.

In these works Anna is portrayed positively, as one would expect for court oratory. Her identity as an intellectual is a recurrent part of her character. Nikephoros is also presented as a highly esteemed intellectual. His penchant for philosophy and education is a consistent part of his character as described in this corpus. We must be cautious in relying on laudatory court oratory for information about personalities. Yet it is quite clear that both Anna and Nikephoros were people worth flattering. For flattery to work it would need to highlight strengths and not point out the flaws in the subject. If Anna and Nikephoros were functionally divorced, forced to live separately while she was imprisoned, gushing about how great their marriage was would not flatter Anna, and so would not win Prodromos another commission. Rather, the consistent portrayal of Anna and Nikephoros as devoted both to each other and to their common intellectual pursuits probably magnifies an aspect of their own self-understanding. The description of them in Manasses, written with the freedom that comes from distance from the subject, confirms the vision of them as mutually devoted married intellectuals.

The image of Anna as a great intellectual is confirmed by other evidence that she was the commissioning patron of a series of commentaries on Aristotle's *Nicomachean Ethics*.[40] Eustratios of Nicaea praised his learned, royal, female patron in the preface to his commentary on book VI of the

Ethics and reveals that she had also commissioned his commentary on book I.[41] Michael of Ephesus complained that working all night on Aristotelian commentaries at Anna's request was ruining his eyesight.[42] Michael was the first scholar to comment on Aristotle's *Parva Naturalia* and zoological texts, and his work may be due to Anna's desire for studies of Aristotelian works that did not yet have commentaries.[43] Anna's active engagement in systematic exposition of Aristotelian thought precludes dismissing other testimony of her intellectual interests as mere flattery. On the contrary, she played a significant role in twelfth-century intellectual history.

Her intellectual reputation was sufficiently secure that two of her poems were preserved in a fourteenth-century collection. Two poems addressing Christ are attributed to Anna, "the most wise *caesarissa porphyrogennete*."[44] One meditates on the daring inherent in trying to draw the Word in the form of Christ as a child. It ends reassuring the artist of the propriety of drawing because Christ was fully alive in both his human and divine natures. This poem probably was inscribed on a frame around an icon. The second poem is an allegorical expression of desire for God, addressed as a chaste bridegroom.[45] Anna may also have written a third poem, inscribed on a reliquary of the hand of John the Baptist that was taken to France in the thirteenth century.[46]

So far the images from court oratory have not indicated that being a great intellectual was in any way difficult for Anna. George Tornikes's funeral oration provides far more detail about how she struggled to obtain her education. His delicate and careful descriptions of her work in ancient literature and philosophy let us know both what she achieved, and how abnormal that behavior was considered. Although Tornikes clearly respected Anna's intellectual activities, and most probably cared about her personally, his task of eulogizing her as a woman of learning was not straightforward. As he reminds his readers on several occasions, Anna was not a typical subject for an encomium. His oration provides significant evidence for the unusual position Anna held in the Constantinopolitan intellectual community. She is deeply admirable, in Tornikes's view, but also prodigious. We can glimpse cultural tensions and a social unease about Anna's intellectualism that closely parallel some of the difficulties Anna encountered in writing a history.

Tornikes's discussions of Anna's education and intellectual activities repeatedly emphasize her moral virtue, her piety, and her modesty. It is the strength of her character that allows her to have the exceptional ability to read ancient texts without becoming morally corrupted. The bedrock of her great piety allows her to engage in philosophical reflection without danger of being led into theological error. Tornikes's emphasis on Anna's moral strength and religious devotion allow him to draw on the common strategy of upholding the gender norms of his culture by presenting an exceptional woman as able to engage in masculine activities.[47] Tornikes also insists strongly on Anna's innate modesty and always presents her intellectual activities as subordinate to her care for her parents, her husband, and her family. The emphasis on Anna's modesty, and her devotion to her family, make her fit some of her culture's primary ideals for virtuous female behavior.

Extensive secular education was considered dangerous for girls such as Anna, and her parents did not initially encourage her studies. Tornikes explained that Eirene and Alexios honored "divine knowledge" but suspected secular learning.[48] Their decision to bar their daughter from further study was presented as an entirely sound and reasonable parenting choice. It was only inappropriate in Anna's case, Tornikes argues, because she was such an extraordinary individual. Tornikes claims that Anna was able to retain her virtue while studying because she approached the matter already armed against the misleading and potentially corrupting aspects of classical literature. He uses martial imagery when explaining how Anna protected herself against the dangers of secular learning while stealthily circumventing her parents' restrictions:

> She knew the judgment of her parents on worldly wisdom and she acquiesced to it, but just as those who have been informed of an ambush by the enemy, who cannot return home by another route, brave the enemy ambush and parry with courage, after arming themselves well and preparing for the attack, in such a way she, after arming herself against the misleading myths and fictions and against the exposition of indecent passions, after bandaging the weakness of her soul to be sure not to be surprised or driven either by the potion of Circe, or the song of the Sirens, but rather closing and opening her ears at the discretion of reason, and proceeding with Odysseus's magic plant, she braved grammar and poetry, and while ensuring that her parents did not know, she took lessons with caution in secret from not ill-educated eunuch servants.[49]

Secular learning is presented a real danger, but one that Anna was able to withstand. Anna's capacity to exercise reason allowed her to open or close her ears against the song of the Sirens just as Odysseus's plant had allowed him to resist the magic of Circe. Tornikes further valorizes Anna's efforts to become educated despite the opposition of her parents, describing her working at night instead of sleeping, and contrasting her zeal and success in learning with those who did not achieve so much despite access to good schools and teachers.[50] Given these adverse circumstances, her very ability to succeed in her studies becomes proof that she was capable of undertaking secular learning.

The strength of Anna's great personal virtue is repeatedly emphasized when Tornikes discusses Anna's interactions with the many men who enabled her intellectual activities. Her virtue is foundational because it allows her to engage men who were not close relatives in conversation without raising suspicions of impropriety. After her marriage, Anna had become a perfect model of morality and progressed in discussions of rhetorical theory. Her lifelong love of learning was shared with her husband, and there were daily discourses on theoretical philosophy in the palace.[51] At this stage, Anna's learning was allowed by her mother, and Anna studied scholarship with a skilled eunuch.[52] The change from clandestine to open study comes with her marriage, and carries the implication that her husband approved of her activities. She conversed with philosophers who were distinguished by their "philosophical habits and by their age."[53] Both the advanced age and the "philosophical habits" of these men marked them as less susceptible to sexual temptation. The change in Anna's study from working exclusively with eunuchs, to also learning from old philosophical men, is presented as corresponding to an increase in her already formidable virtue. At this time in her life Anna grew in "her physical age, her love of secular learning, and the virtue of her habits and deeds, which outshone the others."[54] The description opens and closes with glowing praise for Anna's personal morality. The great strength of her virtue and modesty, in Tornikes's presentation, gives her license to undertake intellectual work.

After the death of Alexios, Tornikes presents Anna's intellectual activities as taking place in the midst of the community of scholars. He says she gathered around her the greatest leaders of all the sciences: "They were many and amazing."[55] He explains that men of letters had been well cultivated in Alexios's reign. Anna gathered both philosophers who disdained money and taught freely and also "more worldly philosophers," "remarkable for their eloquence," who practiced "dazzling rhetoric."[56] Her discussion partners are no longer limited to eunuchs and old men. Here again it is the strength of her virtue that keeps Anna above reproach in such company.

In addition to emphasizing Anna's extraordinary personal virtue, Tornikes cloaks Anna's philosophical practice with Christian piety. Tornikes presents Anna's increasing attention to classical secular learning as a philosophic response to the death of her father, although Anna's actual engagement with philosophy may have started well before Alexios's death. He gives her learning a utilitarian role in the proper cultivation of the Christian spirit by presenting it as a Christian response to grief. The "death of her father and emperor became the beginning of a more perfect and complete philosophy, not only about words and about scientific knowledge and ontological theory, but also philosophy that is able to test whether a character is philosophical or whether a soul is noble or base."[57] Anna, after the death of Alexios, is likened to a ship that is abandoned at sea in a storm. When she was young and her life was calm, Alexios was there to guide her. But just when she most needed help in arranging the marriages for children and directing the affairs of her family, she lost her father's guidance.[58] Anna's response is to turn to God and to learning. Tornikes artfully navigates the careful rhetorical turn from seeking divine help for the suffering soul to secular learning.[59] Anna's deepening engagement in classical scholarship is described as a response to Christian piety.

While her turn to philosophy is presented as a Christian response to grief, the content of her explorations was decidedly pre-Christian. In the company of the learned men and the practitioners of dazzling rhetoric, Anna studied every mode of discourse surviving from antiquity:

> The works of the Stagirite [Aristotle] and Plato, Euclid and Ptolemy, and as much as was not banished by law from the company of Christians, discarding neither public nor theatrical rhetoric, nor dishonoring the usefulness of histories, from which the exercises of the rhetoricians become more persuasive. Always she dwelt with poetry, mourned with the tragedians and played with the comedians, enlivening again with these relaxations the toil from the other philosophy, for while laughing with some matters but mourning and deeming others unhappy, she both praised the laughter of [the cheerful philosopher] Democritus while honoring no less the tears of [the melancholy philosopher] Heraclitus.[60]

Tornikes further discloses that Anna also acquired a perfect knowledge of arithmetic, geometry, and music. She thoroughly studied all of astrology that pertains to the stars and their movements and relationships in space, but rejected all that had to do with prognosticating.[61] Anna is described as wonderfully eloquent and persuasive in conversations and skillfully using discussion as her chief means of expressing her ideas. She could turn a speech any way she wished because of her firm grasp of ancient authors, to the point that she surpassed "Sextus and that Pyrron and whoever else was double-tongued in the manner of Zenon."[62]

Anna's engagement in ancient philosophy was both motivated by pious considerations and entirely consonant with Christian theology. Tornikes frames the discussion of her philosophical interests by pointing out places where she disagreed with ancient philosophers on theological grounds. She agreed with much of Aristotle but disagreed with his view of the uncreated eternity of the world.[63] She admired Plato and his successors but wished to associate their One with God.[64] Her understanding of the soul concurred with much of Platonic thought, but she rejected the idea of the metempsychosis and the uncreated nature of the soul.[65] She maintained a strong belief in divine providence, which led her to disagree with certain aspects of Aristotle's thought.[66] Her belief in providence enabled her to withstand the painful death of her mother and her husband.[67] Because of Anna's careful, deliberate mixing of these studies with Christian theology, "she was never carried off by the folly of the myths or entranced by the Muses of Plato or turned around by the persuasive force of the Stagirite [Aristotle] toward strange doctrines."[68] Tornikes's argument for the maintenance of Anna's piety consistently runs alongside his argument for her mastery of classical learning.

Anna is likened to a bee that would go from flower to flower selecting the best of everything available. Any valuable and worthwhile idea from the classical world, or from among Christian authors, she would accept, while she was able to discern and reject any idea that would be harmful.[69] Her belief in Christian scripture provided a solid foundation for her abode of wisdom.[70] So she preferred the Christian Neo-Platonists Dionysius and Hierotheus to Proclus and Iamblicus, and the Basils and Gregories of the Christian rhetorical tradition to Thucydides and Demosthenes.[71]

Tornikes may be entirely honest in presenting Anna as deeply pious and constantly taking the Christian side in debates between classical and medieval Platonists. Yet the unceasing emphasis on Anna's piety seems a bit defensive. The section of the oration dealing with Anna's philosophical pursuits reads as if Tornikes were trying to convince his audience that philosophy was not incompatible with Christianity, and that one could maintain a pious Christian stance in the midst of classical studies. This defensive stance lends credence to his depiction of Anna as participating in serious philosophical discussions with a number of people. Tornikes is dealing with difficult material here, and his motivation for taking up its challenge presumably stems from his perception that this philosophical community was a significant part of Anna's legacy.

The entire description of Anna's philosophical work is bracketed by mourning, first for her father, and then for her mother and husband. Philosophy is presented as a good response to grief. The connection between philosophy and grief is a standard part of Christian discourse in which true philosophy, that is Christian theology, lessens pain and allows mourners to moderate their emotional response to death. Tornikes uses this valorized connection between mourning and philosophy as a framing mechanism for the discussion of Anna's interests in non-Christian philosophy. While at every key point he presents Anna as siding with the Christian Platonists against the pre-Christian authors, the thrust of this section of the oration is that Anna spent a great deal of time and energy on pagan philosophy. By enclosing this section within mourning for the deaths of her father and mother, Tornikes sets the entire discussion of potentially problematic interest in non-Christian philosophy in a pious Christian context.

Anna's extreme personal modesty returns to the center of attention when Tornikes discusses her authorship. While her skills in oral debate are lauded, Tornikes says that she was not interested in authorship:

> This especially is worthy of admiration . . . that she was not ambitious to leave behind many books, nor writing her name on many pages, annotating the writings of Euclid and Ptolemy and those of the Stagirite and Plato.[72]

Here Tornikes emphasizes Anna's authorial humility.[73] Although she could have written many books, she chose not to because she lacked ambition. This is another way of substantiating Anna's modesty in the midst of discussion of her deep expertise. Tornikes implies that she did compose commentaries on ancient mathematical and philosophical texts, but did not put her name on them. If her commentaries were written down, they presumably circulated anonymously, if at all.

Anna's modesty is further displayed in her reluctance to have her letters circulate. Anna's letters were deeply artful. There one found "grace, what harmony, what rhythm, what readiness, with words, what art in tricks, what beauty in conception, what dignity of scholarly thought!"[74] Anna crafted each letter specifically for the delight of the recipient, never suspecting that they would be performed before audiences.[75] Tornikes takes this as evidence of Anna's modesty, yet "good literature grows to circulate, even if made privately for one person, spreading out everywhere by nature, without delay, like light."[76] Here again Tornikes presents Anna as not seeking fame as an author. Rather her letters come to circulate contrary to her intentions: "And when writings needed to be left to the public, it was not gratifying for her."[77] Anna's memorials rather were the distributions she made for God to the poor in hospitals and old age homes.[78]

The discussion of Anna's reticence to put her name on writings and to have her letters circulate reinforces one of the central claims of the present book: that authorship was considered fundamentally self-aggrandizing and contrary to modesty. Anna's modesty is a key theme throughout the oration. Here Tornikes is careful to stress that she did not desire authorship for the sake of gratifying herself or making a memorial for herself. She commented on the works of others and may not have taken credit even for the commentaries. She wrote letters that were ostensibly for private pleasure only.

When he turns to discuss Anna's major surviving composition, the *Alexiad*, he takes particular care to avoid presenting Anna as working for her own aggrandizement. He opens his discussion by saying she was motivated by fear that time would wipe away the deeds of her father and emperor, using terms closely reminiscent of the opening of the *Alexiad*.[79] He primarily portrays her historical work as an act of devotion to her parents, claiming she earned the titles father-lover and mother-lover. The writing of history is presented as one of many signs of service and devotion she provided to her parents.[80]

Tornikes discloses a second motivation for Anna's historical writing, less clearly articulated in the *Alexiad* itself. Anna was especially interested in writing because of her "zeal for the truth" and her opinion that no one else had a better knowledge about the subject.[81] Tornikes credits Anna with research in oral and written sources: "She gathered infallible testimony from participants with her ears and saw undoubtable investigations with her eyes."[82] His description of the *Alexiad* itself is glowing, but relatively brief, saying that she had created an

> archetype of virtues for both emperors and individuals; relating every-
> thing clearly and in an orderly fashion with suitably beautiful composi-
> tion; matters about piety, politics and wars, about the administration of
> cities, justice in the courts and the distribution of honors, about con-
> cern for subjects, about severity with enemies, about magnanimity with
> ambassadors, about benevolence with conspirators, inner solemnity
> and exterior decorum, generosity in danger, calmness in pain, modera-
> tion in pleasure, generosity with gifts, charm with words, magnificence
> in deeds, and in everything the temperance and humility worthy of the
> emperors.[83]

Tornikes says that he does not need to describe the *Alexiad* further because everybody is able to see it for themselves. The *Alexiad* is acknowledged as one of Anna's accomplishments, but it by no means dominates Tornikes's description of Anna's life. He is far more expansive in his discussions of her philosophical views. The section on Anna's philosophical work takes up eleven pages in the modern edition, whereas the description of Anna's historical work takes nine-teen lines. Had Anna put her name on more philosophical books, the common assessment of her intellectual output may have been very different. It may be that to her contemporaries Anna was better known as a philosopher than as a historian. It may be that Tornikes chose to memorialize her philosophical work more thoroughly because, whereas the *Alexiad* was still available to sub-sequent generations, her philosophical work was a matter of memory within her intellectual community. It is also possible that Tornikes chose not to dwell on Anna's historical work because it was seen as a less appropriate activity for a woman, for any of the reasons explored in chapter 1. The historical precedents of the great female philosophers Hypatia and Theano may have made philoso-phy a somewhat more suitable pursuit for a woman.

Anna's devotion to her mother and father emerges as another consistent theme of Tornikes's oration.[84] Anna understood honoring parents as a law by nature, by scripture, and by spirit, and so she put the service to her par-ents before her children, husband, and the care for her own body.[85] Tornikes describes Anna's character as moderate, selfless, and devoted to caring for others. From her parents Anna received the qualities of temperance, mod-eration, humility, generosity, magnanimity, and gentleness.[86] Anna is cred-ited with great skill in comforting her relatives in their grief.[87] Just as Anna's emphasis on her filial devotion worked in the *Alexiad* to align her with ideal behavior for Byzantine women, here Tornikes emphasizes these same aspects of her character to praise her.

While Tornikes dwells at length on Anna's devotion to her parents and deep mourning for her husband, Anna's children are hardly mentioned. In her history, Anna similarly presents herself as a devoted daughter and loving wife, but her own children are never mentioned. The lack of emphasis on children should not be understood as reflecting an absence of affection, but rather taken within Byzantine culture's extreme discomfort with boasting. Children were not praised because of significant cultural concerns about boasting and malignant envy. The fear that praising children would call out forces that would do them harm is a consistent aspect of ancient and medieval Greek culture, re-envisioned but not fundamentally modified by Christianity.[88] Prodromos breaks the rule against complementing children at the end of his marriage oration for Anna's sons. He calls attention to his breaking of the rules by saying, "Be off, all envy! You have beautiful children married to beautiful girls, we might say the matter is worthy of Apollo."[89] This is a rare moment of unguarded exaltation in beautiful children, and is marked as being in defiance of the cultural rule against exciting envy. Prodromos's explicit evocation and rejection of worry about jealousy lets us know that this moment of praise is an exception that proves the rule. Within Anna's culture, people, particularly mothers, did not boast of their children. Tornikes does not enumerate Anna's children and alludes to them only briefly: "Lift up your eyes, whoever cares to, and see her children, statues who she polished in virtue, not debased metal, but brilliant with virtue and shining in beauty."[90] He describes Anna as devoted to caring for them as well as her parents and her husband, but he does not indulge in descriptions of them. Given this cultural injunction against praising one's children, we should not be surprised that Anna does not mention hers in the *Alexiad* and it is a mistake to say she lacked maternal interests.[91] Anna's allusions to Niobe may be oblique references to her own mourning for her children.[92] Anna's immediate audience would have known that she had endured the deaths of some of her children. By likening herself to Niobe, she may have called her own sorrows to mind.

Tornikes thus ascribes traditional female qualities to Anna and avails himself of the standard technique of saying that Anna's exceptional personal virtue allowed her to have masculine levels of self-control, discernment, and judgment. Yet these familiar methods of valorizing a woman's participation in masculine activities still left Tornikes with a challenging rhetorical problem in praising Anna as a woman. Tornikes appears to admire Anna but emphasizes her singularity in a way that at times seems to question her femininity.

Tornikes is explicit that Anna's endeavors were hampered by her gender. To him, her language was worthy of the Panhellenic theater, but her voice was confined in a female body, which did not allow her to properly display her work.[93] She was a highly skilled doctor who would have healed many people, had not the confinement of women within the house prevented her skills from being known to the public. She therefore lavished her skills on the members of her own household.[94] Tornikes presents these limitations on

Anna's successes as lamentable, but never turns the lament toward any sort of call for cultural change.

Tornikes lays out the essential difficulty in praising Anna in the introduction of his oration, as he explains that Anna presented an entirely novel subject for a eulogy. Tornikes excuses his delay in writing about Anna because he has waited for others to step up to the difficult task of eulogizing her.[95] By Tornikes's reckoning, only a handful of women in history have ever been able to achieve wisdom. Of them, only three studied philosophy. But Anna greatly exceeded their achievements because she alone was able to become learned while distracted by marriage and childrearing "and therefore attacked by waves of difficulties."[96] Anna's wisdom is a marvel because of her gender and her luxurious upbringing:

> Here is a woman belonging by nature to the fragile and delicate sex, only skilled for weaving, distaff and spindle, wrapped first in imperial swaddling clothes, then shining in youth from childhood, by being eldest, by her charm, by the beauty of the body no less than the soul—which is precisely what increases the love and affection of parents—delicately nurtured and raised in the imperial luxury, when just entering puberty girding her head at the same time with the crown of marriage and the imperial crown, and with all the imperial insignia, clothing with pearls and precious stones, thread of woven gold and silver, bracelets and necklaces, crowds of eunuchs, servants in quantity: the ones who mostly enflame covetousness in girls, one after the other offering or giving some new product for beauty. In the midst of such and so many great benefits, a woman, with all that, deploys a manly virtue and reaches the highest peak of wisdom, both human and profane and divine; what is more extraordinary that this miracle?[97]

The impediments to Anna's attainment of wisdom are here described as her gender, which ought to only be good at weaving, her upbringing in luxury (presumably including jewelry such as that pictured) and her maternal commitments. The wealth of the palace is presumed to tempt girls into obsession with physical beauty, while married life and caring for children present a different set of calls to contemplate earthly, fleshly problems. These material and familial concerns are all considered distractions and impediments to attaining wisdom.

The prodigious nature of Anna's intellectual attainments leads Tornikes to liken her to a rare celestial phenomenon. Anna's life deserves study and commentary, as conjunctions of planets and comets rightly attract attention even amidst all the stars of the night.[98] Anna became a new star in the literary firmament of Constantinople:

> So too the city of Constantine was also full of literature-loving men who exercised their ability successfully for any kind of speech, and one could

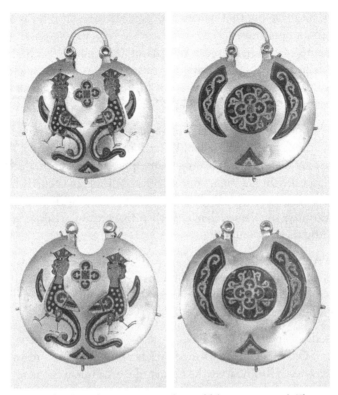

FIGURE 7.1 *Pair of Kolti with Sirens. Enamel on gold (5.3 cm x 5.6 cm). These pendants were affixed to caps so that they hung along the side of the face. Strings of pearls or beads originally were attached to the hoops around the edges. The figures on the front are mythological sirens with the bodies of birds and the heads of women. The backsides have geometric designs.*

© *Dumbarton Oaks, Byzantine Collection, Washington, DC.*

find thousands brilliant in wisdom, shining like stars; but since from the other sex, female, a rival star emerged—though I hesitate to say, out of reverence for men, her brightness exceeds that of men, however, say that there is none less brilliant—a star of beauty that transcends beauty, a grandeur that transcends greatness glittering rays and attractions, a new sun in the world of letters, it is she who should attract all eyes and all have had to describe the qualities of this star, so that the next generation and all the people to come learn the heavenly gift which also swept over us.[99]

Tornikes implies that Anna's brilliance in fact exceeded that of men, but he felt that saying so would be disrespectful to men. In this Tornikes substantiates the understanding that deference to masculine authority was a foundation value of Byzantine culture. There would be something fundamentally inappropriate in saying that Anna's star exceeded the brightness of those of her male contemporaries.

The theme of prodigiousness returns at the end of the oration when Tornikes deliberates about whether to praise Anna as a man or as a woman. The key difficulty is that Anna did not fit his culture's ideas about female behavior. He praises her by ascribing to her some masculine characteristics:

> Oh! What mouth is silenced! What eyes are closed! What intelligence is stopped! What mind is veiled! What charms have vanished! Woman more manly than men, exceeding them in wisdom and prudence! Soul, strong and befitting a man, confined in a delicate and female body! O body, bearing such a greatness of soul, you contain such courage, such magnanimity, such intelligence, such a treasure of wisdom, such an overabundance of thought![100]

Although Anna exceeds men in the masculine characteristics of wisdom and prudence, and possesses a soul fit for a man, she remains a woman, and her accomplishments are thus more remarkable. Anna makes the men look bad by taking up masculine work:

> The deeds of men fail because of you, as much as the female gender prospers. Oh! Hands that wielded tablets and pen instead of wool and spindle; who skillfully wove the beauty of words into a garment.[101]

Tornikes does not know how to properly praise Anna because he cannot settle on a proper comparison. He does not know if he should compare her to women, or to men:

> To whom shall I compare the one who is entirely unsurpassable? A women? But her superiority is not measurable with the word, because splendidly she both had the fairest beauty of the women and was rich with respect to the valorous deeds of men. A man? But she also prevails over them, since with a woman's body she is equal to the best of them, for I am ashamed to say she surpassed them. Oh! Wiser than men, more beautiful than women, and all the world speaks with respect! Oh! Beauty more august than that of women! Oh! Wisdom more graceful than that of men![102]

Anna surpasses men in wisdom, despite the limitations of her body, but equally surpasses women in beauty. She is both masculine and feminine.

In this disruption of gender norms Anna has become an entirely paradoxical creature. Unable to decide whether Anna ought to be praised as a man or a woman, Tornikes solves his dilemma by assimilating Anna to neither category:

> Oh creature, alone in the world as the sun and the moon and each of the stars. . .. For just as the phoenix has grown old with time and

is destroyed, they say another phoenix rises from its ashes, this also unique just as the previous one, ... and so exactly my empress, was a unique creature in this world with no second after her.[103]

Anna, fitting neither the category of women or men, is likened to a phoenix.[104] The strategy of likening Anna to a phoenix, instead of to any man or woman, provided a flattering way of dealing with Anna's transgression of gender norms. Masculine women are usually denigrated in Greek culture, but here Tornikes avoids this trouble by presenting Anna as a different kind of creature entirely.

Tornikes strengthens the disassociation between Anna and examples of masculine women in Greek culture by explicitly invoking, and then rejecting, that comparison. In making his case that Anna was unique, he reminds his audience that among the ancient Greeks there were "manly women and womanish men, base mannishness and womanishness, Teiresias and Penthesilea, and Artemis, an archer among the gods, and Athena, the warlike despoiler god."[105] Tornikes maintains that Anna is nothing like any of these ancient figures. Anna does not lose her proper feminine modesty as she adds masculine virtues.[106]

Tornikes's oration makes clear that Anna's intellectual activities were not normal female behavior in his society. His difficulty in deciding whether he should praise her as a man or as a woman, and ultimate decision that she was neither, reveals how far she did not conform to standard ideals of women's activities. He casts her into the standard valorized roles of the devoted daughter, loving wife, modest woman, and pious woman, all the while describing a wildly unusual and exuberant intellectual career. Tornikes commemorates Anna's striking intellectual achievements in numerous fields: philosophy, medicine, astronomy, history writing, letter writing, as well as extensive study in classical drama, music, and mathematics. He testifies to a stunning academic resume. That he does so while working simultaneously to present Anna as a devoted, demure, pious, and resoundingly modest woman underlines how necessary these virtues were for the good standing of a woman of her era.

Contemporaries probably shared the astonishment and admiration Tornikes expresses for Anna, and also his difficulty in finding a way for her to fit into this highly topologically bound culture, in which she had no real models. In fastening on the singular phoenix as a way of understanding Anna, Tornikes clarifies just how challenging it was for Anna to align her behavior with the models and forms of her society.

A Room of One's Own

Most people who have heard of Anna have been told that she was confined to a monastery following the failure of her attempt to seize power. In the early twentieth century, studies of Anna by Charles Diehl and Ferdinand Chalandon suggested that she retired to a monastery her mother had founded.[1] Other historians however suggested that her monastic retirement was enforced by John and served as a form of mild imprisonment.[2] In the course of the twentieth century the "fact" that Anna was involuntarily confined to a monastery in turn came to be seen as evidence corroborating her role in an attempted plot against John.[3] The strong presumption in scholarship is that Anna would not have wanted to be in a monastery, and that any evidence for her residence in a monastery indicates that she had been denied autonomy and freedom by her brother.

Anna indeed owned several apartments in the precinct of her mother's monastery. Yet nothing suggests her involuntary confinement there. Anna only became a nun on her deathbed, as was common in her culture.[4] Rather than assume a forced internal exile, the consistent role that expressions of deep piety had in enabling women in Anna's culture to act with greater freedom should spark us to consider the advantages Anna may have gained from her residences in monasteries. Extreme piety marked women as demure and supportive, like Mary, rather than as disruptive and sexually enticing, like Eve or harlots.[5] Within such a culture, a woman's ability to associate herself with monastic life would be just the sort of behavior that could give her license for greater autonomy.

Anna owned two sets of apartments in the monastery founded by her mother, yet the details of Eirene's foundation charter make clear that residence in these buildings did not imply adherence to a monastic way of life.

In the early years the twelfth century, Eirene and Alexios founded adjacent monasteries in the northwestern corner of Constantinople. Alexios founded the men's monastery of Christ Philanthropos, while Eirene founded the women's monastery of the Mother of God Full of Grace, "Kecharitomene." Eirene composed the foundation charter for Kecharitomene, probably around 1110, and added an addendum sometime in the later 1120s or 1130s.[6] Anna's apartments are described in the addendum, which altered the testamentary details in light of the death of Anna's sister Eudokia.

Anna had one set of apartments in Kecharitomene that she used while her mother was still alive, located on the wall that separated Kecharitomene from Alexios's Philanthropos monastery.[7] After Eirene's death, Anna was to inherit a second set of palatial buildings that Eirene had originally built for the use of her daughter Eudokia, who was a nun. They are described as "newly built and very sumptuous buildings."[8] Because Eudokia had died by the time of writing, Eirene decreed that these building should be given to Anna after Eirene's death.

What Eirene's various provisions seem to describe is a set of palatial dwellings within the boundary circuit of the monastery, but clearly demarcated as separate from the residences of the nuns. The charter makes clear that "imperial buildings" were separated from the rest of the monastery and not regular monastic cells: "The door which leads into this convent from the direction of imperial buildings will be closed on the inside by the superior and on the

FIGURE 8.1 *Pantokrator Monastery, seen from the east. This is the church of the monastery founded by John II and his wife, Eirene. Nothing survives of the Kecharitomene or Philanthropos monasteries.*

Photo by Bob Ousterhout.

outside by the guardian of the convent."[9] Eudokia's royal buildings were free-standing and apparently not connected to the walls of Kecharitomene.[10]

It is clear from the other provisions in Eirene's charter that the nuns followed a rigorous monastic practice, from which those residing in the sumptuous royal apartments were exempt. Eirene gives instructions about how her male descendants may visit their female relatives who are nuns in the monastery: under the supervision of the superior, only when the other nuns have returned to their dormitory, once or twice a year.[11] This restriction on visitors applies only to the convent and not the imperial buildings. The royal apartments, in contrast, could be frequented by Eirene or Anna, along with their male or female servants or children.[12] Anna or her daughters would have the right to take their meals with the nuns when they were using the apartments, but they could only bring two or three of their serving women.[13] While the nuns could not refuse hospitality to the grand Komnenian women, the women could not impose too large a retinue on the refectory. Unlike the nuns, those dwelling in the imperial building had no requirement to eat in the monastic refectory.

Anna's buildings in Kecharitomene were to be left to her daughter Eirene, and Eirene was given the authority to leave them to any of her children either male or female.[14] The freedom given to Anna's daughter to give these royal apartments to male descendants testifies to the degree to which they were separate from the women's monastery. Eirene specifies that if the line of Anna's descendants fails, control over these buildings was to return to the monastery. In that case, the buildings outside the courtyard were to be rented with the proceeds going to the monastery, while those inside the courtyards were to remain to be used as the monastery wished.[15]

Eirene directed that Anna's dwellings on the wall between the monasteries should be destroyed after Anna's death:

> After the departure from this life of Lady Anna, *porphyrogennete*, only the buildings overhanging the dividing wall and looking towards the garden of the monastery of *Philanthropos* must be destroyed, in which today resides the aforesaid lady, *porphyrogennete*; and this wall must be raised by further two cubits.[16]

Apparently Anna's apartment had a view of the adjacent men's monastery founded by her father. Elsewhere Eirene stipulates that Anna was not to expand these buildings to create a space that looked into the Kecharitomene courtyard.[17] The description of Anna's ability to see into the Philanthropos courtyard, and the concern that future building would allow a view of Kecharitomene, implies that these apartments were situated between the two monasteries, with potential access to both. While this arrangement was acceptable for Anna, once she was gone, these unusual apartments were to be replaced by a higher wall.

As the founder of her monastery, Eirene had financial oversight and own-
ership of it. Upon Eirene's death, the guardianship, *ephoreia*, would pass to
Anna, and in turn to Anna's daughter Eirene, and then to her female descendants. The position of guardian entailed financial control and protection
of the monastery, but not monastic vows or participation in monastic life.
Eirene explicitly banned the holder of the guardianship over her monastery
from entering the monastery except during liturgy.[18] In addition to financial
control and Eudokia's palaces, Anna was to inherit several other structures as
well as rights over water usage and future building in the monastery:

> Furthermore, she should possess the church of St. Demetrius with the
> two bathhouses and a third of the spring water that is brought into the
> buildings of the convent, that is, just as I possess them, and she must
> have complete freedom to build other new buildings, whatever kind
> she wishes, and to change those that exist, both the imperial and the
> other ones, in whatever way she chooses, and to alter them to whatever
> form she wishes, observing this only, namely, not to set a new burden
> of any sort whatsoever on the dividing wall of both monasteries, that
> is of *Philanthropos* and that of *Kecharitomene*, nor to have any place
> overlooking them.[19]

Anna's rights as guardian of the monastery and possessor of these royal buildings exceeded those of the monastery's superior. Eirene forbade the monastic
superior from making further expansions or alterations to the buildings of
the monastery itself. The future superior was only authorized to make necessary repairs to the structures that Eirene had built.[20] Anna and the future
guardians were explicitly given the right to build on the imperial rooms in
any way they pleased, change them as they saw fit, and to rebuild them if they
should happen to fall or burn down. The only restriction on their building
was that they could not make a structure that would allow one in the imperial
rooms to observe the private courtyard of the monastery.[21]

Anna's residence within the property of the monastery in no way implies
that she was subject to monastic discipline. Although at one point Eirene
describes Anna's apartments on the wall as her *kellia*, "cells," residence in
these apartments was not connected with taking monastic vows. Nothing
suggests that the two residences Anna came to own in Kecharitomene were
her only houses. Eirene envisions Anna continuing to possess both her rooms
on the wall between the male and female monasteries and the new buildings constructed for Eudokia. The residences in the monastic compound were
places she could stay when she liked. The section of Anna's will disposing of
property was not preserved, but the existence of the prologue indicates that
Anna had property of considerable value to give away after death.

We know that Anna sometimes lived in her apartments on the dividing
wall between the monasteries even while her husband was alive.[22] The simplest

explanation is that Anna chose to reside in the apartments on the monastery wall only some of the time. The theory that Anna lived at Kecharitomene in a forced internal exile disregards the evidence from court rhetoric that Anna and Nikephoros remained a devoted and loving couple. If Anna and Nikephoros had lived separately in any unusual way, Prodromos's poem in which he extravagantly laments Nikephoros's death in front of Anna would not have been polite.[23] Prodromos's expressions of mourning for Nikephoros go beyond what would be necessary in the context of a funeral oration for Anna's daughter-in-law, and can only be seen as responding to Prodromos's perception that Nikephoros was deeply mourned by Anna.

Given the basic impropriety of men intermingling with women to whom they were not married or related, a monastic residence may have afforded Anna a far greater range of freedom for her intellectual pursuits. As a married woman, Anna's interactions with men other than her husband would be deeply problematic. In those periods in which Nikephoros was serving John outside of the capital, Anna's contacts with other men would have been particularly suspect. Anna would need to be chaperoned. Only a few decades earlier, a general had advised that a man should never let a guest into his house because he would seduce his wife, or boast that he had on the battlefield.[24] Nikephoros did not take his advice on this subject, but both Nikephoros and Anna would have had a strong interest in minimizing the appearance of impropriety engendered by Anna's studies. Moving into her palatial apartments in Kecharitomene while her husband was on campaign may have allowed her greater freedom to continue discussing philosophy and classical literature with men to whom she was not related. Her status as an associate of a monastic community also shielded the men from accusations of inappropriate behavior. Philosophers could visit Anna, and receive visits from her, without incurring suspicion because her reputation for piety was simply above suspicion. Interacting with a princess was presumably safer for reputation and honor when she was staying in a monastery.

As Anna grew to be an older woman, the culturally perceived danger of sexual interaction would have diminished somewhat. Yet the many marriages of the Empress Zoe, continuing well into her middle age, indicate that age itself was not considered to limit a woman's interest in sex. The more Anna could do to desexualize herself, the more socially acceptable her interactions with other men would be. As a widow, Anna would need to clarify her lack of interest in remarriage and her status as beyond interest in sexual relationships. By associating herself with a monastery, Anna helped craft a modest and demure persona for herself.

Anna did not take monastic vows, presumably because she did not wish to submit to the full monastic discipline. Becoming a nun would have curtailed her ability to leave the monastery when she wished and her freedom to talk with men who were not her relatives. The nuns in the monastery of

Kecharitomene were not supposed to be visited by close male relatives, but could only speak with them at the gate under the direction of the superior.[25] Residence in the palatial buildings at Kecharitomene would associate both Eirene and Anna with the piety of monastic devotion, without requiring that they become nuns. Eirene's sumptuous buildings, annexed to a monastery, can be understood as offering both a palatial existence, worthy and appropriate for someone used to the imperial palace, and some aura of monastic piety.[26]

Beyond avoiding the appearance of sexual impropriety, living in a monastery may also have helped Anna deal with the simple transgression of her intellectual predilections. We saw how George Tornikes struggled to present Anna positively as a woman intellectual. One of his main strategies for rendering her interests in classical learning culturally licit was to insist strongly on Anna's great Christian piety. The same strategy could have been at play in Anna's choice to maintain a residence in a monastery.

The appeal for Anna of cloaking aggressive female behavior with a monastic aura is clear from her description of Anna Dalassene in the *Alexiad*. There, Anna uses piety to counter negative associations between women and power, as she describes how her grandmother ruled while Alexios was continually on campaign in the first years of his reign.[27] Anna Dalassene lived in the palace and ruled with great authority, but Anna Komnene rhetorically transformed the palace into a monastery in which her grandmother was able to live humbly. In Anna's description, her grandmother was insulated against accusations of power-lust because she was so far disinterested in power that she turned the whole palace into a monastery. The emphasis on Anna Dalassene's great piety cast her as a properly humble and deferential woman, even though she was running the government.

Anna deploys the same strategy for herself in descriptions of her own authorial power. As we saw in chapter 5, Anna counters every assertion of her research abilities with humbling gestures, including the presentation of herself as isolated and talking only with monks. It is this description of her isolation that provides the strong impetus for scholars to think she lived in a monastery. Yet we have missed how both her rhetorical isolation in the *Alexiad*, and her choice to reside in the precinct of a real monastery, helped to render her boldly transgressive historical and intellectual activities more culturally acceptable.

Dwelling in figurative or physical monasteries seems to have made Byzantine women appear humble and modest, and hence given them greater license for behaviors that fit gender ideals less easily. Maintaining a residence affiliated with a monastery afforded Anna a place to meet with her philosopher friends at those times when her husband was absent for the city, or merely engaged in other activities. Although she was not a nun, Anna's residence in a monastery presumably helped shield her from accusations of sexual impropriety. Residence in a monastery would give Anna ample opportunity to cultivate her intellectual life and write her history, while maintaining an ironclad reputation as a pious woman. Such a reputation could be highly valuable in enabling Anna to maintain close and prolonged ties with a community of male intellectuals. Rather than a place of forced exile, the apartments at Kecharitomene offered Anna greater freedom of action within the constraints of her culture's conceptions of proper female behavior.

{ 9 }

Ambition and Brotherly Love

Another thing that most people who know anything about Anna Komnene have been told is that she *really* hated her brother and wanted to rule the empire. So far we have not seen evidence for either that hatred or ambition. The seeds of both ideas come from thinking that Anna spearheaded an attempt to overthrow her brother. Intense hatred of John and desire for power are provided as the motivations that would make Anna try to murder John. Then, when the *Alexiad* is read with the assumption of those feelings, Anna's emotionalism in the text is interpreted as reflecting real anger and frustration. No one believes that she was that upset about the deaths of her parents and husband after all those years, and so her sadness is interpreted as being really about her political losses and isolation. When she laments the troubles and turmoil in her life, she is taken as alluding to political disappointments. But the key point of the first five chapters is that Anna *performed* misery and anguish in her book in a plea to make her writing more acceptable. We have no way of knowing whether she was actually upset about anything. When the *Alexiad* is read without the assumption that Anna hated her brother, it suddenly does not seem to support that supposition particularly well. Similarly, as we shall see, other texts that are said to reflect the grand conflict between the two siblings do not, in themselves, call for that interpretation.

Anna rarely mentions John in the *Alexiad*. His absence from the history has been interpreted as indicating that Anna disliked him and wanted to erase his memory.[1] John does not appear often in the history, but neither do other people that Anna clearly cared about. If familial affection were the main criteria for inclusion, we would know much more about her children, sisters, and her other brothers. There are plenty of other people whom one might expect to see in the *Alexiad*, who are similarly absent. The subject of the *Alexiad* is Alexios. Robert Guiscard and Bohemond of Taranto are described in detail, not because Anna likes them, but because they provide a worthy foil for Alexios.[2] In combating and defeating such larger-than-life heroes, Alexios is exalted, even when he is losing. Basil, condemned as a Bogomil heretic, plays a striking role in Anna's history. Again this is not due to affection that Anna had for him. His presence allows her to highlight Alexios's care for orthodoxy and proper cultivation of religious propriety within his empire. Attention to a character within Anna's history does not correlate with her affection for that person. John does appear in the *Alexiad* in the places where his presence is needed. To take his absence as an indication of Anna's personal animosity toward him is to bring a set of false expectations to the text.

Anna does give a brief one-line mention of the birth of John's twin children near Thessaloniki in 1106.[3] The mention of the twins comes shortly after the description of how Anna and her mother traveled with Alexios and the army. Apparently John and his wife, Eirene, were also traveling with Alexios at the time. The birth is an anomalous detail in a history that normally does not discuss domestic matters. If Anna had been traveling with the emperor at the time, and Tornikes was truthful about Anna being the family doctor, she may have served as Eirene's midwife. Anna may have thought the births were worthy of mention because John's son offered further stability to the dynasty Alexios had founded. It is also possible that she thought her sister-in-law's accomplishment in giving birth to twins was sufficiently great to get a line recording it for posterity. Regardless of whether this was a compliment to her sister-in-law, it is difficult to see it as reflecting animosity toward John.

FIGURE 9.1 *Mosaic of John II and Eirene bringing offerings to the Mother of God in Hagia Sophia, Istanbul.*

Credit Line © HIP/Art Resource, NY.

Much has been made of Anna's "unflattering" description of John's physical appearance as a man of dark complexion:

> The little boy was of swarthy complexion, with the broad forehead, rather thin cheeks, a nose that was neither flat nor aquiline, but something in between the two, and darkish eyes which, as far as one can divine the appearance of a newborn baby, gave evidence of a lively spirit.[4]

This portrait has been repeatedly taken as unflattering on the presumption that Anna hated her brother. It is not the most idealized description in the *Alexiad*, but neither is there anything particularly insulting about it.[5] Her statement that his nose was "neither flat nor aquiline" is used as evidence of dislike, although in both Byzantine culture and Aristotelian philosophy describing something as the mean between two extremes is a way of saying the thing is perfect. Anna describes her mother's face as neither round, nor long, but slightly oval.[6] If her description of John's nose were in another context, scholars would say that this nose was "just right."

The description of John as dark-skinned was taken by early twentieth-century historians as evidence of Anna's hatred, on the unstated assumption that readers of the twelfth century shared their own dislike of dark skin tones.[7] Somewhat circularly, because Anna is thought to have hated her brother, her description of John as dark has been interpreted as evidence that dark skin was considered unattractive in the twelfth century.[8] John was also described as having a dark complexion by the twelfth-century Latin historian William of Tyre: "John was a man of medium height, with black hair and swarthy skin, and for this reason is still called the Moor."[9] Choniates also describes John's son Manuel as dark in complexion.[10] Apparently Anna did not invent the detail of John's dark skin in order to denigrate her brother.

Throughout her history, Anna took pains to be impartial, including unflattering details as a means of substantiating that she was a trustworthy historian. In her portrait of her father, she included the detail that he was short, even though her other descriptions she consistently holds to the idea that a noble man ought to be tall.[11] Anna insists that, although lacking in stature, Alexios looked imposing when seated on his throne.[12] In saying that Alexios looked impressive when seated, Anna again was trying to be both a loyal daughter and an honest historian. Alexios's height was a good point on which she could substantiate her impartiality, because, since everyone would have known he was short, she would not have been able to get away with fibbing— far better to get the credit for her willingness to point out his flaw. Similarly, John's skin tone would not have been a closely guarded family secret. If John's skin was considered unattractive by his contemporaries, it would have been more flattering for Anna to omit a description of it. Yet had she neglected to point out such a notable aspect of his physical appearance, her history would have been more easily discounted as a work of flattery. Anna was more flattering in other descriptions in her book, and could have done more to make her brother look good. Yet there is nothing objectionable in her description of her brother, and there is considerable space between extreme flattery and eternal hatred.

Anna did not choose to whitewash John's least appealing hour, when he left his dying father to take control of the Great Palace. In the midst of her detailed description of Alexios's slow death, Anna mentions briefly that John had already left the emperor's bedside and that he went quickly to the Great Palace.[13] She then describes her mother as decrying interest in world power and beginning to wail in lamentation. Anna does not blame John for leaving, but her mother's cry to disregard all thought of temporal power calls out John's interest in taking control as inappropriate. It would have been far more flattering to John to omit the detail that he had left his father's side. Anna's choice to mention John's departure can reasonably be taken as showing a lack of affection. Anna of course had the excuse of needing to present the unvarnished truth in her history, but she did not let John's actions be forgotten.

Other readings used to suggest Anna's hatred for her brother are highly tendentious. Anna lists three causes of Alexios's gout: a riding accident during a polo match that injured his knee, the incessant demands of the Westerners who kept him working at all hours, and, perhaps, an unnamed man who remained with Alexios "like the most pernicious humors in the veins."[14] The character of this unnamed man was such that "he was not only a cause of the disease, but he was himself a malady and its most troublesome symptom."[15] Anna demurs from presenting this story in full, saying that she will only sketch it without details. She ends this discussion by saying, "I must bite my tongue and say no more. However eager I may be to jump on these scoundrels, I must not stray off my path. I will reserve what I have to say about him to the appropriate time."[16] She does not return to this topic in any recognizable way. Who was this man whose presence wore down Alexios? Anna's text does not provide enough information to even venture a guess. Yet it has been asserted confidently, and without discussion, that she attributed her father's illness, not to physical injuries, or long-winded Westerners, but to "the ingratitude of her brother John."[17] Anna gives no hints by which we could identify this troublesome man and nothing in this text suggests in any way that it was her brother. The presumed hatred of John is used as a heuristic tool to resolve the mystery in a way that reinforces the postulated hatred.

Elsewhere the meaning of the *Alexiad* is clarified in translation by assuming that obscure sentences somehow refer to John. At the very end of the *Alexiad*, where our text is fragmentary and Anna is engaging in full-on classical lamentation, she says,

> It would have been better for me, it seems, to have been changed into a soulless stone streaming rivers of tears. But still I remain, not insensate

to misfortunes. I must endure so many horrors and now men may stir
up yet other unbearable things which are more unfortunate than even
the ills of Niobe.[18]

The standard English version uses "people in the palace" to translate "men."[19]
This gives a specific political context to Anna's vague expressions of unspecified ills. We are lucky to have such a good English translation of the *Alexiad*,
and it is an excellent guide to Anna's text. But in this case the attempt at clari-
fication introduces politics into a passage where they are absent.

Because of the hatred Anna is presumed to have had for her brother, scholars have taken Anna's criticism of John's policies in the *Alexiad* as motivated
by personal animosity. Yet her policy disagreements with her brother and
nephew need not be connected in any way to an argument in favor of her own
rule. Anna's description of the First Crusade responded directly to the politics
of the mid-twelfth century, and her nephew Manuel's (1143–1180) handling
of the Second Crusade.[20] She made a political argument against her brother
and nephew's policies through her assessment of the empire's natural allies
and enemies. Anna approved of Alexios's relatively accommodationist policy
toward the Turks in Anatolia and with what she presents as his aggressive
stance toward Normans and Crusaders. She supports treaties with Turks and
fighting with Westerners. While both John and Manuel occasionally took a
more bellicose stance toward the Turks in Anatolia than had Alexios, Manuel
was willing to work far more closely with Westerners and eventually led the
empire to a set of alliances with the Crusader states that were underpinned by
notions of a common Christian cause.[21] Anna's evaluation of Alexios's reign
makes clear that she did not approve of these policies. By presenting Alexios
as manipulating the Crusaders and fighting the Normans, Anna argues for a
staunch anti-Western policy.[22]

Anna's most direct and biting criticism of pro-Western policies comes after
she describes how, following the death of Bohemond, Tancred failed to return
Antioch to Alexios. She describes in detail the treacherousness and avari-
ciousness of the counts of the Crusader states, with whom Alexios's payments
and negotiations had come to naught.[23] In contrast to the fruitless diplomatic
efforts to reach an accord with the counts, Anna tells a simple story of Alexios
receiving envoys from Persia (from the Seljuk Sultan of Baghdad) and per-
suading them to come round to his point of view. The next day they signed a
favorable treaty with the empire.[24] The stark contrast makes it clear that Anna
believed the Turks to be far more reasonable diplomatic partners than the
counts of the Crusader states. She describes the Turks' agreement to this treaty
as a significant victory for Alexios, one that brought peace and harmony to
the empire for the remainder of his reign. Anna describes Alexios's concerns
regarding this treaty as entirely those of "Roman sovereignty," perhaps, by
omission, indicating that he did not consider co-religion as a factor that ought

to play a significant role in politics. She explains that once Alexios died, however, this treaty was abandoned and all his efforts came to nothing through
the "stupidity of his successors."[25] This is a strong statement of disagreement
with the policies of John and Manuel, but it is part of a political argument, not
a random insult indicative of personal dislike. While the criticism for allowing treaties with the Seljuks to lapse falls on John, the implicit criticism for
trying to make useful agreements with Westerners falls on Manuel. Anna follows this bald criticism of Manuel's policies with further descriptions of how
dealing with the constant threats of the "Kelts," and the need to listen to their
endless requests, helped bring on Alexios's gout.[26] Here, and elsewhere, Anna
builds a consistent case against trusting Westerners and against cooperation
with the Crusader states. In this, her politics clearly contrast with that of her
nephew Manuel. Later in her text, Anna reveals that Alexios's treaty with
the Seljuks in fact was broken the following year, contradicting her statement
here that it was John's stupidity that caused it to lapse.[27] By blaming Alexios's
successors so robustly for the dissolution of the treaty, she distracts her audience from the fact that it failed on Alexios's watch. Rhetorically she is crafting
a story in which cross-confessional allies are a viable alternative to allying
with Crusaders, but she cannot quite get messy early twelfth-century politics
to fit, and she does not take the step of completely omitting information that
weakens her case.

In maintaining that a good emperor would ignore religious differences
among the empire's enemies, Anna was taking a stand in what was probably one of the central ideological debates of her era. Anna may have been
arguing for political viewpoint that was more common in the beginning
of the twelfth-century than at the time she wrote. As the Romans became
more aware of the theological arguments being put forth in favor of crusad-
ing, some were certainly persuaded that the empire had a moral obligation
to support their co-religionists. Anna did not agree, but her position in this
complex theological and political debate was certainly based on more than
a simple dislike for her brother. Hers was by no means an irrational, or even
unusual, reading of contemporary politics. As such, it makes little sense to
reduce her position to personal animosity.

Another text that has been interpreted in light of the presumed competition between Anna and John is a set of poems entitled the *Alexian Komnenian
Muses*, in which Alexios gives advice on ruling to his son. The first poem contains advice about how a ruler should behave, drawing lessons from Alexios's
own experiences. The second (incomplete) poem dwells on John's prowess
and how he fulfills his father's dreams for his son.[28] In the opening of the first
poem, the author explains that he was presenting the advice that the dying
Alexios had given to his son, indicating that the advice reached its current
form after Alexios's death.[29] It is possible that the author cast into verse ideas
and sentiments that Alexios was remembered as having articulated.[30] Since

John was the emperor when the text was composed, and the author would want another commission, the content of the poems was designed to be pleasing to John. The poems might reflect Alexios's thought, but they equally might reflect what John wished his father had said, or wanted his courtiers to believe his father had said.

For some scholars the poems stand as proof that Alexios always supported John rather than Anna.[31] For others the *Muses* represent John's wishful thinking and his efforts to present himself as having enjoyed his father's support: the poems become John's revisionist ploy for greater legitimization.[32] Yet nothing within the poems alludes to any such contest between John and Anna, nor is such an event required to interpret them. On the contrary, similarities in the characterization of Alexios between the *Muses* and the *Alexiad* indicate a common understanding of Alexios on the part of both authors, as well as common cultural values. The *Alexiad* and the *Muses* are not opposed to each other, and do not counter each other, except in a simple sense that the *Alexiad* emphasizes Anna's love for her father and the *Muses* express John's love for his father (or his father's love for him). Read without the presumption of political discord, these texts support visions of familial solidarity as much as familial rivalry.

The image of Alexios constantly fighting to defend the Roman empire against foreign enemies attacking from all directions is a recurring theme in both the *Muses* and the *Alexiad*.[33] Both texts portray the emperor as a solitary figure who is forced to work continually to combat the perpetual circle of encroaching enemies. The first poem describes Alexios as fighting his encircling enemies in manifold, wily ways, using the epithet of Odysseus, *polytropos*.[34] Odyssean imagery of the clever helmsman using whatever tricks were needed to get out of one tight jam after another form a recurring part of Anna's characterization of Alexios.[35] The Alexios of the *Alexiad* largely made up his own mind even as a green young man. The Alexios of the *Muses* preaches respect for old men, but treasures the advice coming from a young man with an old mind.[36] The Alexios of the *Alexiad* does not spend a lot of time in Constantinople listening to rhetoricians. The Alexios of the *Muses* would have his son provide a forum for clever men, but honor deeds more than words.[37] The Alexios of the *Alexiad* undertakes heartfelt penance for the destruction his revolt caused the city, diligently studies scripture, exercises clemency, and cares for his people with great piety.[38] The Alexios of the *Muses* warns his son that he will be judged as he judges, tells him to learn from Paul, and exhorts him to act always with virtue.[39] Both texts are emphatic that Alexios was a resoundingly successful general who taught his enemies to fear the Romans.[40] The two texts create a common portrait of Alexios as a pious, practical, moral man of action who devoted himself to the vigorous defense of an empire continuously beset by enemies on all sides.

The texts are also similar in what they portray as the major challenges and policies of Alexios's reign. The Alexios of the *Muses* remembers the crusade as a great trial of his reign, as does the *Alexiad*.[41] Alexios's advice in the *Muses* to keep the imperial treasury full, so as to be ready for another onslaught of foreign enemies, accords with Anna's descriptions of Alexios using money to hire mercenaries and pay off enemies.[42] The Alexios of the *Muses* warns his son to be ready to combat a long list of enemies, nearly all of whom Alexios fought in the *Alexiad*.[43] Both texts say that internal revolts presented Alexios with serious challenges, with the *Muses* mentioning revolts on Crete and Cyprus.[44] The Alexios of the *Muses* says that he will not mention "the men from within rising up in arms" who were always trying to topple the emperor, despite his authority "given from on high."[45] The *Alexiad* gives far more detail on the various conspiracies Alexios faces, but concurs with the opinion of the *Muses* that they are "always" taking place.

The *Alexiad* and the *Muses* share a common ideology regarding the roles of religion in politics. Both prize piety and consider military success as dependent upon having the support of God.[46] At the same time, the *Muses* and the *Alexiad* do not portray the empire as naturally driven to ally with Christian nations against infidel nations. In the *Muses*, the empire's enemies are not sorted into Christian and non-Christian groups, nor are the non-Christians described as somehow worse than the Christians. The enemies are distinguished by their military characteristics, and the Christian Westerners were particularly fearsome.[47] The emperor of the *Muses* needs to gain support from on high because he stands alone against the world; the religious affiliations of his enemies are not mentioned. In the *Alexiad*, Alexios is concerned to fight heresy within his empire, but his wars are not driven by desires to fight infidels.[48] He rather deals with foreign enemies as their challenges arise, and some of his greatest challenges came from fellow Christians. In both texts, deep Christian piety is compatible with a politics that is not swayed by confessional considerations. Twelfth-century Western arguments calling all the Christian princes to fight together against all the infidels would have been extremely foreign to viewpoint of the *Alexiad* and the *Muses*.

Both texts share a common sense of morality. The virtue of loving one's parents that Anna strongly articulated in the *Alexiad* is also clear in the *Muses*. The subtitle to the first poem calls Alexios "mother-lover" and John "father-lover," just as Anna proclaimed herself to be "both mother-lover and father-lover" and Anna Dalassene to be a "child-loving mother."[49] Clearly, intergenerational affection was a prized norm. The *Muses* maintain that virtue is a greater glory than the pearls on the imperial crown, mirroring Anna's depiction of her parents' stern morality.[50] The advice to distribute gifts readily and gently fits with Anna's descriptions of Alexios's generosity.[51] Other aspects of the advice in the *Muses* were less specific to Alexios, but such "timeless" ideas were repeated because they were thought to hold true, and they were certainly in keeping with the moral tone of the *Alexiad*. Concern with matters such as just administration, picking wise councilors, and ultimate judgment of a ruler's actions do not differ from the ethical thought in the *Alexiad*.

In terms of memories of Alexios's character, ideas about politics, and moral outlook, Anna and the author of the *Muses* have a great deal in common. One could even think they were siblings. Of course one could presume that every time Anna claimed to love her father, she really meant that she loved him *more than John*. One could also presume that John wanted his courtiers to say that Alexios loved him because, *in reality*, Alexios had disliked and distrusted him. In this way it is possible to understand the *Alexiad* and the *Muses* as representing a refined fight between two siblings over who was the better child. But such a reading is entirely unnecessary, and nothing in the *Muses* hints that this is what was going on. More simply, these texts reflect the common values, current at court, that Anna and John learned from their parents, and common impressions they gained from observing their father struggle against foreign enemies. If the *Muses* reflect John's own views, they and the *Alexiad* seem to testify to the ability of Alexios and Eirene to raise children who shared their sense of morality and values. If John and Anna are presumed to have been enemies, these poems provide no basis to understand what they were fighting about. On the contrary, they demonstrate an absence of disagreement between Anna and John on issues of morality, political ideology, and their father's character.

Anna's supposed coup attempt is normally seen as the product of her own ambition rather than a reasoned political choice. Especially in light of the political consonance between the *Alexiad* and the *Muses*, it is difficult to think what policy would be different, or what party would benefit, if Nikephoros ruled instead of John. Scholars have not been able to establish a compelling political rationale that would have underpinned any efforts to alter the succession away from John. It has been supposed that support for Nikephoros was support for the great aristocratic houses of the eleventh-century, such as the Doukas family, against the Komnenos family.[52] Anna can reasonably be seen as having an affiliation with her mother's Doukas family.[53] But there is no reason to think that Anna would represent that family more than her brother John.[54] Also the role of aristocratic lineages in politics of the early twelfth-century now seems to have been overblown.[55] The strongly pro-Alexios politics of the *Alexiad* complicates alignment of Anna with any kind of anti-Komnenian party.

There is one surviving medieval text that can be read as making a strong case that Nikephoros Bryennios would have been a great emperor. This text is the history Nikephoros wrote. Yet the case he made for the superiority of his own line was systematically refuted by Anna in the *Alexiad*. When Anna's history is compared to her husband's, it makes even less sense to see her ambition as the driving force behind an attempted coup.

Nikephoros Bryennios's history is the work of a man who, I think, would have very much liked to be emperor.[56] Had his grandfather defeated and blinded Alexios, rather than the other way around, he probably would have been emperor. His history tells the story of the fight between his grandfather, Nikephoros Bryennios the Elder, and Alexios in a way that gets the audience to root strongly for his grandfather. Nikephoros presents Alexios as duplicitous, brash, ruthless, and immature. These characteristics are set in contradistinction, on every point, to the courageous, disciplined, honest, and mature men whom Nikephoros portrays as struggling heroically to fight the good fight even as they lose to the treacherous tactics of the Turks and Alexios. Alexios is the winner of Nikephoros's history, but not the hero.

Nikephoros's case that his grandfather was more worthy to rule than Alexios certainly may have provided fuel for rumors that Nikephoros had wanted to succeed Alexios. At the same time his history explains the good working relationship Nikephoros and John seem to have enjoyed. Despite the criticism of Alexios, Nikephoros's history makes a case for Komnenian dynastic legitimacy and argues that aristocratic civil war was one of the causes of imperial decline in the eleventh century.[57] His history is both a vindication of his grandfather's (and presumably his own) supreme qualifications for rule, and an apology for supporting the dynastic rights of the Komnenos family. Nikephoros's valorization of honorable defeat created a stable, meritorious role for himself as a man of great honor who served the legitimate victor. At the time he was writing at least, Nikephoros seems to have been fully reconciled to his role as John's helper.

Anna's insistence on her father's greatness as a ruler undercuts the implicit claim of her husband's history that the empire would have been better off with a Bryennios on the throne. In that Anna presents her father as a morally upstanding and valorous, as well as a great emperor, her history fundamentally disagrees with the politics of her husband's. Anna systematically counters her husband's negative portrait of Alexios. Nikephoros presents Alexios as winning undeserved victories by trickery rather than direct confrontation. Anna accepts this fundamental presentation, but she strives to invert the moral valuation of trickery. Anna agrees that her father preferred to win by guile, but she upholds that propensity for trickery as virtuous behavior that could lead to bloodless victories.[58] In this and other ways she refutes her husband's case that Nikephoros Bryennios the Elder would have made a better emperor than Alexios. There is no rationale by which the *Alexiad* can be seen as supporting Nikephoros's political ambitions.

Choniates's history, which portrays Anna as disputing her father's succession, and Nikephoros upholding it, inverts the political meanings at the heart of the histories Anna and Nikephoros wrote. This discrepancy was not a problem for Choniates because he was not interested in discussing real politics in his section on Alexios's death. He was telling a bad story of family discord at the foundation of the Komnenos dynasty. Such a story did not bother to make sense of the political stances taken in Anna and Nikephoros's histories. Considering the politics of their histories gives us yet more reason to doubt that Choniates's story reflected the reality of Nikephoros and Anna's lives.

Anna's expressions of mourning and misery in the *Alexiad* have been taken as her way of venting her fury with her brother and frustration at her loss of power. The new interpretations of her writing offered in the first half of this book effectively remove the *Alexiad* as evidence for Anna's anger and ambition. When her expressions of misery are given other explanations, there is suddenly less compulsion to see Anna's life as dominated by hatred and desire for rule. She may well have disliked her brother, but there is not much of any reason to think so. She may have liked the thought of being empress (who wouldn't?), but she must have gotten over it because in her history she argued *against* all the reasons her husband had given for thinking he would have been a better emperor. The reevaluation of Anna's authorial strategies significantly readjusts how prominently we should see any political tension in Anna's life.

As for what really happened in 1118, you are now a qualified expert, able to make your own best guess based on the available evidence. What ought to have been a smooth succession certainly seems to have sparked a lot of talk. If Nikephoros and Anna indeed helped Alexios and Eirene with their duties for some period of time, some people at court may have wanted Nikephoros to continue on as emperor. John may have acted to secure his authority before his father died. Yet whatever happened does not seem to have had any lasting impact on John's reign, or Anna and Nikephoros's lives.

{ 10 }

The "Fury of Medea"

Even if you were only half paying attention in the last four chapters, you now have a much larger base of information on which to construct a portrait of Anna Komnene than was available to the scholars of the eighteenth century who established the fundamental narrative of Byzantine political history. They worked almost exclusively from the narrative histories that were the first Byzantine texts to be studied, edited, and translated into modern languages. It also goes without saying that, whatever your approach to reading medieval texts, it is not that of an *Ancien Régime* savant. In this chapter we will explore how Anna has been portrayed since the eighteenth century, but not for the sake of pointing out how scholars from different intellectual worlds have gotten it wrong. Rather we are tracing the feedback loop in which some scholars' readings of the *Alexiad* created negative impressions of Anna's character that then led them to read medieval evidence as showing that Anna was "really" ambitious and arrogant, which then reinforces the disparaging interpretations of the *Alexiad*.

Once a story gets established in scholarship it tends to have staying power because scholars will read evidence in light of the story they already know. The sample of histories examined in this chapter show the story that placed Anna at the center of a coup taking shape in the late eighteenth century, that narrative guiding interpretations of the *Alexiad* and Anna's character in the nineteenth century, and scholars shoehorning their new evidence to fit the existing narrative in the early twentieth century because that story was fundamental to their understanding of Anna. All the while European intellectual culture and historiographic practice were evolving and changing so much that scholars in different sections of this chapter may have had little in common aside from interest in Anna. Despite the changes in academic methodologies, the historians in this chapter are remarkably dependent upon each other's work. Together, over time, they assembled the picture of Anna as a power-hungry, arrogant woman keen on her brother's destruction.

Anna was not always seen so negatively. In 1680, she comes off quite well in the work of one of the founders of Byzantine studies, Charles du Fresne du Cange. He admires Anna and writes approvingly of her education and history:

> Anna Komnene, Porphyrogennete, ... a woman of great spirit, and brilliant distinction in all kinds of knowledge, which is immediately attested by her excellent *Alexiad*. [1]

Du Cange explains that when Alexios was ill, Eirene "inclined more than was fitting to her daughter and son-in-law Bryennios, as outstanding in eloquence, and capable of accomplishing things," and that "Bryennios himself, compelled by his wife Anna, canvassed for a fruitless attempt on the imperial dignity."[2] Du Cange's interpretation that Bryennios was compelled by Anna is presumably based on his reading of Choniates, but he does not follow Choniates in denigrating Nikephoros. Rather he describes Nikephoros as "equally trained in all subjects" and shares his excitement about the recent discovery of Nikephoros's history.[3] Du Cange expresses a genuine admiration for the intellectual activities of Anna and Nikephoros.

Anna was far less sympathetically treated in Charles Lebeau's monumental work, the *Histoire du Bas-Empire*, which was published in 21 volumes from 1757 to 1778 and reprinted frequently throughout the nineteenth century.[4] Lebeau created an edifying and dramatic tale of the whole of Byzantine history.[5] While he usually cleaves closely to the medieval histories he is summarizing, he editorializes his story about Anna. Lebeau's narrative is synthesized from those of Zonaras and Choniates in a way that maximizes the actions of Eirene. He combines Zonaras's description of Eirene's power during Alexios's final years with Choniates's description of Eirene denigrating her son before her husband in an effort to convince him to alter his succession. He includes a version of the speech Choniates gave to Alexios in response to Eirene's badgering. In his story, Eirene and John's competitive positioning intensifies in Alexios's final hours.

Lebeau clarifies the deathbed vignettes presented by Zonaras and Choniates into one story in which John, aware of his mother's plans, entered the room of the dying Alexios and secretly removed his ring from his father's finger without his mother noticing. In a nod to Zonaras's competing stories and Choniates's doubts, he explains that "some said this was done with the will of his father."[6] But where the Greek authors leave the audience guessing, Lebeau immediately assures his audience that Alexios's approval was "very probable."[7] Lebeau includes Zonaras's story of John meeting the Georgian envoys, but then moves to Choniates's story that Eirene tried to motivate Nikephoros to take up arms, to John ignoring his mother's calls to stand down while his father lived, and then to her final appeals to Alexios. Lebeau clarifies Alexios's response, providing a bit of dialog:

> "Dear spouse," she said to him, "you live, and your son snatches the crown." Alexios, who was no longer occupied with this life, raised his eyes to heaven without responding. As she continued to importune him with her cries, the dying prince, casting an agonized smile, "Leave me with God," he said in punctuated words, "I ask his forgiveness for my crimes; the world is no longer anything to me." The despairing princess, leaning over him, could not help saying, "You die as you have lived, always full of deceit."[8]

From this version of Choniates's deathbed scene, Lebeau turns to Zonaras's stories of John's acclamation in Hagia Sophia and his efforts to persuade the Varangians to open the palace to him by claiming Alexios had died, which Lebeau calls "a momentary perjury."[9] He includes Choniates's story of some common people getting inside the palace.

Lebeau enhances Anna's political role in his story of John's accession, which he bases on Choniates. He opens the chapter on John by saying, "A powerful mother, who had given reason to believe that she preferred her son-in-law to her son; an ambitious sister who wanted to put her husband on the throne, gave concern to the legitimate successor."[10] Lebeau compresses the timescale of the narrative, placing the conspiracy as soon as John began appearing in public.[11] The impetus for the conspiracy is entirely placed on Anna: "The intrigues of Anna Komnene, to make the crown fall to her husband, had gained Bryennios a great number of partisans."[12] Choniates attributes the conspiracy to a less specific crowd of jealous relatives and "an evil conspiring swarm."[13] Where Choniates described Nikephoros's good qualities, Lebeau substitutes a comparison of the appearance of Nikephoros and John that implies that the conspirators were swayed by Nikephoros's good looks. Lebeau says they "did not yet have the time to see that [John's] disadvantageous exterior was covering an elevated and generous soul, far superior to that of Bryennios."[14]

Lebeau departs from Choniates to say that Anna rallied all the philosophers of the empire to her husband's cause. Lebeau describes the philosophers as hypocritically protesting against adulation while obsequiously flattering Anna: "Anna Komnene, woman philosopher, had all the philosophers of the Empire in her party, who prostrate at her feet, and showering flattering praise, declaimed incessantly against adulation."[15] This humorous dig at the philosophers Anna interacted with works to undermine her legitimacy as an intellectual. She is surrounded, not by serious moral thinkers, but by hypocritical flatterers. Any philosophy she could have learned from such men would be worthless. Lebeau acknowledged that Anna was learned, but by undercutting the value of that learning, she becomes primarily ambitious.

Lebeau says Anna was "the soul of the plot" working for Nikephoros's elevation. In his judgment the plot "would have succeeded if her husband had resembled her," implicitly attributing to Anna the masculine strength he saw Nikephoros as lacking.[16] Nikephoros, he suggests, let the hour pass because he felt remorse at the thought of killing John. Lebeau includes a desexualized version of Anna's complaint against nature, claiming that Anna said "that nature, in forming the two, had by mistake given to the female the soul intended for the male."[17] Lebeau continues with the story of John Axuch's intercession on Anna's behalf, quoting his dialogue with John, largely as it appears in Choniates.[18]

Lebeau's story cleaves closely to Choniates's narrative line, but makes no effort to convey the sexual undertones of Choniates text. There is little chance that a Hellenist of his extreme skill would have missed them. Rather he chose to write a narrative that was cleaner, either out of his own predilections or the social conventions of his era. Changing Anna's complaint that nature made a mistake in genitals into one about a mistake in souls is the most overt example of Lebeau's desexualization of Choniates. The resulting story has an entirely different tone. It is still a moralizing story, but it is about poor political judgment more than raging emotional and sexual pathologies. Nikephoros emerges far more sympathetically when his lack of action is presented as a choice based simply on moral compunction, rather than metaphorical sexual dysfunction. The general desexualization of the narrative has a consequence in the highlighting of Anna's role. When the other elements of Choniates's rhetoric are removed, Anna's role is proportionately more significant because there is less going on in the story. The resolution of the competing versions of Alexios's deathbed scene into one in which Alexios, most probably, approves of John's seizure of power removes many of the ambiguities about how John's actions were remembered by the medieval historians. John becomes a hero whose decisive actions and great clemency are lauded highly. Lebeau's synthesis of Zonaras and Choniates into a simplified story of good male emperors thwarting the plots of scheming women provided an influential baseline for understanding Anna's life throughout the nineteenth century.

This centrality of Anna to the conspiracy narrative becomes even more acute in the version of the story appearing in chapter 48 of Edward Gibbon's *History of the Decline and Fall of the Roman Empire*, first published in 1788, and continuously in print since then.[19] Gibbon relies on Lebeau's synthesis of Zonaras and Choniates, but his version is more morally judgmental.[20] In his story, Eirene wanted to transfer the succession not to Nikephoros, but to Anna, "whose philosophy would not have refused the weight of the diadem."[21] This mocking of Anna's philosophy negates the validity and merit of Anna's intellectualism, just as had Lebeau's description of the flattering philosophers declaiming flattery. In Gibbon's hands Anna is no longer a conspirator, but rather a traitor. Eirene's plans were thwarted "by the friends of their country," and John is called "the lawful heir."[22] Anna alone is involved in the attempt on John's life, and she is provided with a motivation for the first time: "Anna Komnene was stimulated by ambition and revenge to conspire against the life of her brother."[23] Gibbon does not explain why Anna wanted revenge. Although he usually does not refrain from describing the more salacious aspects of Roman history, Gibbon follows Lebeau in making Anna's complaint about souls rather than genitals: "And when the design was prevented by the fears or scruples of her husband, she passionately exclaimed that nature had mistaken the two sexes, and had endowed Bryennios with the soul of a woman."[24] Gibbon tells the story of John's clemency at the urging of his servant John Axuch, concluding that "the reproach or complaint of an injured brother was the only chastisement of the guilty Princess."[25] The remainder of his description of John is extremely flattering, even likening John to Marcus Aurelius.[26]

Gibbon anticipated the argument I made in chapter 5, in recognizing Anna's description of her isolation as part of a strategy to appear impartial:

Conscious of the just suspicions of her readers, the princess Anna Komnene repeatedly protests, that, besides her personal knowledge, she had searched the discourses and writings of the most respectable veterans: and after an interval of thirty years, forgotten by, and forgetful of, the world, her mournful solitude was inaccessible to hope and fear; and that truth, the naked perfect truth, was more dear and sacred than the memory of her parent.[27]

Gibbon understands Anna's protestations of isolation as a response to the problem of objectivity. He does not accept her argument, however, but rather responds by rejecting the intended effect of Anna's text:

Yet, instead of the simplicity of style and narrative which wins our belief, an elaborate affectation of rhetoric and science betrays in every page the vanity of a female author. The genuine character of Alexios is lost in a vague constellation of virtues; and the perpetual strain of panegyric and apology awakens our jealousy, to question the veracity of the historian and the merit of the hero.[28]

Gibbon does not clarify how the vanity of a female author would differ from the vanity of a male author. Rather he intends to say that women who presume to write were vain by definition. His second statement, that "the genuine character of Alexios is lost in a vague constellation of virtues," is belied by his subsequent description of Alexios, which is a tight summary of Anna's main arguments.[29] In Gibbon's later narrative of the passage of the First Crusade, he is entirely willing to use Anna's *Alexiad* as a corrective to the Western sources.

Gibbon then, does not distrust the *Alexiad* more than other sources, despite saying that Anna's vanity excites suspicion. His distaste for the text appears to be a response to Anna's "affectation of rhetoric and science."[30] It amounts to a personal dislike of an author he sees as vain. His attribution of vanity to Anna, together with "ambition and revenge,"[31] creates a highly negative image of Anna. Gibbon's decision to replace Nikephoros with Anna as the object of Eirene's attempts to alter the succession was taken up by subsequent authors. It may make the story less extreme to think that Eirene favored a daughter over a son, rather than preferring her son-in-law, as the medieval sources maintain. Gibbon's version makes Anna's ambition the point of the story and fits with his assessment of her character in the *Alexiad* as vain.

Gibbon's oblique connection between authorial vanity and political ambition is far more concretely and overtly expressed in Johann Heinrich Krause's 1869 *Die Byzantiner des Mittelalters*. He tells the story of the attempted usurpation twice, once focusing on Eirene in a chapter on the consorts of the emperors and their influence, and again in a section on the education of women in a chapter on Byzantine education where the focus is on Anna.

Krause praises Anna, saying that she surpassed all her female contemporaries in talent, in education, and through "a nearly masculine character."[32] In Krause's mind her masculinity of character is apparent in both her intellectual and political ambitions:

> She emerges with more of a masculine than feminine character, as she asserts by her very decision to make herself a history writer, yet much more through the event of her vigorous operations against her brother, the Emperor John, in which a mild, feminine disposition and sisterly love is completely missing.[33]

Here both history writing and vigorous political action are linked as masculine activities in which Anna engages. Krause says that Choniates presents Anna as the driving force behind the conspiracy and Nikephoros as the cooler head who accurately assessed the political situation.

Krause weaves Choniates's anecdote about Anna's accusation against nature into his story. Acknowledging that Anna's words "cannot be reproduced in our language without violation of literary decorum," he interprets Choniates as saying that nature had mixed up masculine and feminine *beings* in making Anna and Nikephoros.[34] He seems to agree with the assessment that Anna would have made a good man. Krause praises Anna's ability to write military history, which he attributes to her essential masculinity:

> Incidentally her masculine spirit shines also in her descriptions of battles, in which she pictures the deeds of daring courage in the most vivid colors and even with the technical terms of the strategic and tactical art,

showing just as much familiarity as a male author who personally has taken part in campaigns.[35]

In this respect, Krause's view of history was quite similar to that of ancient writers. He considered personal experience and autopsy to be the best means of gaining understanding needed to write accurate descriptions of battles. It is high praise to say that Anna could narrate a battle as well as a man with military experience. His conception of gender also aligned with twelfth-century ideas that exceptional women could become masculine.

The connection between political ambition and masculinity is not consistent for Krause, however, since in his discussion of Eirene, her ambitions are described as a natural consequence of her *feminine* heart. In the discussion of Eirene, she is depicted as the main force for the conspiracy, seeking the throne for Anna, with Nikephoros appearing merely as Anna's husband.[36] His assessment of Eirene is that

> no doubt she was mentally and physically equipped with excellent qualities. But she was not free from those weaknesses arising from ambition to which the female heart is so susceptible. She did not remain alien to the secret tendencies serving intrigue, and always seeking to put her son John in an unfavorable light for her husband, to secure the succession to the throne for her beloved daughter Anna and her husband, which the former sought even more than the latter.[37]

Ambition here is presented as a naturally female characteristic, and associated with intrigue and cunning. Krause does not explain by what logic Eirene's ambition would be better served by having her daughter in power than her son.

Male strength in standing up to female cunning is valorized as Krause approvingly describes the ability of Alexios and John to stand firm and act with energy in the face of Eirene's machinations, concluding, "The intelligent Emperor Alexios, equipped with great wisdom, was not the man to let himself be deceived by the cunning of a woman, because his whole life had been a struggle with foreign trickery and violence."[38] Consistent to both of Krause's versions of the conspiracy story is the association of men's actions with good politics and women's actions with misguided, emotionally driven, bad politics. Eirene was dangerous because she was a scheming woman, whereas Anna was dangerous as an unnaturally masculine woman.

A somewhat more sympathetic view is found in the work of Krause's contemporary, Emil Oster, who published a dissertation on the *Alexiad* in 1868.[39] He explains the efforts to promote Nikephoros as a matter of competing political parties as well as personal resentments. He presents John as open to a possible accord with the West, and puts him at the head of a party supported by his brother Isaac and the army. They were opposed by Anna, her mother,

FIGURE 10.1 *The opulence of the Byzantine court, as imagined by Alexandre Hesse (1806–1879) in "Godefroy de Bouillon faisant acte d'allégeance à l'empereur byzantin Alexis Comnène" for the Hall of the Crusades in the Palace of Versailles. The young woman wearing a diadem, peering inquisitively at the Western knights from behind the throne, presumably represents Anna.*

Credit line: Photo: Gérard Blot. Chateaux de Versailles et de Trianon © RMN-Grand Palais/Art Resource, NY her brother Andronikos, and the "orthodox clerical party."[40] This alignment of the factions in the family with larger political forces places less emphasis on Anna's personal hatred of her brother.

When it comes to the actual course of events, Oster presents a version of the simplified story first articulated by Lebeau. John secretly takes the ring from the dying Alexios and races to the palace. His actions are decried to Alexios, not only by Eirene, but also by Anna and "their followers."[41] Alexios says he is not interested in earthly cares, but Oster clarifies that, "in reality," Alexios wanted to give John a free hand in seizing the empire, a conclusion Oster reaches from "the psychology of [Alexios's] whole character."[42] Anna could not accept to pay homage to her brother, and "ambitious and energetic as she was," she became the "head and soul" of a plot to overthrow John.[43] Nikephoros had support from the strongly orthodox party, on account of his great learning, but allowed the hour to pass. Oster's description of Nikephoros's decision and John's clemency follows Lebeau closely.[44]

Oster differs from his predecessors in paying far greater attention to the *Alexiad*, but he uses information in the *Alexiad* to support Lebeau's basic narrative. Oster is the first of the authors considered here to have Anna end her life in a monastery. He interprets Anna's description of her isolation in her discussion of her sources as evidence that she lived in monastic seclusion. Anna's lamentations for her parents and husband are taken as evidence that she was not happy there.[45] Anna's criticism of John's military policies elsewhere in the *Alexiad* is presented as evidence for their lack of reconciliation.[46] These aspects of Anna's self-presentation are thus brought into line with the developing narrative of her life.

The story of Anna and Eirene conspiring against Alexios and John becomes a tool for the interpretation of the *Alexiad* in the highly influential works of Ferdinand Chalandon on Komnenian history.[47] His works have been valued for their highly detailed reconstructions of events, and are still occasionally cited in scholarship concerned with twelfth-century politics. Chalandon deals with the tension over John's succession first at the end of his volume on Alexios, published in 1900, and again, with a stronger focus on John, at the beginning of the volume dedicated to his reign, published in 1912.

Chalandon thinks that Eirene accompanied Alexios during his final campaigns because he wanted to control his wife and prevent her conspiring in the capital without him:

> Although Anna Komnene claims that her father took Eirene with him to nurse him, she does not hide from us the fact that her mother followed Alexios reluctantly. One must, I think, see in the conduct of the emperor a measure of distrust. Komnenos feared that during his absence from the capital, his wife would be the head of the conspiracy.[48]

This suggestion that Alexios did not trust Eirene enough to leave her in the capital has been often repeated.[49] Chalandon trusts Anna's statement that Eirene did not want to leave the palace but ignores the role of that claim in Anna's construction of her mother as a modest woman.[50] The story of the conspiracy here becomes the historical background that allows Chalandon to get to the "reality" behind Anna's rhetoric.

Chalandon's account of Alexios's death resolves a number of the ambiguities in the narratives of Zonaras and Choniates in favor of a picture in which Alexios and John work in concord to thwart the machinations of Eirene. After dismissing Anna's account of the deathbed events as flattering to Eirene, but different from "reality," Chalandon presents two possible versions of events.[51] In the first, John went to the palace, saw the state of his father, and left to be proclaimed. In the second, a greater role was played by Alexios, "a role much in conformity with his character."[52] Alexios took advantage of the absence of the Empress to call John to him, give him his ring, and order him to be proclaimed before time was lost.[53] Following his father's orders, John was proclaimed by his partisans, and taking advantage of the calm in the city, he hurried to Hagia Sophia where he was crowned by the patriarch. From there he rushed to the sacred palace "whose solid walls would allow him to defy the riots raised by his adversaries."[54] The Varangians, who guarded the palace, "at first opposed the entrance of the son of the emperor; but at the sight of the imperial ring and the announcement of the death of Alexios, ceased their resistance."[55] Back at the Mangana Palace, Eirene redoubled her efforts to get Alexios to recognize Bryennios, "but the emperor, hearing that his son had succeeded, smiled and raised his hands, as in thanks to God."[56] Eirene than utters an accusation of mendacity modeled on that of Choniates.[57]

Although he provides two alternative stories of Alexios's actions, Chalandon clearly marks the story in which Alexios supported John as the one to be believed when he says that Alexios's actions fit his character. In Zonaras's narrative, this is designated as the version John liked, and by implication, the one preferred by flatterers. Alexios is given more agency in Chalandon's version, calling John to him, and ordering him to go off to be proclaimed. The reference to "riots" excuses John from leaving his dying father and blames Anna for disorder. Unlike the previous historians examined, Chalandon explicitly denies the veracity of Anna's account of Alexios's death in the *Alexiad*. Alexios also unambiguously thanks God for John's success, whereas in Zonaras's original it was unclear whether he was cursing John, praising him, or simply past caring.

Chalandon uses mockery to make Anna appear more ferocious in his version of Choniates's story about the attempt to kill John. Several months after John's accession, "Anna Komnene, whom one of her contemporaries calls the fourth Grace and the tenth Muse, exasperated in the failure of her attempt to seize the throne, came to organize a new plot which had as its goal the assassination of her brother."[58] Chalandon uses this allusion to Prodromos's oration for her sons' wedding to heighten his portrayal of Anna as bloodthirsty. In his mocking of Prodromos, Chalandon undercuts the whole corpus of court rhetoric that praised Anna and Nikephoros. He then tells the story of conspirators gathering, their troops entering the grounds at Philopation, and then waiting in vain for the arrival of Nikephoros until they were discovered at dawn.[59] He mentions that at the moment of the failure of the assassination attempt, "she entered into a towering rage and complained in the crudest terms that Providence had given virility to Nikephoros and not to her."[60]

Chalandon politicizes Eirene's monastic foundation, presenting Eirene as founding Kecharitomene as a political refuge for herself, for Anna, and her granddaughters.[61] He sees this refuge as necessary because Anna had fallen into deep disgrace: "Abandoned entirely by the world of courtiers, Anna Komnene lived mostly in the monastery of Our Lady Full of Grace, where no one would trouble her solitude; in effect, she did not have any influence."[62] Chalandon explains that Nikephoros had not shared her disgrace, but does not clarify how exactly Nikephoros continued to live at court while Anna stayed in the monastery. Anna's intellectual activities are considered a diversion she took up to distract her from the memories of her crimes: "After the death of her husband, Anna became yet more isolated, and sought in the cult of letters to forget the evils, whose true creator she had been."[63] In this story, Anna never *really* cared about writing or philosophy, but just did it because she had failed in her real ambition to rule.

Chalandon had access to the works of Prodromos, and knew they implied that Anna continued to be a patron, but he fit that information into the story of Anna's isolation by demoting Prodromos: "Aside of the needy Prodromos, who was reduced to knocking on all doors, for thirty years she had no other relations than with the old companions of her father who had taken the habit."[64] Chalandon alludes here to Anna's description of her isolation in her discussion of her sources. Unlike Gibbon, he took it as a real isolation rather than a claim to impartiality, and reconciled it with the evidence for Anna's continued influence by dismissing Prodromos as a hopeless case. Although Chalandon states clearly that the *Alexiad* cannot be trusted for information about the death of Alexios, here he bends the other sources to fit a section of the *Alexiad* he finds truthful.[65]

The story of Anna's pride, rage, and self-destruction reached dramatic heights in the biography composed by Charles Diehl, first published in 1906 and continuously in print throughout the twentieth century.[66] Diehl's innovation is to create a richly detailed and expressive account of Anna's inner emotional life by reading the *Alexiad* in light of the established synthesis of Zonaras and Choniates. Diehl weaves together hints from all the sources, none noted, into a story of happy childhood, young love, profound ambition, and finally ever-increasing bitterness. The climax and focal point of Diehl's biography is Anna's attempt to overthrow her brother. His descriptions of her childhood, education, and the development of her character, while detailed, all serve to explain how she became a woman so convinced of her right to rule that she tried to kill her brother. His explanations hinge on her overwhelming pride.

Diehl attributes political ambition to Anna from her earliest years: crowned as an infant, and affianced to Constantine, Anna "could dream of the day when she would sit as Empress on the glorious throne of the Caesars."[67] Recalled later, her early years "seemed the happiest of her whole life."[68] Diehl gives an account of Anna's moral and intellectual education in which he declares the *Alexiad* to be the work of "a superior woman."[69] He then connects her intelligence and social class with ambition: "She was much too fully aware of what she was, of her high birth as well as her intellectual superiority, not to be a woman of great ambition."[70] For Diehl, Anna's intellectual abilities are in themselves evidence of political ambition. He writes that Anna's grandmother, Anna Dalassene, and both her father and mother were deeply ambitious. He then attributes to Anna an overwhelming pride:

> Moreover, very proud of having been born to the purple, very proud of being the eldest child of Alexios and Eirene, very proud of the imperial title bestowed on her in her cradle, she deemed anything lower than her lofty dignity as a Porphyrogennete beneath her consideration. Her pride, personal, ancestral, and national, was immeasurable.[71]

The chief evidence Diehl offers for this pride is that she speaks scornfully of the Crusaders.[72] Other reasons are not offered explicitly, but it is reasonable to connect this assessment of her character with the self-assertion Anna undertakes to establish her authority as an author. In reading the *Alexiad* Diehl presumably did not perceive Anna's humbling gestures as such, but saw her boasting of her education, nobility, and family, leading him to present her as overwhelmingly proud and arrogant. In concluding his description of Anna's character, Diehl circles back to "her ambitious and headstrong spirit, her soul of a Porphyrogennete, haughty, proud of her birth and eager for sovereignty that was to sway her destiny."[73] Ambition and pride then are the most significant aspects of Anna's character in Diehl's portrait. She is not so much demonized, as presented as having a tragic flaw.

After this discussion of Anna's formation and character, Diehl turns to the story of her political ambition. He begins with her statement that her misfortunes began when she was eight, and explains that she was referring to the birth of her brother John, which he dates to 1091.[74] Diehl interprets Anna as hating her brother because his birth removed her from succession:

> So for Anna Komnene, the birth of her brother was the great misfortune of her life. It was because of her dreams of sharing the throne with

young Constantine Doukas that she so tenderly cherished his memory. It was because the "dark little boy with the big forehead and the thin cheeks," who was her detested brother, had suddenly come to ruin her ambitions that she hated him so savagely. It was because she hoped to regain the throne through, and with, Nikephoros Bryennios, that she loved him so much.[75]

This blow to her political ambition set her on a course of constant plotting and eventual destruction:

> And it was because she believed herself qualified to reign, by right of seniority, that as long as Alexios lived she plotted, agitated, and used all her influence to push forward her husband, Nikephoros, with the aim of recovering the power that she considered herself unjustly deprived of. This was the constant goal of her ambition, the justification of all her acts; this one, tenacious, dream filled her whole existence—and explains it—up until the day when, having finally failed to attain her goal, she understood that she had, at the same time, wrecked her life.[76]

Acknowledging that Diehl worked in an era with markedly different methodologies for reading sources than my own, which led him to accept far more information at face value than I would, it yet seems that he is here adding a great deal to the story that does not derive from medieval evidence. Diehl here has filled out the sketchy information in our sources with his own ideas about what kind of woman Anna was and provided her with a consistent, if not entirely coherent, motivation grounded in his belief that she was overwhelmingly ambitious.

In the story of the conspiracy that follows, Anna was aided by her mother's affection for Nikephoros and "the two women resolved to oust the legitimate heir."[77] Eirene exercised her influence over the emperor, and "soon, thanks to these intrigues, Bryennios was all-powerful at the palace."[78] Diehl writes that at the betrothal of Bryennios's son "the official orators extolled in pompous epithalamiums the qualities of the young bridegroom, who seemed destined to the Empire."[79] He refers here to the work of Prodromos, but places it before the death of Alexios, and takes it as evidence that Anna was expected to succeed. Diehl then opens his discussion of Alexios's death by describing in detail the scene as depicted by Anna and noting "in all this beautiful account, there is not a word that could lead one even to suspect the intrigues and ambitions at work in that sickroom."[80] He then describes in quick succession sordid details loosely compiled from Zonaras and Choniates's histories: "Eirene's violent attempts to make the emperor disinherit his son"; her "fury" when John took his father's ring; the "outburst of wild rage on the part of these ambitious women" when John took control of the palace; "Eirene [urging] Bryennios also to proclaim himself emperor, and to take up arms against his brother-in-law;"

Eirene throwing herself on Alexios's "agonizing body," entreating him to recognize Bryennios; Alexios's vague gesture; "Eirene, exasperated, burst[ing]
into reproaches," accusing Alexios of being a deceiver; and finally Alexios's
body left almost entirely unattended and buried without ceremony.[81] While
Diehl makes quick work of his summary of the events, he is expansive in his
description of the emotional impact they had on Anna:

> Anna's plots had failed: her brother was emperor. For the proud prin-
> cess this was a terrible and unexpected blow. For many years she had
> lived in the hope of inheriting the Empire. She considered the throne
> legitimately and essentially hers, she thought herself so superior to
> her detested younger brother. Now, all her dreams had crumbled.
> The audacity of John Komnenos and the hesitancy of Bryennios had
> overturned at a single stroke the whole edifice of intricate schemes so
> cleverly constructed by Anna and Eirene. The daughter of Alexios was
> inconsolable, and her frustrated ambition, obliterating all other senti-
> ments, kindled in her heart the fury of Medea.[82]

Diehl does not explain what Anna's plots had been, or the nature of "the
whole edifice of intricate schemes" she and her mother had "so cleverly constructed." Such details were unnecessary because scheming and plotting were
consistent aspects of the type of woman he thought Anna to be. Once Diehl
had constructed Anna as a woman of extreme ambition, intelligence, and
pride, it would go without saying that she would be scheming.

This pride and ambition also provides the fuel that gives her "the fury of
Medea," which propels her to the next plot: "The year had not run its course
before she attempted to seize the power by means of a plot to assassinate her
brother John."[83] This plot failed because her husband "was rather weak . . .
and not really ambitious," and "his scruples and his weakness paralyzed the
zeal of the other conspirators."[84] Diehl lauds John's clemency, which he characterizes as "the supreme humiliation for this proud princess."[85] Diehl then
turns to the story of Anna's disgust with her husband:

> When she saw her whole enterprise brought to nothing by the shilly-
> shallying of Bryennios, she, so chaste and proper, swore at her husband
> like a trooper. Cursing his cowardice, she declared that nature had made
> a pretty mess of things, clothing her masculine spirit with a woman's
> body and Bryennios's timid and indecisive soul with man's. Decency
> obliges me to paraphrase the actual terms she used, which were very
> different, much coarser and more vigorous. But Anna Komnene must
> indeed have felt cruelly stricken, to have stooped, literary and well-bred
> as she was, to utter words of such crudity.[86]

Diehl's shock seems not to be so much about the gender inversion expressed,
as about the vulgarity of Anna's language. The incongruity of Anna speaking

in these terms does not prompt him to question how Choniates knew what Anna had said, but rather becomes more evidence of the extremity of her disappointment.

Diehl sees the attempt on the throne as structuring the whole of Anna's life: "Anna Komnene was only thirty-six years old, but her life was over."[87] Diehl draws together Anna's expressions of personal tragedy in the *Alexiad* and attributes them to Anna's emotional state created by "the collapse of her great ambitions."[88] He thought that "this long last chapter of her existence was, for her, mortally sad."[89] Diehl's knowledge of Anna's emotional life does not end: "Every day she became more gloomy and morose; she saw herself more and more as the victim of an unjust fate."[90] Diehl elaborates on John's forgiveness, explaining how this "gentle and merciful Prince" forgave his sister everything, "hoping by this chivalrous magnanimity to awaken some remorse in her troubled soul and reviving in it some feelings of affection."[91] Diehl describes Anna as deeply and increasingly embittered by the failure of her ambitions, driven to ever-greater isolation because of her unwillingness to humble herself by forgiving John. Diehl's Anna has the passions, frustrations, and ultimate tragedy of a heroine of a late Victorian novel.

Diehl's narrative concretizes Anna's vague expressions of personal tragedy and gives them an explicit political meaning. Diehl seems to have originated the idea that Anna nursed a grudge against John continually throughout her life. He provides a new motivation for Anna's ambition, suggesting that she had grown accustomed to the idea of being empress in her childhood, and later merely tried to return to that position. Diehl's theory is attractive because it provides something of a recognizable emotional cause for Anna's ambition, and hence an explanation for the attempted coup.

The dramatic story constructed by Diehl is quite similar to a longer and more sympathetic version published by Louis du Sommerard in 1907. Sommerard differs from his predecessors in pointing out that Anna's complaint against nature originated in a much later text. He attributes the story of Anna's anger with Nikephoros explicitly to Choniates: "Nature, he would have her say, had mistaken the sexes."[92] He then observes that the phrases used do not all resemble the fine moral and literary tenor of the *Alexiad*, and explains that Choniates was writing in the thirteenth century. For the first time, these are not Anna's words, but Choniates's. He suggests that Choniates's story came from "a legend" that had formed around Anna because she lived the last thirty years of her life in disgrace.[93] He considers that legend unfortunate because Anna was for the most part virtuous, humane, and sensible, but had been led to crime by her passionate ambition.

In his concluding assessment of Anna's historical work, Sommerard praises Anna's research and use of sources but says that she had two or three causes of error. The most significant was her "need to ennoble her own role" and lead readers to "admire her as a loving daughter whose actions were always selfless and devoted."[94] Her filial partiality, which led her to constantly glorify Alexios, "also falsified her testimony."[95] These aspects of Anna's self-presentation, which I believe were designed to make her more appealing to her twelfth-century audience, are interpreted here as causing flaws in her historical methodology.

The works of Diehl, Chalandon, and Sommerard added the information about Anna and Eirene living in Eirene's monastic foundation to the story of Anna's life. Diehl and Chalandon are both careful to say that Anna lived in the monastery "most of the time" and present her as withdrawing from society as much out of her own bitterness and pique as from John's displeasure. Sommerard interprets Anna staying at Kecharitomene as a form of involuntary confinement, which he considers a lenient punishment.[96] Sommerard's version was seen as a more satisfying, however, and through the twentieth century it was largely accepted that Anna's monastic retirement was a form of internal exile.[97]

Once Anna's character was firmly established as vain, ambitious, and bloodthirsty, historians could be even more blithe about dismissing her testimony in the *Alexiad*. Joseph McCabe, writing in 1913, based his story far more on Diehl than any of the medieval sources. Yet he says that Zonaras and Choniates are trustworthy while "Anna Komnene crowns her work with a masterpiece of deliberate lying."[98] His negative judgment of Anna's character leads to his judgment of the *Alexiad*:

> That work—affected, insincere and ambitious—reflects the character of its author, nor can its lavish use of the art of suppressing some facts and enlarging others efface from our memory the ignoble attitude of Eirene and Anna by the bedside of the dying Alexios and towards his legitimate heir.[99]

Here we see an echo of the ancient principle that a history could only be trusted if its author was believed to have good moral character. McCabe dislikes both Anna and her history. He derives strong moral lessons from history, and makes Anna a grand villainess.[100]

Perhaps not surprisingly, the feminist author and political advocate Naomi Mitchison created a somewhat different image of Anna in her 1928 biography. She considers Anna to have been an industrious historian, who nevertheless "did manage to write—as history—a curiously bad history book."[101] Mitchison's story of Anna's life follows the basic plot line established by Diehl with the striking exception that she attributes Anna's ambition not to her pride, but to the confinement of women in Byzantine society:

> Too much shutting up in the home, combined with a quite reasonable education, had done it. If women are to be kept behind bars it is silly to compromise about it as the later Byzantines did and allow them to be

intelligent beings at all. It must lead to discontent and when possible
violent ambition.[102]

Mitchison praises Nikephoros for refusing to participate in his wife's plot and
John for his mercy.[103] She dwells far less on Anna's rage and jealousy than
other writers, however. She does not include a paraphrase of Choniates's line
about Anna's complaint against nature and frustration with Nikephoros,
merely saying, "She seems to have lost her temper furiously with him after
the failure of the plot."[104]

Mitchison departs most forcefully from previous readings of Anna's life
in suggesting that Anna enjoyed the last decade of her life because she was
writing history. Whereas for Diehl, Anna has no enjoyment in life but only
ever-increasing bitterness after her failed coup, Mitchison speculates that the
writing the *Alexiad* must have been quite a lot of fun. She imagines Anna vis-
iting the palace to copy letters and treaties, receiving her father's old friends,
and enjoying reading over her book with "the admiring friends, the old generals delighted to listen to the sound of their own names, paying elaborate
complements to the faded Princess."[105] Of course Mitchison is just guessing,
but it is striking that it took so long for someone to suppose that Anna enjoyed
writing the *Alexiad*.

Another significant dissenting voice to the emerging consensus on Anna's
biography was that of Georgina Buckler, who published a long and detailed
book on Anna in 1929.[106] Overall Buckler presents an extremely positive evaluation of Anna's abilities as a historian.[107] Buckler opened her discussion of
Anna's life with the assumption that her readers already knew that Anna was
a wildly ambitious woman who disputed her brother's right to rule. At the
beginning of her book, Buckler sets out to challenge this view, which she presents as unjustifiably negative:

> First, as to the ambition which her critics cast in her teeth. The "bitter-
> ness" of which she herself is conscious and the very last word of her work
> must surely be attributed less to her griefs than to cheated hopes. As a
> child she had been taught to reckon on being Empress; she never was,
> and it soured her against her hated brother and successor John. But it is
> not necessary to assume that she contested the legitimacy of his claim.[108]

Buckler argues that it would have been simply illogical for Anna to dispute
her brother's rights to inherit the Empire:

> The principle of heredity was too strong in her for her really to think
> that she and Nikephoros Bryennios had superior rights to the throne. . . .
> Under the circumstances she could hardly without stultifying herself
> have hoped to mount her father's throne in preference to John, and we
> have no adequate reason for believing that she did so.[109]

Buckler maintains that the principle of inheritance by the eldest son was strong in Byzantine political thought, and that throughout the *Alexiad* Anna resoundingly supported the rights of legitimate heirs. Once Constantine Doukas had died, Anna may have been unhappy, but she did not deny that John was next in line.[110] Buckler does not discuss the stories in Zonaras or Choniates directly, but considers them sufficiently refuted through her discussion of the political illogic of opposing John.[111]

Since Buckler does not believe that Anna revolted against her brother, she has a harder time explaining why Anna presented herself in the *Alexiad* as suffering. She systematically reviews all the passages in the *Alexiad* in which Anna speaks about herself, and points out how they do not easily cohere into a logical narrative. Buckler sees the expressions of woe as inconsistent with the events of Anna's life: "We can sympathize with her over the loss of parents and husband, but not with the exaggerated frenzy into which it throws her."[112] Anna's sorrow is an enduring mystery:

> What then was this carking sorrow that for nearly threescore years, from her eighth year to her sixty-fifth, "engulfed" Anna Komnene? After eight centuries we cannot tell . . . and we cannot gauge the depth of feeling beneath her hysterical bombast. One thing is, however, self-evident . . . Anna's [woes] were emphatically not great except in her own self-centered, self-satisfied mind.[113]

Ultimately, for Buckler, Anna had no real reason to be upset. Expressions of misery that I think Anna intended to make herself seem humble and worthy of pity, Buckler interprets as making Anna seem vain and self-absorbed.

Despite Buckler's dissenting voice, the story constructed by Diehl and Chalandon simply seems to have been more appealing to modern sensibilities. At least theirs was the story that entered the great twentieth-century textbooks of Byzantine history, by Alexander Vasiliev in 1928 and George Ostrogorski in 1940.[114] These two texts were the gateway to Byzantine studies throughout the twentieth century, and with them, Anna's failed conspiracy and forced monastic retirement became received knowledge among Byzantinists. Historians of the later twentieth century did not study these events in depth, because they were well-known and understood. For example, when it comes to Anna, Konstantinos Varzos dispenses with the footnotes to primary sources that normally follow every sentence in his exhaustive prosopography of the Komnenos family. He copies Chalandon's joke contrasting Prodromos's praise of Anna with her bloodthirstiness, and quotes Cavafy's poem on Anna as providing insights to her character.[115] Changing attitudes toward female empowerment in the later twentieth century led to new valuations of Anna's biography, with some historians seeing Anna's attempt to seize power as a good thing.[116] The underlying synthesis of sources, however, remained relatively unchanged. Other textbooks and surveys written since the middle of the twentieth century repeat the received wisdom.[117] Even in 2011, the entry on Anna published online for the *International Encyclopedia for the Middle Ages* includes the story of early childhood ambition dashed by John's birth, plotting by both Anna and Eirene, Nikephoros's loyalty to "the family," and forced retirement to Kecharitomene as a result of the conspiracy.[118]

Anna's preferred image of herself as demure, modest, yet intellectually brilliant, has thus lost out resoundingly to an image of her as consumed by anger, arrogance, and violent ambition. Issues of historical sources, and how those sources ought to be read, played important parts in the development of the standard narrative of her life. In addition, however, there is something about the conspiracy story that seems particularly compelling for modern audiences.

As for sources, scholars working in earlier eras did not have access to all of the information we do. Many of the texts discussed in chapters 7 and 9 were not published until the twentieth century, and only studied systematically beginning in the 1970s.[119] Perhaps most importantly, the manuscript of George Tornikes's funeral oration for Anna was first described in 1916, but not published until 1970.[120] Had these texts been available to Lebeau and Gibbon, they may have established a different fundamental narrative of Anna's life. That Anna would be flattered and pleased with Prodromos's image of her joyfully watching John lead her sons' marriage procession is not easily compatible with the idea that she had just tried to murder him. But by the time Prodromos's oration was published, the narrative of Anna's plot against John's life was established as fact. The same can be said of the vast trove of information about Anna revealed in Tornikes's oration.

As for how medieval texts can be read, scholars such as Lebeau seem to have treated the medieval histories as relatively straightforward transcripts of events that all actually happened just as described. Even when Choniates tells his readers that his reliable information begins with the events of his own lifetime, it may not have occurred to Lebeau to ask why he then included the stories about Alexios and John, and what role these unreliable stories played in the structure of Choniates's argument. By contrast, I expect Byzantine writers to express truth through the arrangement, design, and expression of the story, as well as through what is said on the surface of the text, because that is how I understand their historiographical tradition as working. My approach is shaped by relatively recent research on the methods of ancient and medieval historians.[121]

Most of the modern historians we have discussed also were not willing to engage with the sexuality of Choniates's characterizations, presumably out of their own sense of propriety and modesty. They have Anna accuse nature of giving her and Nikephoros the wrong souls, the wrong beings, the wrong spirits; some say they cannot talk about it; none admit that the Greek text talks about the wrong genitals. These scholars do not see, or do not interact with, the rest of the sexuality of Choniates's narrative. This is not the only sentence in Choniates's narrative with a sexual meaning. It is merely the only one that cannot be translated without admitting a sexual meaning. For the other sentences, historians have been able to either ignore or gloss over sexual connotations and metaphors. By sanitizing Choniates, and then pulling out details pertaining to events from his narrative, they create a far simpler narrative of political rivalry.

These historians also worked without help of recent research on Byzantine culture. The eighteenth- and nineteenth-century historians fundamentally missed what Anna was doing by presenting herself as miserable, in part because we have only recently learned enough about Byzantine literary culture to see how Anna's misery was a performance of humility. Gibbon understood that Anna claimed to be isolated in order to substantiate the impartiality of her sources, but subsequent historians preferred to take her protestations of isolation literally as revealing that she was imprisoned. Historians working in earlier eras were acting in good faith in trying to come up with explanations for Anna's self-pity and why she would live in a monastery. The study of Byzantine gender that clarifies how having an apartment in a monastery would be empowering for Anna is recent. In Choniates's story of Alexios's succession, everyone, except John Axuch, behaves in ways diametrically opposed to Byzantine gender ideals for them. Yet this is only easily apparent with the benefit of considerable research into how Byzantine people perceived ideal behavior. Without this background research, it was easy for earlier scholars to see Anna as the only character expressing gender inversion. There remains much we do not understand. Previous generations of historians cannot be faulted for the state of the field in their era. Nonetheless, it is now possible to see that these interpretations are based fundamentally on misunderstandings of Anna's text and our other medieval evidence for her life.

Beyond all these reasons having to do with the state of the field in earlier eras and changes in historical methodology, some of the interpretations of Anna as proud, ambitious, and scheming clearly derive from eighteenth- to twentieth-century beliefs about women, power, and history writing. Although most of these scholars were uncomfortable with the sexuality of Choniates's text, they were nearly all drawn to Anna's complaint against nature as expressing something true about her character. She seemed like a woman who would wish that she were a man. For Krause, Anna's masculinity was shown "by her very decision to make herself a history writer."[122] Krause's view that history writing was an activity for men accords perfectly with medieval and ancient thinking on the matter. Chapters 3 and 4 argued that Anna deliberately performed the femininity her culture expected in the *Alexiad* through various feminizing discourses. These strategies of feminization apparently did not work for Krause and other historians of his era who thought that Anna must have been a lot like a man because she wrote a history.

Some of Anna's modern readers seem to have shared negative attitudes about women in politics. Lebeau's synthesis of the highly ambiguous medieval narratives about John's accession into a simple story of good men warding off the intrigues of bad women would be appealing to those who held such views. Both Krause and McCabe tell the story through the prism of a strong prejudice against any woman's involvement in politics. Since within this moral system, a woman involved in politics was a bad woman, and as a historian Anna was interested in politics, these scholars were naturally inclined to accept the story that Anna was eager to murder her brother.

In several narratives, most overtly in Diehl's, Anna's political ambition is driven by her overweening pride. The view that she was overly proud can be firmly attributed to her authorial activities. Anna's claims to education and strength of judgment, which I understand as attempts to substantiate her abilities as an author before an audience that did not expect educated women, were taken by the modern readers as simple boasts. These boasts led historians to see her as vain and proud. The places where Anna claims impartial judgment, access to sources, and the education necessary to write history were perceived clearly by her eighteenth- to twentieth-century readers. Within the totality of her text, this is a small strand of her self-presentation, and one that she never asserts without simultaneously making humbling and self-abasing gestures. Yet since those gestures were invisible to modern readers, they saw her authorizing discourse as prideful and distastefully self-aggrandizing. A woman's authorial self-aggrandizement, while perhaps less of a problem in the eighteenth century than it had been in the twelfth, was still seen as bad. Gibbon thought Anna was vain *because* she wrote a history. Anna's obvious intellectual ambition in choosing to write a history seems to have led some scholars inexorably to see her as also politically ambitious. It appears that Anna was instinctively perceived as interested in power because she wrote a history.

Ideas about proper female behavior common from the eighteenth to twentieth centuries thus created some of the same problems that Anna had expected in her twelfth-century audience. She anticipated that her audience would think history writing was an activity only for men and that a woman who wrote history would be arrogant and transgressive. She tried to address these issues by presenting herself as feminine, humble, appropriately devoted to her parents, and isolated from the halls of power. The strategies Anna used in her self-presentation were ineffective for these more modern audiences, however. Her efforts to present herself as a devoted daughter merely made her seem biased and lacking in proper historical objectivity. Ancient and medieval ways of humbling oneself through a presentation of self as sufferer were completely lost on Anna's more modern audiences. Whereas I see Anna's piteous and tragic self-presentation as a self-abasing gesture designed to evoke condescending pity among the audience—and it may have worked that way for much of her twelfth-century audience—more recent readers understood her as genuinely upset and blamed her sadness on thwarted ambition. Anna's lamentations and protestations of misery do nothing to get pity from eighteenth- to twentieth-century readers. For Georgina Buckler, who was otherwise quite sympathetic to Anna, they were entirely distasteful and a sign of "hysterical bombast."[123] This is an aspect of Anna's self-presentation that fails completely to prompt its intended affect among modern audiences.

For Anna to be perceived as both a virtuous woman and a reliable historian, her self-presentation in the *Alexiad* needs to elicit goodwill from her audience. As audiences change their cultural presuppositions over time, they change in how they see Anna's character and what meanings they take from her text. With the probable exception of Choniates, Anna's strategies for sympathetic self-presentation seem to have worked for her near contemporaries. Readers of the eighteenth, nineteenth, and twentieth centuries brought different perceptions of appropriate gender roles and proper historical methodology to the *Alexiad*. For them, Anna's attempts to make herself seem like a modest and virtuous woman failed. Yet the cultural imperative for a woman writing history to be perceived as modest and virtuous was hardly less compelling in the nineteenth century than it had been in the twelfth. For these later audiences, then, Anna seemed to be transgressively masculine, overwhelmingly arrogant, proud, and politically ambitious. As McCabe put it, the "character of the author" is reflected in the *Alexiad*: "affected, insincere and ambitious."[124] Evaluations of Anna's character vary among these historians, with some expressing considerable sympathy and others clear revulsion. They were nearly all inclined to believe she was the sort of woman would be willing to murder her brother in order to seize the throne.

This negative readers' response to Anna's character, as expressed in the *Alexiad*, combined with multiple small misunderstandings of our medieval evidence, worked together to create the standard narrative that emerged in the early twentieth century. Slight misperceptions and misunderstandings were compounded when they were woven together in a way that made sense in the context of the culture and society of the eighteenth, nineteenth, and early twentieth centuries. The bones of this narrative were accepted and repeated by subsequent generations of scholars. So long as the *Alexiad* prompted readers to think Anna was arrogant and ambitious, the standard narrative seemed to make sense of her character.

Conclusion

In Anna's culture, the deeds of men in war and politics were commemorated by men. These were inappropriate subjects for women to talk about, let alone write about. A woman who wrote about such matters could only be deeply transgressive, immodest, and concerned with male things rather than female things. A woman who would dare to impose her judgment and organizational view on the deeds of men, and tell others what to think of them, could only be arrogant and inappropriately conceited.

Anna did not shy away from these problems. She could have written under a pseudonym, or she could have used her rhetorical powers to gloss over or submerge the challenges of writing history as a woman. Rather she opted to address her unique challenges openly. She did not smooth over problems, but held them up for her audience to see the tensions. In trying to write with the power and authority necessary to preserve Alexios's memory, and yet exhibit proper feminine humility, Anna was striving to write politely and with tactful deference to her culture's conceptions of correct behavior. The study of how she endeavored to write in a tactful manner has illuminated some fundamental structures of her society: "Tact, after all, is merely the play of light on the surface of a culture's submerged ideology: even the most superficial appearances depend ultimately upon profound structural tensions."[1] Anna's writing exposes the tensions at the heart of her project, and her society, as she invites her audience to observe her deft weaving of contradictory cultural impulses.

Tension aptly characterizes Anna's need to present herself as a good daughter, naturally displaying deep affection for her father, and to disregard her natural love for her father in order to write truthful history. While Anna's historical impartiality causes her to write negatively about her father, when she deems it appropriate, she does prove herself to be a devoted daughter. Wherever possible she strives to make Alexios personally look good, even when he is experiencing failures.

There was tension in any Byzantine author's dual mandate to be a provider of moral exemplars (and hence to some extent, the moral model himself) and to remain humble and self-effacing. For Anna, this tension was unusually acute because, as a woman, she needed to insist more strongly on her moral and intellectual qualifications while enacting a level of humility appropriate for a modest, good woman. Anna's extreme concern to present herself as a pitiable woman indicates her understanding of the difficulties she faced as a female author, given the negative associations between self-aggrandizement and authorship in Byzantine culture. However hard her contemporaneous male rhetoricians worked to efface their authorship and present themselves modestly, writing was far less problematic for them than for Anna. Further, Byzantine culture held strong negative associations between women and power. Female empowerment was considered the source of discord and trouble. Anna's choice to write history was transgressive, not merely in a general sense that women did not write histories in the twelfth century, but in that the assertion of authority inherent in writing set her up against the strong cultural imperative for women to avoid placing themselves in positions of power. For Anna to exert the power of authorship and have any hope of not being seen as deeply objectionable, she needed to present herself as profoundly humble. Anna's self-presentation as the object of pity is always in tension with the strength and authority she does exert through the act of narrating men's deeds in the public sphere. Framing her history with lamentation and proclamations of personal suffering mitigates some of the effrontery of her act of history writing. It does not resolve or eliminate the inherent tension, but endeavors to deal with it tactfully.

Tact also seems to be the pervasive guiding principle in Anna's interactions with her culture's fundamental conception that authority should rest with men. She does not combat this ideology, but uses traditional strategies that empower women while upholding prevailing ideas of proper authority. Like the women discussed in chapter 1, whose financial self-determination was enabled through their performances of extreme feminine weakness that constrained men to help them, Anna's calls for pity were calls for her audience to support her efforts. In evoking support from her audience by playing the piteous widow, Anna used the moral logic of her culture to enable her authorial creativity. Anna also freely takes the opposite tact of transcending her natural female weaknesses through strength of character and innate nobility. Just as every female saint was an extraordinary exception to the rule of women's weak nature, and just as every woman undertaking a legally binding transaction had the exceptional strength to act without "womanly simplicity," Anna had the exceptional strength of character that allowed her to overcome her natural female emotionalism to write dispassionately.

Anna could not resolve these tensions, but she treated them with great tact, and masterfully wove them into a strong, taut textual fabric. All her methods and strategies—her presentation as a mourning widow and object of pity, her balancing of historical impartiality with familial devotion, her careful policing of the boundaries of the discourse of history, her use of documents to efface and strengthen her authorship, her efforts to humbly and modestly substantiate her historical abilities—work to help Anna craft an authorial persona as both a good woman and a good historian. If this book has in any way enabled readers to approach Anna's history with a better understanding of the cultural difficulties that led to the emotional peculiarities of her text, it will have succeeded.

The failure of later readers to understand Anna's efforts at tact have led to negative interpretations of her character. Although our medieval evidence does not allow us to *prove* much of anything about who felt or did what on the night that Alexios died, modern depictions of Anna as wholly consumed with imperial ambition are not supported by current interpretations of medieval evidence or the politics of her era. Anna's efforts to appear humble and modest may well have worked for her contemporaries, but they have not for most of her modern readers. To Gibbon her history everywhere expressed the "vanity of a female author," and to many of her nineteenth- and early twentieth-century readers, pride and arrogance were her chief characteristics, along with ambition. These modern readers shared a dislike of female power with Anna's contemporaries, but were worlds away from the other aspects of her culture that allowed her humbling strategies to function. "Modern" and medieval cultures of historiography were different enough that much of Anna's rhetoric did not work for her modern readers, yet they were sufficiently alike in attitude toward female authorship that Anna's great fear—that by writing history she would be seen as transgressive, arrogant, and unnatural woman—has been realized by readers' responses to her work for the past several centuries.

Now, in the second decade of twenty-first century, we read ancient and medieval texts with far more attention to the rhetorical purposes of their authors' exposition and growing awareness of the differences between ancient and contemporary historical practices. Scholars of ancient historiography are developing ever-more refined understandings of what truth and lying meant for the writers of ancient history, and how these ideas differ from those of the contemporary academy. Lebeau seems to have worked with the assumption that everything an ancient history said was true, in the same way that he understood truth, and his job was to fit all the bits together. That is not the approach scholars would now take to Choniates, Zonaras, or any of the other sources for Anna's biography. Lebeau's intellectual world is nearly as foreign to us as Anna's. It is time to let our interpretations of the medieval material be freed from a narrative of political history developed in the 1770s.

Our judgments about whether Anna's history writing made her arrogant are also, for the most part, no longer constrained by a cultural prejudice that women's intellectualism is a sign of vanity. While women academics continue to cite their own research in footnotes at significantly lower rates than their male colleagues in order to avoid the appearance of self-aggrandizement,[2] Anna may at last have found an audience that would not presume that a woman who liked writing history would be conceited. We now are able to perceive clearly how diligently she worked to be considered modest and gracious. With these changes—in our methods of analysis, contemporary academic culture, and understanding of Anna's authorial strategies—Anna can emerge primarily, not as a thwarted and embittered bloodthirsty schemer, but as one of the greatest intellectuals of her era and a woman who succeeded in creating a masterwork of history.

I have used the metaphor of Anna weaving the tense and conflicting threads of her discourse into a taut, strong fabric because I think Anna would have liked it. The norms of her culture told her that as a woman she was fit only for weaving with spindle and distaff. Yet she skillfully wove with words, creating a textual fabric of such strength and power that it has successfully stayed the onrush of the river of time and saved the memory of Alexios's glorious deeds from oblivion for eight centuries and counting. Working with supple, silken strength, Anna succeeded in creating a history of her father and her era that will endure for centuries yet to come.

{ ACKNOWLEDGMENTS }

Studying the obstacles Anna Komnene faced in writing history has made me even more grateful for the support I enjoy from my family, university, and intellectual community. This project is an outgrowth of recent progress in our understanding of Byzantine authorship and gender made especially by Derek Krueger, Stratis Papaioannou, and Aglae Pizzone, who have my deepest thanks. The audience at the 2011 Byzantine Studies Conference was instrumental in setting the project on the right track. I also benefited from comments and discussion following presentations at the Byzantine Studies Conference in 2013, 2014, and at the Leeds International Medieval Congress in 2015. Anthony Kaldellis commented with insightful enthusiasm on an early draft.

Funding for research was generously given by the Wisconsin Alumni Research Foundation annual competition at the University of Wisconsin Madison. History department staff (Nic Hauge, Scott Burkhardt, and Leslie Abadie) were invaluable in helping me balance administrative work with history writing. Marlina Polk McGiveron's careful reading helped ensure the book's accessibility. The librarians and Interlibrary Loan staff at the University of Wisconsin's Memorial Library ensured that America's dairy-land remains a great place to do Byzantine history. William James Conlin and Kerry Lefebvre, outstanding students at the University of Wisconsin, assisted by creating a small database of the grammatical gender and number of all of Anna's self-referential statements. Irina Tamarkina took part in the seminar on Byzantine women in which I first began to understand the *Alexiad*, and has been a delightfully vigorous interlocutor throughout the project. I enjoyed discussing some of Anna's more ambiguous sentences with Laura McClure, Jeffrey Beneker, and William Brockliss. Stefan Vranka consistently supported this project and Sarah Svendsen skillfully saw it though production. The patient and expert copyediting of Hank Southgate greatly improved the final version. John Rowe encouraged this project through his delight in Byzantine history and unwillingness to accept easy answers, as well as by providing the financial resources for my professorship. All have my deep thanks.

As always Stephen Rhody was a stalwart supporter and astute advisor, graciously helping our children grow into people who take pride in their mother's intellectual accomplishments. Anna Komnene and Theodore Prodromos together could not praise him adequately. This book is dedicated to my parents in gratitude for their many acts of encouragement and their belief that, of course, it would be a lovely thing for their daughter to be a historian.

{ NOTES }

Introduction

1. The idea that large portions of the *Alexiad* were written by Anna's husband Nikephoros has been resoundingly rejected. For the suggestion, see James Howard-Johnston, "Anna Komnene and the *Alexiad*," in *Alexios I Komnenos*, ed. Margaret Mullett and Dion Smythe (Belfast: Belfast Byzantine Enterprises, 1996), 232–302. For the rebuttal: Ruth Macrides, "The Pen and the Sword: Who Wrote the *Alexiad*?," in *Anna Komnene and Her Times*, ed. Thalia Gouma-Peterson (New York: Garland, 2000), 63–81; Diether Roderich Reinsch, "Women's Literature in Byzantium? The Case of Anna Komnene," in *Anna Komnene and Her Times*, ed. Thalia Gouma-Peterson (New York: Garland, 2000), 83–105; Leonora Neville, *Heroes and Romans in Twelfth-Century Byzantium: The "Material for History" of Nikephoros Bryennios* (Cambridge: Cambridge University Press, 2012), 182–93. On the art of the *Alexiad*, see Penelope Buckley, *The* Alexiad *of Anna Komnene: Artistic Strategy in the Making of a Myth* (Cambridge: Cambridge University Press, 2014); Jakov Ljubarskij, "Why Is the Alexiad a Masterpiece of Byzantine Literature?," in *Leimon: Studies Presented to Lennart Rydén on His Sixty-Fifth Birthday*, ed. Jan Olof Rosenqvist (Uppsala: Acta Universitatis Upsaliensis, 1996), 127–41.

2. John was born on September 13, 1187. In her history Anna says that John was crowned immediately, but documents preserved in the archives of Naples count 1092 as the first year in his reign. *Alexiad*, 6.8.5; Antonio Spinelli, ed., *Regii neapolitani archivi monumenta edita ac illustrata* (Neapoli: ex Regia Typographia, 1845), vol. 5, nos. 457–58, 462, 464–67. For Alexios and Eirene's children, see Alexander Kazhdan, "Die Liste der Kinder des Alexios I in einer Moskauer Handschrift (UBV 53/148)," in *Beiträge zur alten Geschichte und deren Nachleben*, ed. Ruth Stiehl and Hans Erich Stier (Berlin: De Gruyter, 1969), vol. 2, 233–37.

3. T. Büttner-Wobst, ed., *Ioannis Zonarae epitomae historiarum libri xviii*, vol. 3, Corpus scriptorum historiae Byzantinae (Bonn: Weber, 1897), 747. Hereafter "Zonaras."

4. Jean-Claude Cheynet, *Pouvoir et contestations à Byzance (963–1210)* (Paris: Publications de la Sorbonne, 1990), 76–90.

5. Zonaras, 738; *Alexiad*, 6.8.3; Paul Gautier, *Nicephore Bryennios Histoire; Introduction, Texte, Traduction et Notes* (Bruxelles: Byzantion, 1975), 63–67; Demetrios I. Polemis, *The Doukai: A Contribution to Byzantine Prosopography* (London: Athlone, 1968), 62.

6. Although Anna was betrothed at her birth, she mentions in her history that she joined Maria of Alania's household when she was seven: *Alexiad*, 3.4. Age seven was the legal age at which girls could be betrothed. It was also the normal time for education to begin. Anna similarly was in charge of raising her own daughter-in-law Theodora, as described in her funeral lament by Theodore Prodromos: Wolfram Hörandner,

Theodoros Prodromos. Historische Gedichte, Wiener Byzantinistische Studien 11 (Vienna: Österreichische Akademie der Wissenschaften, 1974), 383–84, poem number 39, lines 20–62. On age seven as a moment of transition, see Evelyne Patlagean, "L'enfant et son avenir dans la famille byzantine (IV–XIIe siècles)," in *Structure sociale, famille, chrétienté à Byzance, IVe–XIe siècle* (London: Variorum, 1981), 87; Cecily Hennessy, *Images of Children in Byzantium* (Farnham: Ashgate, 2008), 11–13; Eve Davies, "Age, Gender and Status: A Three-Dimensional Life Course Perspective of the Byzantine Family," in *Approaches to the Byzantine Family*, ed. Leslie Brubaker and Shaun Tougher (Farnham: Ashgate, 2013), 159.

7. *Alexiad*, 9.5.5.

8. Polemis, *The Doukai*, 63; *Alexiad*, 9.5.4.

9. Lynda Garland and Stephen Rapp, "Mary 'of Alania': Woman and Empress Between Two Worlds," in *Byzantine Women: Varieties of Experience 800–1200*, ed. Lynda Garland (Aldershot: Ashgate, 2006), 110–11; Peter Frankopan, "Kinship and the Distribution of Power in Komnenian Byzantium," *English Historical Review* 122 (2007): 17–20.

10. Diether Roderich Reinsch, "Der Historiker Nikephoros Bryennios, Enkel und nicht Sohn des Usurpators," *Byzantinische Zeitschrift* 83 (1990): 423–24.

11. *Alexiad*, 14.8.2.

12. She mentions going on campaign at *Alexiad*, 12.3.7 and 14.7.4.

13. The names of Andronikos, Constantine, and Maria are known only from their commemoration in the *typikon* of the monastery of Christ Philanthropos. Andronikos died on September 21, Constantine died on October 30, and Maria on April 18, all in unknown years. Matoula Kouroupou and Jean-François Vannier, "Commémoraisons des Comnènes dans le typikon liturgique du monastère du Christ Philanthrope (ms. Panaghia Kamariotissa 29)," *Revue des études byzantines* 63, no. 1 (2005): 49–51, 61.

14. Paul Gautier, ed., "Theodore Prodomus: Epithalamium fortunatissimis caesaris filiis," in *Nicéphore Bryennios. Histoire*, Corpus Fontium Historiae Byzantinae (Brussels: Byzantion, 1975), 341–55.

15. Kouroupou and Vannier, "Commémoraisons des Comnènes," 59.

16. Hörandner, *Theodoros Prodromos, Historische Gedichte*, 382–89, poem number 39.

17. Gautier, "Theodore Prodomus: Epithalamium fortunatissimis caesaris filiis," 351.

18. Ibid. 353.

19. Anna's daughter Eirene used the surname Doukaina. Paul Gautier, "Le typikon de la Théotokos Kécharitôménè," *Revue des études byzantines* 43, no. 1 (1985): 132, 139; Kōnstantinos Varzos, *Hē genealogia tōn Komnēnōn* (Thessalonikē: Kentron Vyzantinōn Ereunōn, 1984), 326–30.

20. Polemis, *The Doukai*, 113–14; Varzos, *Hē genealogia tōn Komnēnōn*, 308–26; Kouroupou and Vannier, "Commémoraisons des Comnènes," 59–60; Jean Darrouzes, *George et Demetrios Tornikes. Lettres et Discours* (Paris: Editions du Centre national de la recherche scientifique, 1970), 163.

21. Gautier, "Kécharitôménè," 14, 145, line 2242.

22. Stratis Papaioannou, "Anna Komnene's Will," in *Byzantine Religious Culture: Studies in Honor of Alice-Mary Talbot*, ed. Denis Sullivan, Elizabeth Fisher, and Stratis Papaioannou (Leiden: Brill, 2012), 107–9.

23. Darrouzes, *Tornikes*, 221–323.

24. *Alexiad*, 10.9.8.

25. Paul Gautier, ed., *Lettres et discours: Michel Italikos* (Paris: Institut français d'études byzantines, 1972), 154.

26. Nikephoros is commemorated as deceased in the Typikon of Pantokrator, which was created in 1136. His name was probably a later addition. Paul Gautier, "L'obituaire du typikon du Pantokrator," *Revue des études byzantines* 27, no. 1 (1969): 251–52.

27. Paul Stephenson, "Anna Comnena's Alexiad as a Source for the Second Crusade?," *Journal of Medieval History* 29 (2003): 41–54; Paul Magdalino, "The Pen of the Aunt: Echoes of the Mid-Twelfth Century in the Alexiad," in *Anna Komnene and Her Times*, ed. Thalia Gouma-Peterson (New York: Garland, 2000).

28. Darrouzes, *Tornikes*, 309–15.

29. C. P. Cavafy, *Collected Poems*, rev. ed., trans. Edmund Keeley and Philip Sherrard, ed. George Savidis (Princeton: Princeton University Press, 1992), 109.

30. Charles Diehl, *Figures Byzantines* (Paris: A. Colin, 1906); Charles Diehl, *Byzantine Empresses*, trans. Harold Bell and Theresa de Kerpely (New York: Knopf, 1963), 190.

31. There were four Byzantine female hymnographers, three in the ninth century and one in the fourteenth. Eva Catafygiotu Topping, "Women Hymnographers in Byzantium," *Diptycha* 3 (1982–83): 98–111; Maria Mavroudi, "Learned Women of Byzantium and the Surviving Record," in *Byzantine Religious Culture: Studies in Honor of Alice-Mary Talbot*, ed. Denis Sullivan, Elizabeth Fisher, and Stratis Papaioannou (Leiden: Brill, 2012), 64–65. Anna also wrote the preface to her will, preserved among the writings of Michael Italikos, and two or three poems: Papaioannou, "Anna Komnene's Will"; Anneliese Paul, "Dichtung auf Objekten. Inschriftlich erhaltene griechische Epigramme vom 9. bis zum 16. Jahrhundert: Suche nach bekannten Autornamen," in *Byzantinische Sprachkunst: Studien zur Byzantinischen Literatur gewidmet Wolfram Hörandner zum 65. Geburtstag*, ed. Martin Hinterberger and Elisabeth Schiffer (Berlin: De Gruyter, 2007), 250; J. Sola, "De Codice Laurentiano X Plutei V," *Byzantinische Zeitschrift* 20 (1911): 373–83.

32. Pamphile of Epidaurus wrote a *Miscellany of Historical Notes* in the first century CE. According to Photios's description (in the *Bibliotheke*, a set of descriptions and notes on various texts composed in the ninth century), it was a collection of anecdotes and useful sentences compiled without order as she encountered them. Pamphile's project, while of great interest, was not that of writing a historical narrative, in which the author imposes organizational structure on material. It is possible that other women in antiquity wrote histories that no longer survive. Starting in the late nineteenth century, Greek women, such as Penelope Delta, wrote historical fiction. Others wrote didactic texts about folk traditions and events of importance for national consciousness, largely published as articles in women's and children's journals. Some of these texts could be categorized as histories. But the conclusion from preliminary research seems to be that for a formal history, fitting the era's conception of proper practice (as Anna's had), we must wait for the generation of women historians active after the Second World War. I am grateful to Despina Christodoulou for her research and insight into this question. *Bibliothèque, Photius*, ed. René Henry (Paris: Société d'édition Les Belles Lettres, 1959), 2:170–71, codex number 175; A. Adler, ed., *Suda Lexicon*, Vol. 4 (Leipzig: Teubner, 1931), 15, entry number 139 under *pi*; *Suda On Line*, s.v. "Pamphile," trans. Malcom Heath, 16 May 2002, http://www.stoa.org/sol-entries/pi/139.

33. Some exceptions: Alexander Riehle, "Authorship and Gender (and) Identity. Women's Writing in the Middle Byzantine Period," in *The Author in Middle Byzantine*

Literature Modes, Functions, and Identities, ed. Aglae Pizzone (Berlin: De Gruyter, 2014), 245–62; Reinsch, "Women's Literature"; Thalia Gouma-Peterson, "Gender and Power: Passage to the Maternal in Anna Komnene's Alexiad," in *Anna Komnene and Her Times,* ed. Thalia Gouma-Peterson (London: Garland Publishing, 2000), 107–24; Thalia Gouma-Peterson, "Engendered Category or Recognizable Life: Anna Komnene and Her Alexiad," *Byzantinische Forschungen* 23 (1996): 25–34; Peter Frankopan, "Perception and Projection of Prejudice: Anna Comnena, the Alexiad and the First Crusade," in *Gendering the Crusades* (Cardiff: University of Wales Press, 2001), 59–76; Barbara Hill, "A Vindication of the Rights of Women to Power by Anna Komnene," *Byzantinische Forschungen* 23 (1996): 45–53. For James Howard-Johnston, Anna's natural female interests and capabilities meant she must have gotten the extensive military material in the *Alexiad* from another author. Howard-Johnston, "Anna Komnene and the Alexiad." Howard-Johnston's theory has been robustly criticized in Macrides, "The Pen and the Sword"; Reinsch, "Women's Literature"; Neville, *Heroes and Romans,* 182–93.

34. Of course there was great variation and change in conceptions of gender and authorship among the historians here collectively called "modern."

35. Diehl, *Byzantine Empresses,* 196.

36. Derek Krueger, *Writing and Holiness: The Practice of Authorship in the Early Christian East* (Philadelphia: University of Pennsylvania Press, 2004); Glenn W. Most, "The Stranger's Stratagem: Self-Disclosure and Self-Sufficiency in Greek Culture," *Journal of Hellenic Studies* 109 (1989): 114–33; Andrew Stone, "The Panegyrical Personae of Eustathios of Thessaloniki," *Scholia: Studies in Classical Antiquity* 18 (2009): 107–17; Aglae Pizzone, "Narrating Is Not for the Weak of Heart. Some Remarks on John Kaminiates' Capture of Thessaloniki," (Lecture, General Seminar of the Centre for Byzantine, Ottoman and Modern Greek Studies, University of Birmingham, October 27, 2011).

37. Emmanuel C. Bourbouhakis, "The End of ἐπίδειξις. Authorial Identity and Authorial Intention in Michael Chōniatēs' Πρὸς τοὺς αἰτιωμένους τὸ ἀφιλένδεικτον," in *The Author in Middle Byzantine Literature: Modes, Functions, and Identities,* ed. Aglae Pizzone (Berlin: De Gruyter, 2014), 201–24; Emmanuel C. Bourbouhakis, "'Political' Personae: The Poem from Prison of Michael Glykas: Byzantine Literature between Fact and Fiction," *Byzantine and Modern Greek Studies* 31 (2007): 53–75.

38. Sarah McNamer, *Affective Meditation and the Invention of Medieval Compassion,* Middle Ages Series (Philadelphia: University of Pennsylvania Press, 2010); Derek Krueger, *Liturgical Subjects: Christian Ritual, Biblical Narrative, and the Formation of the Self in Byzantium* (Philadelphia: University of Pennsylvania Press, 2014).

39. Stratis Papaioannou, "Voice, Signature, Mask: The Byzantine Author," in *The Author in Middle Byzantine Literature: Modes, Functions, and Identities,* ed. Aglae Pizzone (Berlin: De Gruyter, 2014), 26–28; Stratis Papaioannou, *Michael Psellos: Rhetoric and Authorship in Byzantium* (Cambridge: Cambridge University Press, 2013), 132–40; Stone, "The Panegyrical Personae of Eustathios of Thessaloniki." Byzantine rhetorical training manuals give us clues about how they expected audiences to react. Examples of such manuals: George Alexander Kennedy, trans., *Invention and Method: Two Rhetorical Treatises from the Hermogenic Corpus,* vol. 15, Writings from the Greco-Roman World (Atlanta: Society of Biblical Literature, 2005); George Alexander Kennedy, trans., *Progymnasmata: Greek Textbooks of Prose Composition and Rhetoric* (Atlanta: Society of Biblical Literature, 2003); Christian Waltz, ed., "Gregorius Pardus: Commentarium

in Hermogenis librum περὶ μεθόδου δεινότητος," in *Rhetores Graeci*, vol. 7.2 (Stuttgart: Cotta, 1834), 1090–1352.

40. For an exemplary journey from analysis of authorial self-presentation to understanding the context of composition, see Aglae Pizzone, "Anonymity, Dispossession and Reappropriation in the Prolog of Nikēphoros Basilakēs," in *The Author in Middle Byzantine Literature: Modes, Functions, and Identities*, ed. Aglae Pizzone (Berlin: De Gruyter, 2014), 225–45.

41. Diehl, *Byzantine Empresses*, 196

42. Cavafy, *Collected Poems*, 109.

Chapter 1

1. See Introduction, note 32.

2. Anna was a Greek historian in that she wrote in Greek and participated in the tradition of Greek history writing begun in antiquity. Greek was the language of expression of Anna's Roman culture and Roman political identity. On the Roman-ness of Byzantine society see Anthony Kaldellis, *Hellenism in Byzantium: The Transformations of Greek Identity and the Reception of the Classical Tradition* (Cambridge: Cambridge University Press, 2007).

3. Vicki Leon, *Uppity Women of Medieval Times*, 5th ed. (New York: Fine Communications, 1998), 114–15.

4. Angeliki Laiou, "Women in the Marketplace of Constantinople (10th–14th Centuries)," in *Byzantine Constantinople: Monuments, Topography and Everyday Life*, ed. Nevra Necipoğlu (Leiden: Brill, 2001), 261–73; Angeliki Laiou, "The Role of Women in Byzantine Society," *Jahrbuch der Österreichischen Byzantinistik* 31 (1981): 233–60; Liz James, "The Role of Women," in *The Oxford Handbook of Byzantine Studies*, ed. Elizabeth Jeffreys, John F. Haldon, and Robin Cormack, Oxford Handbooks (New York: Oxford University Press, 2008), 643–51; Ioli Kalavrezou, ed., *Byzantine Women and Their World* (Cambridge: Harvard University Art Museum, 2003); Joëlle Beaucamp, "Incapacité féminine et rôle public à Byzance," in *Femmes et pouvoirs des femmes à Byzance et in Occident (VIe–XIe siècle)*, ed. Stéphane Lebecq et al. (Lille: Villeneuve d'Ascq, 1999), 23–36; Joëlle Beaucamp, *Le statut de la femme á Byzance, 4e–7e siècle*. Vol.1. *Le droit impérial* (Paris: De Boccard, 1990); Joëlle Beaucamp, *Le statut de la femme à Byzance, 4e–7e siécle*. Vol.2. *Les practiques sociales* (Paris: De Boccard, 1992); Alice-Mary Talbot, *Women and Religious Life in Byzantium* (Aldershot: Ashgate, 2001); Judith Herrin, *Unrivalled Influence: Women and Empire in Byzantium* (Princeton: Princeton University Press, 2013); Leonora Neville, "Taxing Sophronia's Son-in-Law: Representations of Women in Provincial Documents," in *Byzantine Women: Varieties of Experience, 800–1200*, ed. Lynda Garland, (Aldershot: Ashgate, 2006), 77–89.

5. Judith Herrin, *Women in Purple: Rulers of Medieval Byzantium* (London: Weidenfeld & Nicolson, 2001); Barbara Hill, *Imperial Women in Byzantium, 1025–1204: Power, Patronage and Ideology* (New York: Longman, 1999); Liz James, *Empresses and Power in Early Byzantium* (London: Leicester University Press, 2001).

6. Charalambos Messis, "La construction sociale, les 'realités' rhétoriques et les représentations de l'identité masculine à Byzance" (PhD diss., L'École des hautes etudes

en science sociales, 2006), 435–40; Stratis Papaioannou, *Michael Psellos: Rhetoric and Authorship in Byzantium* (Cambridge: Cambridge University Press, 2013), 202; Eustratios N. Papaioannou, "On the Stage of Eros: Two Rhetorical Exercises by Nikephoros Basilakes," in *Theatron: Rhetorische Kultur in Spätantike und Mittelalter/Rhetorical Culture in Late Antiquity and the Middle Ages,* ed. Michael Grünbart (Berlin: De Gruyter, 2007), 373–74; Liz James, "Men, Women, Eunuchs: Gender, Sex and Power," in *The Social History of Byzantium,* ed. John F. Haldon (Malden: Blackwell, 2009), 31–50; Liz James, *Women, Men, and Eunuchs: Gender in Byzantium* (London: Routledge, 1997); Charles Barber, "Homo Byzantinus?," in *Women, Men and Eunuchs: Gender in Byzantium* (London: Routledge, 1997), 185–99; Mathew Kuefler, *The Manly Eunuch: Masculinity, Gender Ambiguity, and Christian Ideology in Late Antiquity* (Chicago: University of Chicago Press, 2001); Myles Anthony McDonnell, *Roman Manliness: Virtus and the Roman Republic* (Cambridge: Cambridge University Press, 2006).

7. Susan Ashbrook Harvey, "Women in Early Byzantine Hagiography: Reversing the Story," in *That Gentle Strength: Historical Perspectives on Women in Christianity,* ed. Lynda L. Coon, Katherine J. Haldane, and Elisabeth W. Sommer (Charlottesville: University Press of Virginia, 1990), 41.

8. Catia Galatariotou, "Holy Women and Witches: Aspects of Byzantine Conceptions of Gender," *Byzantine and Modern Greek Studies* 9 (1984): 55–94; Stamatina McGrath, "Women in Byzantine History in the Tenth and Eleventh Centuries: Some Theoretical Considerations," in *Byzantine Religious Culture: Studies in Honor of Alice-Mary Talbot,* ed. Denis Sullivan, Elizabeth A. Fisher, and Stratis Papaioannou (Leiden: Brill, 2012), 85–98; James, "Gender, Sex and Power"; Messis, "L'identité masculine à Byzance," 575–77; Harvey, "Women in Early Byzantine Hagiography: Reversing the Story"; Martha Vinson, "The Christianization of Sexual Slander: Some Preliminary Observations," in *Novum Millennium: Studies on Byzantine History and Culture Dedicated to Paul Speck* (Aldershot: Ashgate, 2001), 415–24; Dion Smythe, "Gender," in *Palgrave Advances in Byzantine History,* ed. Jonathan Harris (New York: Palgrave, 2005), 157–65.

9. Messis, "L'identité masculine à Byzance," 575.

10. Maria Dora Spadaro, *Raccomandazioni e consigli di un galantuomo (Strategikon)* (Alessandria: Edizioni dell'Orso, 1998), 148–50.

11. Pierre Noailles and Alphonse Dain, eds., *Les Novelles de Léon VI, Le Sage* (Paris: Société d'édition Les Belles Lettres, 1944), 189–90; Messis, "L'identité masculine à Byzance," 574–75.

12. Laiou, "Women in the Marketplace of Constantinople (10th–14th Centuries)," 263–64.

13. Ibid. 264–65.

14. The reality of women's confinement within the home has been questioned: Laiou, "Role of Women," 249. Yet the ideal of seclusion of aristocratic women seems to have had wide support. How many people enacted this ideal is simply unknown. Scholars of classical Athens also question how far the normative seclusion of women was actually practiced. Laura McClure, *Women in the Ancient World: A New Approach* (Malden: Blackwell, forthcoming 2017).

15. Thucydides, 2.45.2.

16. Messis, "L'identité masculine à Byzance," 435–40.

17. Harvey, "Women in Early Byzantine Hagiography: Reversing the Story," 40.

18. Ibid. 41.

19. Papaioannou, *Michael Psellos*, 215–18.

20. Lynda L. Coon, Katherine J. Haldane, and Elisabeth W. Sommer, eds., *That Gentle Strength: Historical Perspectives on Women in Christianity* (University of Virginia Press, 1990), 4–5.

21. Paul Gautier, ed., "Theodorus Prodromos: Epitaphius in Theodoram nurum Bryennii," in *Nicéphore Bryennios. Histoire* (Brussels: Byzantion, 1975), 347.

22. Jean Darrouzes, *George et Demetrios Tornikes. Lettres et Discours* (Paris: Editions du Centre national de la recherche scientifique, 1970), 267, lines 20–25.

23. Helen Saradi-Mendelovici, "A Contribution to the Study of the Byzantine Notarial Formulas: The Infirmitas Sexus of Women and the Sc. Velleianum," *Byzantinische Zeitschrift* 83 (1990): 72–90.

24. Leonora Neville, "The Adventures of a Provincial Female Founder: Glykeria and the Rhetoric of Female Weakness," in *Female Founders in Byzantium and Beyond*, ed. Margaret Mullett, Michael Grünbart, and Lioba Theis, vols. 50–51, Wiener Jarhbuch Für Kunstgeschichte (Vienna, 2010), 159.

25. Nicolas Oikonomides, ed., *Actes de Docheiariou* (Paris: P. Lethielleux, 1984), 67–73, document number 3. Neville, "Taxing Sophronia's Son-in-Law: Representations of Women in Provincial Documents," 88–89.

26. The widow wearing down men in power by persistently asking for help was already a stock character at the time she appears in Jesus's parable in Luke 18:1–8. The poor and needy cry for help, and God and the righteous hear them; for example: Psalms. 12:5, 35:10, 41:1–3, 7:5, 86:1, 109:22, 113:7, 140:12. On the formation of character via participation in religious observances, see Derek Krueger, *Liturgical Subjects: Christian Ritual, Biblical Narrative, and the Formation of the Self in Byzantium* (Philadelphia: University of Pennsylvania Press, 2014).

27. Eudokia's husband, Stephen, was still alive and adds his own declaration of his support. He held the imperial rank of *protospatharios*, which, while not a grand title in 1112, still indicated that they were not peasants. The land Eudokia sold was only a portion of her dowry, and she would remain a not-insignificant landowner. Several unusual aspects of Eudokia's deed of sale seem designed to prevent her from later renouncing the sale on the common legal grounds of ignorance of the law, coercion, deception, and womanly simplicity. The passage from the medieval code of Roman law, that banned the sale of dowry land was quoted in the opening of Eudokia's deed, so she could not claim ignorance of the law. The monks convened a council of prominent local men to judge whether Eudokia's appeal to the governor reflected her own intentions, so she could not claim coercion, deception or female simplicity. They tested whether she knew what she was doing, not whether she was poor.

28. The moral obligation of caring for and defending widows recurs in many of the theological texts that structured Byzantine morality; for example: Isaiah 1:16–23, Exodus 22:22–23, Deuteronomy 27:19. Defending widows is a characteristic of God; for example: Psalms 68:5, 146:9, Deuteronomy 10:18.

29. Throughout the sale, Eudokia repeatedly and emphatically reiterates her desire to sell her property, and the freedom and self-determination with which she is able to make this choice. Yet that choice is legally enabled by her performance of complete helplessness and her portrayal as a victim of inescapable necessity in her petition to the governor.

Because dowry land could only be sold in circumstances of extreme need, she had to convincingly be utterly desperate and helpless before the governor. Because sales were only legally binding if undertaken with complete free will, Eudokia had to be convincingly authoritative, reasonable, and willing before the witnesses of the sale.

30. Paul Lemerle et al., *Actes de Lavra*, vol. 1 (Paris: Lethielleux, 1970), 141–44, document number 16.

31. Neville, "Rhetoric of Female Weakness."

32. In denying her local bishop authority over the monastery she had founded on her land, Glykeria was acting in defiance the fourth canon of the Council of Chalcedon (451) that gave bishops authority over monasteries. Ibid. 153–54.

33. Cyril A. Mango and Roger Scott, eds., *The Chronicle of Theophanes Confessor: Byzantine and Near Eastern History, AD 284–813* (Oxford: Clarendon Press, 1997), 626–27; James, *Empresses*, 68.

34. Martha Vinson, "Gender and Politics in the Post-Iconoclastic Period: The Lives of Antony the Younger, the Empress Theodora, and the Patriarch Ignatios," *Byzantion* 68 (1998): 492–93.

35. The ongoing process of working out these differences has been one of the great achievements of classical scholarship since the 1990s. For essential orientation to this research, see John Marincola, ed., *Greek and Roman Historiography* (Oxford: Oxford University Press, 2011); John Marincola, *A Companion to Greek and Roman Historiography* (Malden: Blackwell, 2007); A. J. Woodman, *Rhetoric in Classical Historiography: Four Studies* (Portland: Areopagitica Press, 1988). The study of medieval Greek history writing has far fewer practitioners, but with every study it becomes more evident that the practices of the medieval historians were similar to those of the ancient historians. I apply scholarship on ancient historiography to medieval histories with great confidence. On medieval historiography in Greek, see Ralph-Johannes Lilie, "Reality and Invention: Reflections on Byzantine Historiography," *Dumbarton Oaks Papers* 68 (2014): 157–210; Ruth Macrides, ed., *History as Literature in Byzantium* (Farnham: Ashgate, 2010); Ruth Macrides, "The Historian in the History," in *Philellēn: Studies in Honour of Robert Browning*, ed. C. N. Constantinides, Nikolaos Panagiōtakēs, and Elizabeth Jeffreys (Venice: Istituto ellenico di studi bizantini e postbizantini di Venezia, 1996), 205–24; Dimitris Krallis, *Michael Attaleiates and the Politics of Imperial Decline in Eleventh-Century Byzantium* (Tempe: ACMRS, 2012); Anthony Kaldellis, "The Corpus of Byzantine Historiography: An Interpretive Essay," in *The Byzantine World* (London: Routledge, 2010), 211–22; Alicia Simpson and Stephanos Efthymiades, eds., *Niketas Choniates: A Historian and a Writer* (Geneva: La Pomme d'Or, 2009); Paolo Odorico, Panagiotis A. Agapitos, and Martin Hinterberger, eds., *L'écriture de la mémoire: la littérarité de l'historiographie*, Dossiers byzantins 6 (Paris: Centre d'études byzantines, néo-helléniques et sud-est européennes, École des Hautes Études en Sciences Sociales, 2006); Athanasios Markopoulos, *History and Literature of Byzantium in the 9th–10th Centuries* (Aldershot: Ashgate, 2004).

36. The ninth-century history of George the Monk was an exception that dealt with many topics beyond the standard politics and war. But while his history was highly popular, his model was not followed. Dimitry E. Afinogenov, "Some Observations on Genres of Byzantine Historiography," *Byzantion* 62 (1992): 13–33; Jakov Ljubarskij, "George the Monk as a Short-Story Writer," *Jahrbuch der Österreichischen Byzantinistik* 44 (1994): 255–64; Kaldellis, "The Corpus of Byzantine Historiography," 212.

37. Paul Magdalino, "Byzantine Historical Writing, 900–1400," in *The Oxford History of Historical Writing*, ed. Sarah Foot, Chase F. Robinson, and Daniel R. Woolf, vol. 2 (Oxford: Oxford University Press, 2012), 218–37. An increasing focus on the deeds of the emperors in tenth- and eleventh-century historiography led Greek history writing to take on a somewhat biographic cast. Athanasios Markopoulos, "From Narrative Historiography to Historical Biography. New Trends in Byzantine Historical Writing in the 10th–11th Centuries," *Byzantinische Zeitschrift* 102 (2010): 697–715.

38. John Marincola, *Authority and Tradition in Ancient Historiography* (Cambridge: Cambridge University Press, 1997), 86, 133–48; Charles Fornara, *The Nature of History in Ancient Greece and Rome* (Berkeley: University of California Press, 1983), 47–50.

39. Polybius, 12.28a.8–10, quoted in Marincola, *Authority and Tradition*, 73.

40. On Attaleiates see Krallis, *Michael Attaleiates and the Politics of Imperial Decline in Eleventh-Century Byzantium*, 52–69.

41. Hans-Georg Beck, "Die Byzantinische 'Mönchschronik,'" in *Ideen und Realitäten in Byzanz* (London, 1972), 188–97; Kaldellis, "The Corpus of Byzantine Historiography," 212.

42. Angeliki Laiou, "Law, Justice, and the Byzantine Historians: Ninth to Twelfth Centuries," in *Law and Society in Byzantium: Ninth–Twelfth Centuries* (Washington, DC: Dumbarton Oaks, 1994), 151–86; Anthony Kaldellis, "Byzantine Historical Writing, 500–920," in *The Oxford History of Historical Writing*, ed. Daniel Woolf, Sarah Foot, and Chase F. Robinson, vol. 2 (Oxford: Oxford University Press, 2012), 204; Magdalino, "Byzantine Historical Writing, 900–1400," 233.

43. Marincola, *Authority and Tradition*, 128.

44. Ibid. 6–7.

45. Psellos, for instance, wrote his *Historia Syntomos* with the didactic purpose of educating a future emperor. Stratis Papaioannou and John Duffy, "Michael Psellos and the Authorship of the Historia Syntomos: Final Considerations," in *Byzantium, State and Society: In Memory of Nikos Oikonomides*, ed. A. Abramea, Angeliki Laiou, and Evangelos Chrysos (Athens: Hellenic National Research Foundation, 2003), 219–29.

46. Athanasios Markopoulos, "Byzantine History Writing at the End of the First Millennium," in *Byzantium in the Year 1000*, ed. Paul Magdalino (Leiden: Brill, 2003), 186.

47. Leonora Neville, *Heroes and Romans in Twelfth-Century Byzantium: The "Material for History" of Nikephoros Bryennios* (Cambridge University Press, 2012), 140–49.

48. Translation by Nigel Wilson, *The Bibliotheca: A Selection* (London: Duckworth, 1994), 157–58; *Bibliothèque, Photius*, ed. René Henry (Paris: Société d'édition Les Belles Lettres, 1959), 2:170–171, codex number 175.

49. Wilson, *The Bibliotheca*, 158.

50. Karl Müller, Theodor Müller, and Victor Langlois, eds., *Fragmenta historicorum graecorum*, (Paris: Ambrosio Firmin Didot, 1841–1938; repr. Frankfurt: Minerva, 1975), vol. 3, 520–22; citation refers to reprint edition.

51. Wilson, *The Bibliotheca*, 158. The attribution of her work to her husband is recorded in the Suda, a tenth-century dictionary: A. Adler, ed., *Suda Lexicon*, vol. 4 (Leipzig: Teubner, 1931), 15, entry number 139 under *pi.*; *Suda On Line*, s.v. "Pamphile," trans. Malcom Heath, 16 May 2002, http://www.stoa.org/sol-entries/pi/139.

52. Papaioannou, *Michael Psellos*, 200–201.

53. Ibid. 192.

54. Harvey, "Women in Early Byzantine Hagiography: Reversing the Story," 37–38; Susan Ashbrook Harvey, "Including the 'Despised Woman': Jacob of Serug at the Nativity Feast," in *Byzantine Religious Culture: Studies in Honor of Alice-Mary Talbot*, ed. Denis Sullivan, Elizabeth A. Fisher, and Stratis Papaioannou (Leiden: Brill, 2012), 14–19; Papaioannou, *Michael Psellos*, 135–36.

55. Papaioannou, *Michael Psellos*, 135–36.

56. Ibid. 52.

57. Glenn W. Most, "The Stranger's Stratagem: Self-Disclosure and Self-Sufficiency in Greek Culture," *Journal of Hellenic Studies* 109 (1989): 131.

58. Floris Bernard highlights the tensions between the established "discourse of modesty" and the "discourse of display" used among self-made intellectuals working in a highly competitive intellectual marketplace in the eleventh century. Floris Bernard, "The Ethics of Authorship: Some Tensions in the 11th Century," in *The Author in Middle Byzantine Literature: Modes, Functions, and Identities*, ed. Aglae Pizzone (Berlin: De Gruyter, 2014), 41–60. In certain circumstances, the discourse of modesty would lead to what Pizzone terms "poetics of anonymity." Aglae Pizzone, "Anonymity, Dispossession and Reappropriation in the Prolog of Nikēphoros Basilakēs," in *The Author in Middle Byzantine Literature: Modes, Functions, and Identities*, ed. Aglae Pizzone (Berlin: De Gruyter, 2014), 225–45.

59. Derek Krueger, *Writing and Holiness: The Practice of Authorship in the Early Christian East* (Philadelphia: University of Pennsylvania Press, 2004), 98.

60. Ibid. 94–109.

61. Papaioannou, *Michael Psellos*, 233.

62. Ibid. 132.

63. Ibid.

64. Most, "The Stranger's Stratagem," 131.

65. Plutarch, *Moralia*, 539–47.

66. George Alexander Kennedy, *Invention and Method: Two Rhetorical Treatises from the Hermogenic Corpus*, vol. 15, Writings from the Greco-Roman World (Atlanta: Society of Biblical Literature, 2005), 244–47; Christian Waltz, ed., "Gregorius Pardus: Commentarium in Hermogenis librum περὶ μεθόδου δεινότητος," in *Rhetores Graeci*, vol. 7.2 (Stuttgart: Cotta, 1834), chapter 24, pages 1298–1301. *Eustathii archiepiscopi Thessalonicensis Commentarii ad Homeri Iliadem pertinentes ad fidem codicis Laurentiani editi*, ed. Marchinus van der Valk (Leiden: Brill, 1971), vol.1, 188. I thank Aglae Pizzone for bringing Eustathius's discussion to my attention.

67. Most, "The Stranger's Stratagem," 130.

68. Martin Hinterberger, *Phthonos: Missgunst, Neid und Eifersucht in der byzantinischen Literatur* (Wiesbaden: Dr. Ludwig Reichert Verlag, 2013); Martin Hinterberger, "Envy and Nemesis in the Vita Basili and Leo the Deacon: Literary Mimesis or Something More?," in *History as Literature in Byzantium* (Farnham: Ashgate, 2010), 187–203; Martin Hinterberger, "Emotions in Byzantium," in *A Companion to Byzantium* (Malden: Wiley-Blackwell, 2010), 121–34.

69. Glenn W. Most, "The Stranger's Stratagem," 114–33; Aglae Pizzone, "Narrating Is Not for the Weak of Heart. Some Remarks on John Kaminiates' Capture of Thessaloniki," (Lecture, General Seminar of the Centre for Byzantine, Ottoman and Modern Greek Studies, University of Birmingham, October 27, 2011).

70. *Alexiad*, 15.9.1.

Chapter 2

1. Iordanis Grigoriadis, *Linguistic and Literary Studies in the Epitome Historion of John Zonaras* (Thessalonike: Center for Byzantine Research, 1998), 31.

2. See page 27.

3. See page 28.

4. See page 16–17.

5. *Alexiad*, P.1.1.

6. Sophocles, *Ajax* 646–47. Modified translation of Richard C. Jebb, *The Tragedies of Sophocles* (Cambridge: Cambridge University Press, 1904).

7. *Alexiad*, P.1.2.

8. Herodotus, 1.1, trans. A. D. Godley, *Herodotus* (Cambridge: Harvard University Press, 1920).

9. Thucydides, 1.1, trans. Richard Crawley, *History of the Peloponnesian War* (London, J.M. Dent: 1910).

10. John Duffy, "Hellenic Philosophy in Byzantium and the Lonely Mission of Michael Psellos," in *Byzantine Philosophy and Its Ancient Sources* (Oxford: Clardenon Press, 2002), 139–56; Katerina Ierodiakonou and Dominic J. O'Meara, "Philosophies," in *The Oxford Handbook of Byzantine Studies*, ed. Elizabeth Jeffreys, John F. Haldon, and Robin Cormack, Oxford Handbooks (New York: Oxford University Press, 2008), 711–20.

11. Averil Cameron, *The Byzantines* (Malden: Blackwell, 2006), 133–45; Liz James, "The Role of Women," in *The Oxford Handbook of Byzantine Studies*, ed. Elizabeth Jeffreys, John F. Haldon, and Robin Cormack, Oxford Handbooks (New York: Oxford University Press, 2008), 646; Maria Mavroudi, "Learned Women of Byzantium and the Surviving Record," in *Byzantine Religious Culture: Studies in Honor of Alice-Mary Talbot*, ed. Denis Sullivan, Elizabeth Fisher, and Stratis Papaioannou (Leiden: Brill, 2012), 53–84.

12. *Alexiad*, 12.3.3.

13. E. Kurtz, "[Monodies on Nikephoros Komnenos by Eustathios of Thessaloniki and Constantine Manasses]," *Vizantiĭskiĭ Vremennik* 16 (1922): 307.

14. On the Pythagorean tradition of female philosophers, see Sarah B. Pomeroy, *Pythagorean Women: Their History and Writings* (Baltimore: Johns Hopkins University Press, 2013). I thank Anthony Kaldellis for bringing these precursors to Anna's philosophical activity to my attention.

15. Iordanis Grigoriadis, *Linguistic and Literary Studies in the Epitome Historion of John Zonaras* (Thessalonike: Center for Byzantine Research, 1998), 42.

16. John Marincola, *Authority and Tradition in Ancient Historiography* (Cambridge: Cambridge University Press, 1997), 87.

17. Ibid. 89–90.

18. Ruth Macrides, "The Historian in the History," in *Filellen: Studies in Honour of Robert Browning* (Venice: Instituto ellenico di studi bizantini e postbizantini di Venezia, 1996), 218.

19. Stratis Papaioannou, *Michael Psellos: Rhetoric and Authorship in Byzantium* (Cambridge: Cambridge University Press, 2013), 216.

20. *Alexiad*, P2.3.

21. *Alexiad*, P2.2.

22. *Alexiad*, P2.3.

23. She uses a phrase "οὐ γὰρ περιαυτολογία τὸ πρᾶγμα" from Psellos's encomium for his mother. There Psellos askes that he not be blamed if he talks about himself on the grounds that doing so would not be a discourse about himself but about the causes of his mother's virtue: "εἰ δέ τι καὶ περὶ ἐμαυτοῦ διηγοίμην, μεμφέσθω μηδείς, οὐ γὰρ περιαυτολογία τὸ πρᾶγμα, ἀλλ᾽ αἰτιολογία, ὅπη παρείκοι, τῶν τῆς μητρὸς καλῶν" (Ugo Criscuolo, ed., *Autobiografia: Encomio per La Madre: Michele Psello* [Naples: M. D'Auria editore, 1989], lines 260–62). He again denies "περιαυτολογία" in the midst of self-description in *Chronographia* Book 6.46.11.

24. See page 27.

25. *Alexiad*, P1.1.

26. *Alexiad*, P1.2.

27. *Alexiad*, P2.1.

28. *Alexiad*, P3.3.

29. Marincola, *Authority and Tradition*, 237–41.

30. Aglae Pizzone, "Narrating Is Not for the Weak of Heart. Some Remarks on John Kaminiates' Capture of Thessaloniki," (Lecture, General Seminar of the Centre for Byzantine, Ottoman and Modern Greek Studies, University of Birmingham, October 27, 2011).

31. This may allude to Christian and pre-Christian philosophy.

32. *Alexiad*, P4.1.

33. Glenn W. Most, "The Stranger's Stratagem. Self-Disclosure and Self-Sufficiency in Greek Culture," *Journal of Hellenic Studies* 109 (1989): 114–33; Pizzone, "Kaminiates."

34. *Alexiad*, P4.2.

35. *Alexiad*, P4.3.

Chapter 3

1. See T. J. Luce, "Ancient Views on the Causes of Bias in Historical Writing," *Classical Philology* 84 (1989): 16–31; John Marincola, *Authority and Tradition in Ancient Historiography* (Cambridge: Cambridge University Press, 1997), 128–74; Iordanis Grigoriadis, "A Study of the Prooimion of Zonaras' Chronicle in Relation to Other 12th-Century Prooimia," *Byzantinische Zeitschrift* 91 (1998): 327–44.

2. Marincola, *Authority and Tradition*, 158.

3. *Alexiad*, P2.3.

4. *Alexiad*, 1.16.9.

5. *Alexiad*, 1.16.9.6–11.

6. *Alexiad*, 14.7.3.

7. *Alexiad*, P2.2.

8. *Alexiad*, P2.2, quoting Homer *Iliad* 11.653.

9. Genesis 9:20–27.

10. Ludwig August Dindorf, ed. *Ioannis Zonarae Epitome Historiarum* (Leipzig: Teubner, 1886), vol.1, 22; Philo of Alexandria, *On Sobriety*, section 32; James L. Kugel, *Traditions of the Bible: A Guide to the Bible as It Was at the Start of the Common Era* (Cambridge: Harvard University Press, 1998), 222.

11. Basil of Caesarea, sermon 11, *Patrologiae Graeca*, vol. 31 (Paris: Excecudebatur et venit apud J-PMigne, 1857), 640.

12. Athanasios Kambylis, "Zum Programm der byzantinischen Historikerin Anna Komnene," in *Dōrēma: Hans Diller zum 70. Geburtstag: Dauer und Überleben des antiken Geistes*, ed. Kōnstantinos Vourverēs and Aristoxenos D. Skiadas (Athens: Griechische Humanistische Gesellschaft, 1975), 138.

13. Ancient ideas of truth and impartiality in history are not the same as modern ideas about historical objectivity. In the ancient historiographic tradition, the virtue of impartiality was essential because it was the main guard against inventing the stories that would help a biased author prove his point. The modern discourse of objectivity concerns the ability of a historian to judge between competing evidence. See Charles Fornara, *The Nature of History in Ancient Greece and Rome* (Berkeley: University of California Press, 1983), 91–141; Marincola, *Authority and Tradition*, 158–74; Luce, "Ancient Views on the Causes of Bias in Historical Writing."

14. *Alexiad*, 1.10.2.5–8.

15. Jean Darrouzes, *George et Demetrios Tornikes. Lettres et Discours* (Paris: Editions du Centre national de la recherche scientifique, 1970), 265.

16. Ibid. 317, lines 14–21.

17. Stratis Papaioannou, "Anna Komnene's Will," in *Byzantine Religious Culture: Studies in Honor of Alice-Mary Talbot*, ed. Denis Sullivan, Elizabeth Fisher, and Stratis Papaioannou (Leiden: Brill, 2012), 105–6, 111.

18. Alexios was called "mother-lover" and his son John a "father-lover." P. Maas, "De Musen des kaisers Alexios I," *Byzantinische Zeitschrift* 22 (1913): 349; Diether Roderich Reinsch, "Abweichungen vom traditionellen Byzantinischen Kaiserbild im 11. und 12. Jahrhundert," in *L'éducation au gouvernement et à la vie: la tradition des "règles de vie" de l'antiquité au moyen âge*, ed. Paolo Odorico (Paris: École des hautes études en sciences sociales, Centre d'études byzantines, néo-helléniques et sud-est européennes, 2009), 116.

19. *Alexiad*, 7.3.9–12.

20. *Alexiad*, 7.3.12.

21. Anthony Kaldellis, "The Military Use of the Icon of the Theotokos and Its Moral Logic in the Historians of the Ninth-Twelfth Centuries," *Estudios Bizantinos: Revista de La Sociedad Española de Bizantinística* 1 (2013): 56–75.

22. *Alexiad*, 7.3.10.

23. *Alexiad*, 7.3.9, 7.3.11.

24. *Alexiad*, 11.10.4.

25. *Alexiad*, 10.9.

26. *Alexiad*, 2.12.4.

27. *Alexiad*, 3.5.

28. *Alexiad*, 6.8.1.

29. Perhaps most explicitly at *Alexiad*, 14.7.

30. Eirene: *Alexiad*, 3.3.3–4, 12.3.2–10; Anna Dalassene: 3.8.1–3.8.11.

31. At three different points in her encomiastic description of her grandmother, Anna insists that she is not writing an encomium: *Alexiad*, 3.8.1.5–8; 3.8.5.1–6; 3.8.11.3–6.

32. *Alexiad*, 6.8.2.

33. *Alexiad*, 15.3.4.

34. *Alexiad*, 14.9.5.

35. *Alexiad*, 12.3.10.

36. *Alexiad*, 7.2.6.4–10.

37. *Alexiad*, 7.2.6.3–4.

38. *Alexiad*, 7.2.6.10–21.

39. *Alexiad*, 10.9.8.

40. *Alexiad*, 10.9.8.

41. Leonora Neville, *Heroes and Romans in Twelfth-Century Byzantium: The "Material for History" of Nikephoros Bryennios* (Cambridge: Cambridge University Press, 2012), 89–103, 121–38, 159–70.

42. Ibid. 182–93.

43. *Alexiad*, P2.2.

44. *Alexiad*, 12.5.1; 13.10.7; 15.10.4.

45. Martin Hinterberger, *Phthonos: Missgunst, Neid und Eifersucht in der byzantinischen Literatur* (Wiesbaden: Dr. Ludwig Reichert Verlag, 2013); Martin Hinterberger, "Envy and Nemesis in the Vita Basili and Leo the Deacon: Literary Mimesis or Something More?," in *History as Literature in Byzantium* (Farnham: Ashgate, 2010), 187–203; Martin Hinterberger, "Phthonos als treibende Kraft in Prodromos, Manasses und Bryennios," *Medioevo Greco* 11 (2011): 1–24.

46. The perceived need to protect infants from the malignant forces of envy is well-attested in both late antique and early modern Greek culture. In the surviving excerpts of his discussion of the baby-devouring demon, Michael Psellos does not make an explicit connection with envy. He describes the *gillo* as a malignant power that offered itself to old women who would secretly kill babies by suckling them. Within the later and earlier traditions, it is the jealousy of the old woman for the young mother that calls out the malignant agencies that cause the death of infants. Because of the strong continuities of other elements of this tradition, I take envy, *phthonos*, as the driving force for the twelfth-century as well. See John M. Duffy and Dominic J. O'Meara, eds., *Michaelis Pselli Philosophica minora* Vol. 2. *Opuscula psychologica, theologica, daemonologica* (Leipzig: B. G. Teubner, 1992), 164; Irene Sorlin, "Striges et Geloudes. Histoire d'une croyance et d'une tradition," *Travaux et Mémoires* 11 (1991): 411–36. For late antiquity: James Russell, "The Archaeological Context of Magic in the Early Byzantine Period," in *Byzantine Magic*, ed. Henry Maguire (Washington, DC: Dumbarton Oaks, 1995), 35–50; Matthew W. Dickie, "The Fathers of the Church and the Evil Eye," in *Byzantine Magic*, ed. Henry Maguire (Washington, DC: Dumbarton Oaks, 1995), 9–34. On the early modern tradition: Karen Hartnup, *"On the Beliefs of the Greeks": Leo Allatios and Popular Orthodoxy* (Leiden: Brill, 2004), 146–49.

47. *Alexiad*, 12.3.4.9–11.

48. *Alexiad*, 3.1.3.

49. *Alexiad*, 6.7.

50. *Alexiad*, 1.13.3. On the story see Emily Albu, "Viewing Rome from the Roman Empires," *Medieval Encounters* 17, no. 4/5 (2011): 499–500.

51. The *Dogmatiki Panoplia* by Zygabenos.

52. *Alexiad*, 15.9.1–5.

53. *Alexiad*, 12.3.3.

54. *Alexiad*, 12.3.4.

55. *Alexiad*, 12.3.6.

56. *Alexiad*, 12.3.6.

57. On the damage to a woman's honor from being seen by men, see Charalambos Messis, "La construction sociale, les 'realités' rhétoriques et les représentations de l'identité masculine à Byzance" (PhD diss., L'École des hautes etudes en science sociales, 2006), 574–75.

58. It is possible that it may not have been so unusual for twelfth-century women to accompany the emperor on campaign. A set of poems describing the tent of the Sevastokratorissa Eirene indicates that she accompanied her brother-in-law Manuel to at least some of his military camps. Another story used to adduce the regular presence of female relatives in camps is that of Andronikos Komnenos nearly getting caught in bed with his cousin Eudokia by a group of her angry and armed relatives. J. van Dieten, ed., *Nicetae Choniatae historia, pars prior*, Corpus Fontium Historiae Byzantinae (Berlin: De Gruyter, 1975), 103–5. The behavior of Eudokia and Andronikos was seen as outrageous and perhaps should not be used to argue that women were normally present in camp. Rather, this evidence may reflect the lax sexual morality of the court of Manuel Komnenos, against which Anna may be reacting. For the view that women normally may have traveled with the court see Michael Jeffreys, "Manuel Komnenos' Macedonian Military Camps: A Glamorous Alternative Court?," in *Byzantine Macedonia: Identity Image and History*, ed. John Burke and Roger Scott (Queensland: Australian Association for Byzantine Studies, Australian Catholic University, 2000), 184–91; Jeffrey Anderson and Elizabeth Jeffreys, "The Decoration of the Sevastokratorissa's Tent," *Byzantion* 64 (1994): 8.

59. *Alexiad*, 12.3.7.

60. *Alexiad*, 12.3.7, quoting Homer, *Iliad* 11.653.

61. Buckley convincingly argues that the discussion of Eirene traveling with Alexios is placed at this point, at the opening of book 12, because it marks a shift in the image of Alexios from a more bellicose, fearsome warrior emperor, toward a more holy image of emperor as bringer of peace. The constant accompaniment of his gentle, charitable wife—whose name means "peace"—is a way of signaling this change. Penelope Buckley, *The Alexiad of Anna Komnene: Artistic Strategy in the Making of a Myth* (Cambridge: Cambridge University Press, 2014), 228–31. Chalandon used Anna's description of Eirene's reluctance to accompany Alexios as evidence that she was forced to go because Alexios did not trust her enough to leave in the capital. Angold builds on this theory, arguing that because Zonaras mentioned Eirene traveling with Alexios after a serious illness, she must have been brought along as "a way of keeping an eye on her." This case would be greatly weakened if the evidence for women normally traveling with the imperial camp is accepted. Ferdinand Chalandon, *Essai sur le règne d'Alexis Ier Comnène (1081–1118)* (Paris: A. Picard et fils, 1900), 274. Michael Angold, "Alexios I Komnenos: An Afterword," in *Alexios I Komnenos*, edited by Dion Smythe and Margaret Mullett, Belfast Byzantine Texts and Translations 4.1 (Belfast: Belfast Byzantine Enterprizes, 1996), 404–5.

62. *Alexiad*, 4.7.2.

63. *Alexiad*, 4.7.3–4.

64. *Alexiad*, 4.8.1.

65. *Alexiad*, 4.8.1.

66. The Suda defines *sobades* as "chasing harlots." A. Adler, ed., *Suda Lexicon*, vol. 4 (Leipzig: Teubner, 1931), 394, entry number 754 under *sigma*; *Suda On Line*, s.v.

"Sobades," trans. David Whitehead, 24 April 2003, http://www.stoa.org/sol-entries/
sigma/754. Niketas Choniates describes Andronikos Komnenos as traveling with a group
of courtesans, as Dionysius escorted Thyades, Sobades, Maenads, and Bacchantes. J. van
Dieten, ed., *Nicetae Choniatae historia, pars prior*, Corpus Fontium Historiae Byzantinae
(Berlin: De Gruyter, 1975), 321.

67. See page 27–28.

68. Homer, *Odyssey* 20.339.

69. Aligning herself with Telemachos fits nicely with Anna's overarching presentation
of her father as an Odysseus.

Chapter 4

1. *Alexiad*, 15.9.1.

2. Stratis Papaioannou, *Michael Psellos: Rhetoric and Authorship in Byzantium*
(Cambridge: Cambridge University Press, 2013), 192.

3. Hugo Rabe, ed., *Aphthonii Progymnasmata*, Bibliotheca Scriptorum Graecorum
et Romanorum Teubneriana (Leipzig: B. G. Teubner, 1926), 35–37; George Alexander
Kennedy, trans., *Progymnasmata: Greek Textbooks of Prose Composition and Rhetoric*
(Atlanta: Society of Biblical Literature, 2003), 116–17.

4. Gregory of Nyssa's sermon on the Widow of Nain: *Patrologiae Graeca*, vol. 44
(Paris: Excecudebatur et venit apud J-P. Migne, 1863), 220–21; A. Pignani, ed., *Niceforo
Basilace. Progimnasmi e monodie* (Naples: Bibliopolis, 1983), 169–80, exercise number
41. Henry Maguire, *Art and Eloquence in Byzantium* (Princeton: Princeton University
Press, 1981), 91–96. On the liturgical contexts of the laments of the Virgin, see Nancy P.
Ševčenko, "The Service of the Virgin's Lament Revisited," in *The Cult of the Mother of God
in Byzantium*, ed. Leslie Brubaker and Mary Cunningham (Burlington: Ashgate, 2011),
247–62.

5. Eva Catafygiotu Topping, "Women Hymnographers in Byzantium," *Diptycha* 3
(1982–83): 64–65; Eva Catafygiotu Topping, "Thekla the Nun: In Praise of Women," *Greek
Orthodox Theological Review* 25, no. 4 (1980): 353–70; Anna M. Silvas, "Kassia the Nun
c.810–c.865: An Appreciation," in *Byzantine Women: Varieties of Experience, 800–1200*,
ed. Lynda Garland (Aldershot: Ashgate, 2006), 17–39.

6. Luke 7:36; Eva Catafygiotu Topping, "Kassiane the Nun and the Sinful Woman,"
Greek Orthodox Theological Review 26, no. 3 (1981): 201–9.

7. Leonora Neville, *Heroes and Romans in Twelfth-Century Byzantium: The "Material
for History" of Nikephoros Bryennios* (Cambridge: Cambridge University Press, 2012),
140–51.

8. Martha Vinson, "Gender and Politics in the Post-Iconoclastic Period: The Lives of
Antony the Younger, the Empress Theodora, and the Patriarch Ignatios," *Byzantion* 68
(1998): 469–515.

9. James Amelang, "Mourning Becomes Eclectic: Ritual Lament and the Problem of
Continuity," *Past and Present* 187 (2005): 3–32; Margaret Alexiou, *The Ritual Lament in
Greek Tradition* (Cambridge: Cambridge University Press, 1974).

10. Laura McClure, *Spoken like a Woman: Speech and Gender in Athenian Drama*
(Princeton: Princeton University Press, 1999), 40.

11. Nicole Loraux, *The Invention of Athens: The Funeral Oration in the Classical City* (Cambridge: Harvard University Press, 1986); Nicole Loraux, *Mothers in Mourning; with the Essay, Of Amnesty and Its Opposite*, trans. Corinne Pache (Ithaca: Cornell University Press, 1998); Nicole Loraux, *The Mourning Voice: An Essay on Greek Tragedy* (Ithaca: Cornell University Press, 2002); Helene P. Foley, *Female Acts in Greek Tragedy* (Princeton: Princeton University Press, 2001); Laura Swift, *The Hidden Chorus: Echoes of Genre in Tragic Lyric* (Oxford: Oxford University Press, 2010); Karen Stears, "Death Becomes Her: Gender and Athenian Death Ritual," in *The Sacred and the Feminine in Ancient Greece*, ed. Sue Blundell and Margaret Williamson (London: Routledge, 1998), 113–27; Christine Sourvinou-Inwood, "Gendering the Athenian Funeral: Ritual Reality and Tragic Manipulations," in *Greek Ritual Poetics*, ed. Dimitrios Yatromanolakis and Panagiotis Roilos (Cambridge: Harvard University Press, 2004), 161–88; McClure, *Spoken like a Woman*; A. P. M. H. Lardinois and Laura McClure, *Making Silence Speak: Women's Voices in Greek Literature and Society* (Princeton: Princeton University Press, 2001).

12. Suter points out that men also cried and lamented in classical tragedy. Yet the presence of men's tears does not obviate the primary point of the scholarship on female lamentation, which explored how women in antiquity spoke. Ann Suter, "Tragic Tears and Gender," in *Tears in the Graeco-Roman World*, ed. Thorsten Fögen (Berlin: De Gruyter, 2009), 60–83; Ann Suter, "Male Lament in Greek Tragedy," in *Lament: Studies in the Ancient Mediterranean and Beyond* (Oxford: Oxford University Press, 2008). Weeping had a significant religious function in demonstrating contrition of the soul in medieval Christianity. The tears of emperors before battle were particularly important because they were a sign of the penitence that would win God's favor. Martin Hinterberger, "Tränen in der byzantinischen Literatur. Ein Beitrag zur Geschichte der Emotionen," *Jahrbuch der österreichischen Byzantinistik* 56 (2006): 27–51; Michael Grünbart, "Der Kaiser weint: Anmerkungen zur imperialen Inszenierung von Emotionen in Byzanz," *Frühmittelalterliche Studien* 42 (2008): 89–108; Martin Hinterberger, "Emotions in Byzantium," in *A Companion to Byzantium* (Malden: Wiley-Blackwell, 2010), 121–34; Elina Gertsman, ed., *Crying in the Middle Ages: Tears of History* (Abingdon: Routledge, 2012); Symeon the New Theologian, *The Discourses*, trans. C. J. de Catanzaro (New York: Paulist Press, 1980), 88–89.

13. Rabe, *Aphthonii Progymnasmata*, 35–37; Kennedy, *Progymnasmata*, 116–17; D. A. Russell and Nigel Guy Wilson, *Menander Rhetor* (Oxford: Clarendon Press, 1981), 200–203.

14. Luke 7:11–17; Gregory of Nyssa *Patrologiae Graeca* 44: 220–21; Maguire, *Art and Eloquence*, 95–96; Russell and Wilson, *Menander Rhetor*, 200–207.

15. Maguire, *Art and Eloquence*, 96.

16. Ibid. 91–101. On the liturgical contexts of the laments of the Virgin, see Ševčenko, "The Service of the Virgin's Lament Revisited," 247–62.

17. Sharon Gerstel, "Painted Sources for Female Piety in Medieval Byzantium," *Dumbarton Oaks Papers* 52 (1998): 102. See also Henry Maguire, "The Depiction of Sorrow in Middle Byzantine Art," *Dumbarton Oaks Papers* 31 (1977): 123–74.

18. Russell and Wilson, *Menander Rhetor*, 203.

19. Ibid., 204–7.

20. *Alexiad*, P4.1.2–7.

21. *Alexiad*, 1.12.3.5–8.

22. *Alexiad*, 15.5.4.4–8.

23. Alexiou, *Ritual Lament*: for past and present, 165; light, 187–89; antithetical imagery, 151–60.

24. Ibid., 171–77.

25. *Alexiad*, P.4.3.5–6; cf. Euripides, *Hecuba* 518.

26. *Alexiad*, 15.5.4.

27. *Alexiad*, 15.11.12.10–13; cf. Sophocles, *Oedipus Coloneus* 1250–51.

28. *Alexiad*, 15.11.21.11–12; citing Euripides, *Orestes* 1–3.

29. *Alexiad*, 15.11.23.

30. *Alexiad*, P.4.3.

31. *Alexiad*, 15.5.4.

32. *Alexiad*, 15.11.17.8–10, 15.11.19.3–4. On the ritual gestures of archaic lamentation, see Sourvinou-Inwood, "Gendering the Athenian Funeral: Ritual Reality and Tragic Manipulations," 167–69.

33. Sheila Murnaghan, "The Survivors' Song: The Drama of Mourning in Euripides' 'Alcestis,'" *Illinois Classical Studies* 24 (1999): 107–16; Alexiou, *Ritual Lament*, 182–84.

34. Sophocles, *Electra. 77*.

35. Homer, *Iliad* 24.725–45.

36. *Alexiad*, P4.1.1–2.

37. *Alexiad*, 1.12.3.1–3, 8–9.

38. *Alexiad*, 15.5.4.

39. Swift, *The Hidden Chorus*, 308–9.

40. Alexiou, *Ritual Lament*, 180–81.

41. *Alexiad*, 15.11.22.9–12.

42. *Alexiad*, 15.11.23.

43. *Alexiad*, 15.11.23.1.

44. *Alexiad*, 15.11.21.5–15; Euripides, *Orestes* 1–3.

45. *Alexiad*, 15.11.21.1–5.

46. *Alexiad*, 15.11.24.

47. Euripides, *Medea* 928.

48. Papaioannou, *Michael Psellos*, 192–231.

49. Ibid. 208.

50. Glenn W. Most, "The Stranger's Stratagem: Self-Disclosure and Self-Sufficiency in Greek Culture," *Journal of Hellenic Studies* 109 (1989): 114–33.

51. See page 27–28.

52. *Alexiad*, 1.10.2; 1.12.3.

53. *Alexiad*, P.4.1.7–12.

54. *Alexiad*, P 4.1.12–17; see page 39.

55. Homer, *Iliad* 3.156; *Odyssey*. 1.350. For a different interpretation of this passage, see Ellen Quandahl and Susan C. Jarratt, "'To Recall Him … Will Be a Subject of Lamentation': Anna Comnena as Rhetorical Historiographer," *Rhetorica* 26 (2008): 319.

56. *Alexiad*, 13.6.3. Translation modified from Frankopan and Sewter: E. R. A. Sewter and Peter Frankopan, trans., *The Alexiad*, Revised (London: Penguin Classics, 2004), 373.

57. John Marincola, *Authority and Tradition in Ancient Historiography* (Cambridge: Cambridge University Press, 1997), 148–58.

58. Richard Rutherford, "Tragedy and History," in *A Companion to Greek and Roman Historiography*, ed. John Marincola (Malden: Blackwell, 2007), 508.

59. For a notable exception, see the lamentations of Josephus for the capture of Jerusalem: Josephus, *Bellum Judaicum* 1.9–11; *Bellum Judaicum* 5.19–20.

60. *Alexiad*, 15.5.4.9.

61. *Alexiad*, 1.12.3.1–4, alluding to Demosthenes, *De corona* 27.

62. *Alexiad*, 4.8.1. See page 58–59.

63. The first-century historian Flavius Josephus similarly broke from his historical narrative of the Jewish War to lament the fate of the Jewish people, at one point directly addressing Jerusalem. He then returns to his historical discourse saying, "Emotions must be restrained according to the law of the work, since this is the occasion not for one's own lamentations, but for the narration of deeds." Josephus, *Bellum Judaicum* 5.19–20. This allows Josephus "to express himself with full emotion, while at the same time indicating his knowledge of the genre's conventions." Marincola, *Authority and Tradition*, 168.

64. Athanasios Kambylis, "Zum Programm der byzantinischen Historikerin Anna Komnene," in *Dōrēma: Hans Diller zum 70. Geburtstag: Dauer und Überleben des antiken Geistes*, ed. Kōnstantinos Vourverēs and Aristoxenos D. Skiadas (Athens: Griechische Humanistische Gesellschaft, 1975), 140–41.

65. *Alexiad*, 1.16.7.

66. *Alexiad*, 5.9.3.4–5; 5.9.3.19.

67. *Alexiad*, 3.8.1.

68. *Alexiad*, 3.8.1.5–8; 3.8.5.1–6; 3.8.11.3–6.

69. *Alexiad*, 3.8.5.

70. *Alexiad*, P.4.2.7–8.

71. *Alexiad*, 1.12.3.2–3.

72. *Alexiad*, 15.11.15.5–6.

73. *Alexiad*, 15.11.16.3–4.

74. *Alexiad*, P4.3.12–13.

75. *Alexiad*, P4.3.4.

76. *Alexiad*, 1.12.3.

77. *Alexiad*, 15.5.4.9–10.

78. Demosthenes, *De corona* 27.

79. See page 18–19.

80. *Alexiad*, 15.11.1.2–3.

81. *Alexiad*, 15.11.1.3–4.

82. *Alexiad*, 15.11.1.6–7.

83. *Alexiad*, 15.11.2.6–7.

84. Diether R. Reinsch and Athanasios Kambylis, ed., *Alexiad* (Berlin: De Gruyter, 2001), 13–28.

Chapter 5

1. See page 21–22.

2. *Alexiad*, 3.6.4–8, 3.10.3–8, 13.12.

3. Penelope Buckley thinks it probable that the text of the treaty of Devol in the *Alexiad* was actually written by Anna, but, so far, her view is exceptional. Penelope Buckley, *The Alexiad of Anna Komnene: Artistic Strategy in the Making of a Myth* (Cambridge: Cambridge University Press, 2014), 243. Ralph-Johannes Lilie considers it a separate text because it differs from Anna's style: Ralph-Johannes Lilie, "Reality and Invention: Reflections on Byzantine Historiography," *Dumbarton Oaks Papers* 68 (2014): 190–93. Some studies treat the quoted texts as independent texts. On the Treaty of Devol see: Ralph-Johannes Lilie, *Byzantium and the Crusader States, 1096–1204* (Oxford: Oxford University Press, 1994), 75–82; Paul Stephenson, *Byzantium's Balkan Frontier: A Political Study of the Northern Balkans, 900–1204* (Cambridge: Cambridge University Press, 2000), 182–83. On Anna Dalassene see: Élisabeth Malamut, "Une femme politique d'exception à la fin du XIe siècle: Anne Dalassène," in *Femmes et pouvoirs des femmes à Byzance et en occident (VIe–XIe siècles)*, ed. Stéphane Lebecq et al. (Lille: Centre de Recherche sur l'Histoire de l'Europe du Nord-Ouest, 1999), 103–20; Ludwig Burgmann, "Lawyers and Legislators: Aspects of Law-Making in the Time of Alexios I," in *Alexios I Komnenos*, ed. Dion Smythe and Margaret Mullett, Belfast Byzantine Texts and Translations 4.1 (Belfast: Belfast Byzantine Enterprises, 1996), 185–98. On the letter to Henry see: Jonathan Harris, *Byzantium and the Crusades* (London: Hambledon and London, 2003), 39.

4. Attributed quotation of documents was not unprecedented among classical historians, and was common in Church histories, but among histories of the tenth–twelfth centuries, Anna's practice stands out. P. J. Rhodes, "Documents and the Greek Historian," in *A Companion to Greek and Roman Historiography*, ed. John Marincola (Malden: Blackwell, 2007), 56–66.

5. "In the course of the work's sermons, [the author] Antony displaces his teaching into the mouth of [the saint] George. This ventriloquism models humility, since Antony does not claim the teaching of virtue as his own but attributes it to another." Derek Krueger, *Writing and Holiness: The Practice of Authorship in the Early Christian East* (Philadelphia: University of Pennsylvania Press, 2004), 102, see also 94–109.

6. Malamut, "Une femme politique d'exception à la fin du XIe siècle: Anne Dalassène"; Steven Runciman, "The End of Anna Dalassena," *Annuaire de l'institut de philologie et d'histoire orientales et slaves* 9 (1949): 517–24.

7. Zonaras, 746. The idea that Alexios's reliance on his mother made him a weak man was taken up into modern scholarly discourse as well. See Paul Lemerle, *Cinq études sur le XIe siècle byzantin* (Paris: Centre national de la recherche scientifique, 1977), 298. This is disputed by Barbara Hill, "Alexios I Komnenos and the Imperial Women," in *Alexios I Komnenos*, ed. Dion Smythe and Margaret Mullett, (Belfast: Belfast Byzantine Enterprises, 1996), 37–54.

8. *Alexiad*, 3.6.4–8.

9. Marin Cerchez, "Religion in the Alexiad" (PhD diss., University of Wisconsin–Madison, 2014), 35–62.

10. On the Byzantine policy of using money to gain allies, including a discussion of this letter, see Harris, *Byzantium and the Crusades*, 33–51.

11. For a more nuanced analysis of their characterization and its function in the *Alexiad*, see Buckley, *The Alexiad of Anna Komnene*.

12. Athanasios Kambylis, "Zum Programm der byzantinischen Historikerin Anna Komnene," in *Dōrēma: Hans Diller zum 70. Geburtstag: Dauer und Überleben des antiken*

Geistes, ed. Kōnstantinos Vourverēs and Aristoxenos D. Skiadas (Athens: Griechische Humanistische Gesellschaft, 1975), 133–46.

13. *Alexiad,* 14.7.1–2.

14. *Alexiad,* 14.7.3.

15. Aristotle, *Nicomachean Ethics* 1.1096.a16

16. *Alexiad,* 14.7.4.

17. John Marincola, *Authority and Tradition in Ancient Historiography* (Cambridge: Cambridge University Press, 1997), 63–86.

18. *Alexiad,* 14.7.4.

19. *Alexiad,* 12.3.7.

20. See page 53–55.

21. *Alexiad,* 12.3.3–8.

22. *Alexiad,* 12.3.2.

23. *Alexiad,* 14.7.4.

24. See, for example, M. Jeffreys et al., *Prosopography of the Byzantine World* (2011), s.v. Konstantinos 107531, http://db.pbw.kcl.ac.uk/pbw2011/entity/person/107531; Charles Diehl, *Byzantine Empresses,* trans. Harold Bell and Theresa de Kerpely (New York: Knopf, 1963) 184–85.

25. For both boys and girls at age seven, betrothal was legal, formal education began, and they could be liable for murder. Evelyne Patlagean, "L'enfant et son avenir dans la famille byzantine (IV–XIIe siècles)," in *Structure sociale, famille, chrétienté à Byzance, IVe–XIe siècle* (London: Variorum, 1981), 87; Cecily Hennessy, *Images of Children in Byzantium* (Farnham: Ashgate, 2008), 11–13; Eve Davies, "Age, Gender and Status: A Three-Dimensional Life Course Perspective of the Byzantine Family," in *Approaches to the Byzantine Family,* ed. Leslie Brubaker and Shaun Tougher (Farnham: Ashgate, 2013), 159; Anthony Kaldellis, *Mothers and Sons, Fathers and Daughters: The Byzantine Family of Michael Psellos* (Notre Dame: University of Notre Dame Press, 2006), 60; Ugo Criscuolo, ed., *Autobiografia: Encomio per la Madre: Michele Psello* (Naples: M. D'Auria editore, 1989), 292–95; Günter Prinzing, "Observations on the Legal Status of Children and the Stages of Childhood in Byzantium," in *Becoming Byzantine: Children and Childhood in Byzantium,* ed. Arietta Papaconstantinou and Alice-Mary Talbot (Washington, DC: Dumbarton Oaks, 2009), 25–28.

26. *Alexiad,* 14.7.5.

27. *Alexiad,* 14.7.5.

28. Marincola, *Authority and Tradition,* 148–57.

29. *Alexiad,* 14.7.6.

30. Paul Magdalino, "The Pen of the Aunt: Echoes of the Mid-Twelfth Century in the Alexiad," in *Anna Komnene and Her Times,* ed. Thalia Gouma-Peterson (New York: Garland, 2000), 21.

31. *Alexiad,* 14.7.6.

32. The great preponderance of Anna's references to herself are in the singular. With the assistance of William James Conlin and Kerry Lefebvre, I have counted seventy-five passages where Anna presents herself in the singular, and twelve where she uses the plural. Given the length of the text, it is possible that we missed something, but the general proportions would remain. Anna shifts to a plural voice when she acts as historical narrator, in phrases such as "let us digress" or "we have said enough about this." Digressions: *Alexiad,*

6.7.2, 6.7.6, 14.8.9; discussions of contents: 7.2.2, 7.2.6, 7.5.3, 10.10.4, 14.8.2, 15.8.7, 3.8.5, 1.10.2, 14.4.9, 1.12.4. An illustrative exception: 1.12.4. Anna's plural narrator's voice is usually not marked for gender: 1.12.4, 3.8.5, 6.7.2, 6.7.6, 7.2.2, 7.2.6, 7.5.3, 10.10.4.4 (switch from singular to plural), 14.4.9, 15.8.7. Feminine plural: 1.10.2 (fem. pl. pronoun). She uses the masculine plural twice for the phrase "as we have been saying": 1.12.2.4, 14.8.9.1. A more significant exception is 3.2.5.

33. *Alexiad*, 14.7.7.

34. *Alexiad*, 14.7.7.

35. Kambylis, "Zum Programm der byzantinischen Historikerin Anna Komnene," 141–46.

36. On Anna's actual sources, see Peter Frankopan, "Turning Latin into Greek: Anna Komnene and the Gesta Roberti Wiscardi," *Journal of Medieval History* 39, no. 1 (2013): 80–99.

Chapter 6

1. Ruth Macrides, "The Pen and the Sword: Who Wrote the Alexiad?," in *Anna Komnene and Her Times*, ed. Thalia Gouma-Peterson (New York: Garland, 2000), 73; Ruth Macrides and Paul Magdalino, "The Fourth Kingdom and the Rhetoric of Hellenism," in *The Perception of the Past in Twefth-Century Europe*, ed. Paul Magdalino (London: The Hambledon Press, 1992), 117–56; Dimitry E. Afinogenov, "Some Observations on Genres of Byzantine Historiography," *Byzantion* 62 (1992): 13–33.

2. Zonaras, 747.

3. Zonaras, 748.

4. Zonaras, 748.

5. Zonaras, 748.

6. Zonaras, 748.

7. Zonaras, 748–49.

8. Zonaras, 754.

9. Zonaras, 754.

10. Zonaras's text does *not* support the contention that John "was losing out in the struggle for the succession to his sister Anna Komnene, whom Zonaras singles out as the driving force behind Bryennios." Michael Angold, "Alexios I Komnenos: An Afterword," in *Alexios I Komnenos*, Belfast Byzantine Texts and Translations 4.1 (Belfast: Belfast Byzantine Enterprizes, 1996), 405.

11. Zonaras, 754–55.

12. Zonaras, 755–58.

13. Zonaras, 758.

14. Zonaras, 761.

15. Zonaras, 761. She was a daughter of King David II of Georgia. Matoula Kouroupou and Jean-François Vannier, "Commémoraisons des Comnènes dans le typikon liturgique du monastère du Christ Philanthrope (ms. Panaghia Kamariotissa 29)," *Revue des études byzantines* 63, no. 1 (2005): 59.

16. Zonaras, 761–62.

17. Zonaras, 762.

18. Zonaras, 762.
19. Zonaras, 764.
20. Zonaras, 764–65.
21. Zonaras, 748.
22. Philipp Meyer, *Die Haupturkunden für die Geschichte der Athosklöster: Grösstentheils zum ersten Male* (Leipzig: Hinrich, 1894), 163–84; Rosemary Morris, *Monks and Laymen in Byzantium, 843–1118* (Cambridge: Cambridge University Press, 1995), 275–80; Krausmüller, "The Athonite Monastic Tradition during the Eleventh and Early Twelfth Centuries," in *Mount Athos and Byzantine Monasticism*, ed. Anthony Bryer and Mary Cunningham (Aldershot: Variorum, 1996), 58–59; Margaret Mullett, "Novelisation in Byzantium: Narrative after the Revival of Fiction," in *Byzantine Narrative: Papers in Honour of Roger Scott*, ed. J. Burke, et.al., (Melbourne: Australian Association for Byzantine Studies, 2006), 21–27; Margaret Mullett, "In Search of the Monastic Author. Story-Telling, Anonymity and Innovation in the 12th Century," in *The Author in Middle Byzantine Literature: Modes, Functions, and Identities*, ed. Aglae Pizzone (Berlin: De Gruyter, 2014), 171–98; Morris, *Monks and Laymen*, 275–80; Krausmüller, "The Athonite Monastic Tradition during the Eleventh and Early Twelfth Centuries," 58–59.
23. Meyer, *Haupturkunden*, 178–80.
24. Ibid. 182. While this part of the story is narrated after the discussion of John's actions, it must have taken place before the death of the patriarch in 1111.
25. Ibid. 181.
26. Ibid. 169.
27. Ibid. 180. The text does *not* say that "Alexios persuaded the dying patriarch . . . to bless his son's succession to the throne." Angold, "Alexios I Komnenos: An Afterword," 403.
28. This text also provides a rare indication that John served Alexios. When the Patriarch Nicholas was dying, Alexios sent his son-in-law the Caesar and his son John to him, before deciding to go himself as well. Meyer, *Haupturkunden*, 178. Medieval Greek has one word for son-in-law and brother-in-law, so the man identified as Alexios's *gambros* the Caesar could be either Nikephoros Bryennios or Nikephoros Melissenos, who is mentioned earlier at page 173.
29. Michael Glykas, *Michaelis Glycae Annales*, ed. Imanuel Bekker (Bonn: Weber, 1836), 622.
30. See page 122–24.
31. Jean Darrouzes, *George et Demetrios Tornikes. Lettres et Discours* (Paris: Éditions du Centre national de la recherche scientifique, 1970), 220–323, oration number 14.
32. He was elected Metropolitan of Ephesus in 1155. Ibid. 7–20.
33. Ibid. 253.6–14.
34. Ibid. 261.25–26.
35. Ibid. 261.16–21.
36. Ibid. 261.21–26.
37. Ibid. 263.1–3.
38. Ibid. 267.20–25.
39. Ibid. 267.25–269.1.
40. Ibid. 269.3.

41. Ibid. 269.3–12.

42. Ibid. 269.12–18.

43. Alicia J. Simpson, *Niketas Choniates: A Historiographical Study* (Oxford: Oxford University Press, 2013), 11–23.

44. Alicia Simpson, "Before and After 1204: The Versions of Niketas Choniates' 'Historia,'" *Dumbarton Oaks Papers* 60 (2006): 189–221; Simpson, *Niketas Choniates*, 80–102.

45. Alicia Simpson, "Niketas Choniates: The Historian," in *Niketas Choniates: A Historian and a Writer* (Geneva: La Pomme d'Or, 2009), 17; Simpson, *Niketas Choniates*, 147–48.

46. Simpson, *Niketas Choniates*, 197–203.

47. Ibid. 124–25.

48. Stephanos Efthymiades, "Niketas Choniates: The Writer," in *Niketas Choniates: A Historian and a Writer* (Geneva: La Pomme d'Or, 2009), 46.

49. Ibid. 39.

50. Ibid.

51. The civil war ensuing upon Darius's death drives the action of the story. Cyrus was supported by his mother in attempted usurpation. Efthymiades, "Niketas Choniates: The Writer," 43; Anthony Kaldellis, "Paradox, Reversal and the Meaning of History," in *Niketas Choniates: A Historian and a Writer* (Geneva: La Pomme d'Or, 2009), 78.

52. J. van Dieten, ed., *Nicetae Choniatae historia, pars prior*, Corpus Fontium Historiae Byzantinae (Berlin: De Gruyter, 1975), 5, lines 7–9. προπετῆ τοῦτον ἀποκαλοῦσα καὶ ὑγρὸν τὸν βίον παλίνστροφόν τε τὸ ἦθος καὶ μηδαμῇ μηδὲν ὑγιές. On στρόφος used in contexts of incipient defecation, see Jeffrey Henderson, *The Maculate Muse: Obscene Language in Attic Comedy* (Oxford: Oxford University Press, 1991), 197.

53. Choniates, 5.

54. Choniates, 5.

55. Magoulias's translation adds Anna into the sentence. Harry J. Magoulias, trans. *O City of Byzantium: Annals of Niketas Choniates* (Detroit: Wayne State University Press, 1984), 5.

56. Nikephoros's family was from Macedonia; Choniates, 5–6.

57. Bravo Garcia sees this speech as deliberately parallel to that made by John as he is dying justifying his choice to elevate his younger son, Manuel, as emperor. Antonio Bravo Garcia, "Politics, History and Rhetoric: On the Structure of the First Book of Nicetas Choniates' History," *Byzantinoslavica* 56, no. 2 (1995): 423–28.

58. Choniates, 6.

59. Choniates, 6, lines 14–19.

60. Riccardo Maisano, ed., *Niceta Coniata—Grandezza e catastrofe di Bisanzio: narrazione cronologica*, trans. Anna Pontani, vol. 1. Libri I–VIII (Milan: Fondazione Lorenzo Valla, A. Mondadori, 1994), 515, note 24.

61. Choniates, 6, lines 19–21.

62. Efthymiades, "Niketas Choniates: The Writer," 46; Kaldellis, "Paradox, Reversal."

63. Choniates, 6.

64. Homer, *Iliad* 9.14, 16.3.

65. Choniates, 6–7.

66. Choniates, 7.

67. Choniates, 7.

68. Choniates, 8.

69. Choniates, 8.

70. Choniates, 8.

71. Choniates, 10, lines 4–6.

72. Kaldellis, "Paradox, Reversal," 74–84.

73. Choniates, 10.

74. Choniates, 10, lines 16–22.

75. "χαλαρὸν" is related to the verb used by Aristophanes to mean 'loosen up' by sexual penetration. Aristophanes, *Lysistrata*, 419; Jeffrey Henderson, *The Maculate Muse: Obscene Language in Attic Comedy* (Oxford: Oxford University Press, 1991), 177. It was used by Plato of Ionic and Lydian musical modes whose laxity made them inappropriate for warriors. Plato, *Republic* 398e. It is glossed in the Suda as 'loose' or 'open' and illustrated with a quotation and equates it with femaleness. "Χαλαρά: χαῦνα ... χαλαρὸν ἦν αὐτῷ καὶ θῆλυ τὸ σπλάγχνον πρὸς τοὺς δεομένους, εἴπερ τινὶ τῶν καθ᾽ αὐτὸν ἀνθρώπων." "If ever anyone of his kind had an heart open and female towards those in need, it was he." A. Adler, ed., *Suda Lexicon*, vol.4 (Leipzig: Teubner, 1931), 779, entry number 7 under *chi*; *Suda On Line*, s.v. "chalara," trans. Roger Travis, 22 June 1999, http://www.stoa.org/sol-entries/chi/7.

76. Choniates, 10, lines 22–25.

77. χαῦνον: Henderson, *Maculate Muse*, 211. φύσις: John J. Winkler, *The Constraints of Desire: The Anthropology of Sex and Gender in Ancient Greece* (New York: Routledge, 1990), 217–20.

78. Choniates, 10, lines 22–25.

79. Choniates, 11.

80. Choniates, 11.

81. Choniates, 12, lines 3–4.

82. Choniates, 8.

83. Simpson, *Niketas Choniates*, 16. Citing Spyridōn Lampros, ed., *Michaēl Akominatou tou Chōniatou ta Sōzomena* (Groningen: Bouma's Boekhuis, 1968), vol. 1, 351.22–25.

84. Simpson believes it is likely he had read the *Alexiad*. But, judging from the index locorum in van Dieten's edition, he did not cite it. Simpson, *Niketas Choniates*, 253, note 171.

85. Albert Abouna, trans., *Anonymi Auctoris Chronicon Ad A[nnum] C[hristi] 1234 Pertinens II*, vol. 354, Corpus Scriptorum Christianorum Orientalium (Louvain: Secrétariat du Corpus SCO, 1974), vii, 63.

86. *Alexiad*, 15.11.17.

87. Warren T. Treadgold, *A History of the Byzantine State and Society* (Stanford: Stanford University Press, 1997), 629; Timothy E. Gregory, *A History of Byzantium* (Oxford: Blackwell, 2005), 302; Paul Magdalino, "The Empire of the Komnenoi (1118–1204)," in *The Cambridge History of the Byzantine Empire c.500–1492* (Cambridge: Cambridge University Press, 2008), 629; Michael Angold, *The Byzantine Empire, 1025–1204: A Political History* (London: Longman, 1997), 181–83; Robert Browning, *The Byzantine Empire* (Washington, DC: The Catholic University of America Press, 1980), 165; George Ostrogorski, *History of the Byzantine State*, trans. Joan Hussey, rev.

(New Brunswick: Rutgers University Press, 1969), 377; J. M. Hussey, *The Byzantine World* (New York: Harper, 1961), 60.

Chapter 7

1. Paul Gautier, ed., "Theodore Prodomus: Epithalamium fortunatissimis cae-saris filiis," in *Nicéphore Bryennios. Histoire*, Corpus Fontium Historiae Byzantinae (Brussels: Byzantion, 1975), 341–55.

2. Matoula Kouroupou and Jean-François Vannier, "Commémoraisons des Comnènes dans le typikon liturgique du monastère du Christ Philanthrope (ms. Panaghia Kamariotissa 29)," *Revue des études byzantines* 63, no. 1 (2005): 59.

3. Wolfram Hörandner, *Theodoros Prodromos. Historische Gedichte*, Wiener Byzantinistische Studien 11 (Vienna: Österreichische Akademie der Wissenschaften, 1974), 382–89, text number 39.

4. Gautier, "Theodore Prodomus: Epithalamium fortunatissimis caesaris filiis," 353.

5. Ibid. 347, lines 2–15.

6. Ibid. 340, note 1.

7. E. Kurtz, "Unedierte Texte aus der Zeit des Kaisers Johannes Komnenos," *Byzantinische Zeitschrift* 16 (1907): 86.

8. Hörandner, *Theodoros Prodromos. Historische Gedichte*, 387, text number 39, lines 161–76.

9. Ibid. 183–90, text number 2, lines 10–17.

10. Ibid. 383–84, text number 39, lines 20–62.

11. Zonaras, 761.

12. Paul Gautier, ed., *Lettres et discours: Michel Italikos* (Paris: Institut français d'études byzantines, 1972), 87–88, oration number 3.

13. Ibid. 154, letter number 17, line 3. Anna herself related that her Nikephoros died of an illness he contracted while participating in John's campaigns in Syria, which took place in 1137 and 1138.

14. Ibid. 151, oration number 15. Gautier dates the encomium to between 1118 and 1138.

15. Hörandner, *Theodoros Prodromos. Historische Gedichte*, 188, text number 2, lines 95–97.

16. Gautier, *Lettres et discours: Michel Italikos*, 88, oration number 3, lines 1–4.

17. Hörandner, *Theodoros Prodromos. Historische Gedichte*, 382–89, text number 39.

18. Gautier dates it to 1140. Paul Gautier, ed., "Theodorus Prodromos: Epitaphius in Theodoram nurum Bryennii," in *Nicéphore Bryennios. Histoire* (Brussels: Byzantion, 1975), 354–55.

19. Hörandner, *Theodoros Prodromos. Historische Gedichte*, 383, text number 39, lines 43–50.

20. Ibid. 377–81, text number 38.

21. Ibid. 377–81, text number 38, lines 1–10 and 110–19.

22. Tzetzes describes him as the son-in-law of a heretic, Tzourichos. John Tzetzes, *Epistulae*, ed. Pietro Luigi Leone (Leipzig: B. G. Teubner, 1972), 75–77, letter number 55. Michael Grünbart, "Prosopographische Beiträge zum Briefcorpus des Ioannes Tzetzes," *Jahrbuch der Österreichischen Byzantinistik* 46 (1996): 207.

23. Tzetzes, *Episulae*, 77, letter number 55, lines 1–6.

24. Gautier, *Lettres et discours: Michel Italikos*, 151, oration number 15, lines 12–14.

25. Ibid. 151, oration number 15, lines 18–24.

26. Hörandner, *Theodoros Prodromos. Historische Gedichte*, 377-81, text number 38, lines 1–10 and 110–19.

27. Gautier, "Theodore Prodomus: Epithalamium fortunatissimis caesaris filiis," 347–49.

28. Ibid.

29. Barbara Hill, "The Ideal Komnenian Woman," *Byzantinische Forschungen* 23 (1996): 13.

30. Aristotle, *Nicomachean Ethics* 2.1103a19. I thank Michele Trizio for alerting me to the Aristotlean allusion. Michele Trizio, *Il neoplatonismo di Eustrazio di Nicea*, Biblioteca filosofica di Quaestio 23 (Bari: Pagina soc. coop., 2016).

31. Gautier, "Theodore Prodomus: Epithalamium fortunatissimis caesaris filiis," 347–49.

32. A. Majuri, "Anecdota Prodromea dal Vat. Gr. 305," in *Rendiconti della Reale Accademia dei Lincei: Classe di Scienze Morali, storiche e filologiche*. Series 5, vol. 17 (Rome: Tipografia della Accademia, 1908), 523, lines 10–11.

33. Gautier, *Lettres et discours: Michel Italikos*, 141–44, 152, 153–54, letters 14, 16, and 17.

34. Ibid. 142, letter number 14, lines 16–19.

35. Eustathios of Thessaloniki also wrote a funeral oration for Nikephoros Komnenos, but did not describe his grandparents. Nikephoros held the title *epi ton deison*. E. Kurtz, "[Monodies on Nikephoros Komnenos by Eustathios of Thessaloniki and Constantine Manasses]," *Vizantiĭskiĭ Vremennik* 16 (1922): 283–322.

36. Ibid. 306.

37. Ibid. 307, lines 145–58.

38. Ibid. 307, lines 149–54.

39. Ibid. 308, lines 161–64.

40. Commentaries were written on books I and VI of the *Nicomachean Ethics* by Eustratios of Nicaea, on books V, IX, and X by Michael of Ephesus, and on book VII by an anonymous author. Anthony Kaldellis, "Classical Scholarship in Twelfth-Century Byzantium," in *Medieval Greek Commentaries on the* Nicomachean Ethics, ed. Charles Barber and David Jenkins (Leiden: Brill, 2009), 37; Gustav Heylbut, ed., *Eustratii et Michaelis et anonyma in Ethica Nicomachea commentaria*. (Berlin: Typis et Impensis G. Reimeri, 1892); Charles Barber and David Jenkins, eds., *Medieval Greek Commentaries on the Nicomachean Ethics* (Leiden: Brill, 2009).

41. Heylbut, *Ethica Nicomachea commentaria*, 256–57; Peter Frankopan, "The Literary, Cultural and Political Context for the Twelfth-Century Commentary on the *Nicomachean Ethics*," in *Medieval Greek Commentaries on the* Nicomachean Ethics, ed. Charles Barber and David Jenkins (Leiden: Brill, 2009), 46.

42. Jean Darrouzes, *George et Demetrios Tornikes. Lettres et Discours* (Paris: éditions du Centre national de la recherche scientifique, 1970), 283, oration number 14.

43. I thank Michele Trizio for calling attention to the importance of these commentaries in the history of Aristotelian scholarship. See his forthcoming *Il neoplatonismo di Eustrazio di Nicea* for a thorough discussion of Anna's role in the study of Aristotle. We are informed of Anna's interest in new commentaries in Tornikes's oration: Darrouzes, *Tornikes*, 283.4–8. Citations are to page and line numbers.

44. J. Sola, "De Codice Laurentiano X Plutei V," *Byzantinische Zeitschrift* 20 (1911): 375–76.

45. The central image of sleeping among trees of pine, cypress, and cedar may have been prompted by Isaiah 60:13.

46. Anneliese Paul, "Dichtung auf Objekten. Inschriftlich erhaltene griechische Epigramme vom 9. bis zum 16. Jahrhundert: Suche nach bekannten Autornamen," in *Byzantinische Sprachkunst: Studien zur Byzantinischen Literatur Gewidmet Wolfram Hörandner zum 65. Geburtstag*, ed. Martin Hinterberger and Elisabeth Schiffer (Berlin: De Gruyter, 2007), 250. Some scholars have assumed that this Anna is the same as our author, and that she wrote the poem. Nothing absolute associates this poem with our Anna, however, and a reasonable case has been made that the patron was John's daughter Anna, the wife of Stephen Kontostephanos, and that she hired another to write the poem. Brigitte Pitarakis, "Female Piety in Context: Understanding Developments in Private Devotional Practices," in *Images of the Mother of God: Perceptions of the Theotokos in Byzantium* (Aldershot: Ashgate, 2005), 160–62.

47. See page 17–19.

48. Darrouzes, *Tornikes*, 243, oration number 14. Citations are to page and line numbers.

49. Ibid. 245.

50. Ibid. 245.27–247.4.

51. Ibid. 263.13–17.

52. Ibid. 263.17–19.

53. Ibid. 263.19–20.

54. Ibid. 263.20–22.

55. Ibid. 281.4–5.

56. Ibid. 281.5–14.

57. Ibid. 271.17–21.

58. Ibid. 271.21–273.19.

59. Ibid. 273–81.

60. Ibid. 281.14–283.3.

61. Ibid. 297.6–18.

62. Ibid. 301.10–14.

63. Ibid. 281.14–283.3.

64. Ibid. 287.

65. Ibid. 289.

66. Ibid. 291.

67. Ibid. 295.

68. Ibid. 285.10–13.

69. Ibid. 299.

70. Ibid. 299.

71. Ibid. 299–301. The Basils and Gregories Tornikes had in mind are presumably Basil of Caesarea, Basil of Seleucia, Gregory of Nyssa, and Gregory of Nazianzus. I thank Derek Krueger for helping me identify the most likely other Basil.

72. Ibid. 301.14–17.

73. This passage was discussed as an example of the importance of authorial humility by Aglae Pizzone in "Eaten by the Moths: Dispossession and Reappropriation in Nikephoros Basilakes' Autobiography" (Byzantine Authorship: Theories and Practices, Durham University, July 23–25, 2012).

74. Darrouzes, *Tornikes*, 301.20–303.6.

75. Ibid. 303.2–3.
76. Ibid. 303.3–6.
77. Ibid. 303.6–7.
78. Ibid. 303.7–12.
79. Ibid. 303.13–14.
80. Ibid. 303.3–12.
81. Ibid. 304.15.
82. Ibid. 303.16–17.
83. Ibid. 303.18–305.2.
84. Ibid. 257.20–23, 261.17–21, 265.20–267.17, 269.23–271.17.
85. Ibid. 267.19–26.
86. Ibid. 243.
87. Ibid. 225.
88. See page 52–53.
89. Gautier, "Theodore Prodomus: Epithalamium fortunatissimis caesaris filiis," 351, lines 16–18.
90. Darrouzes, *Tornikes*, 265.5–8.
91. As does Barbara Hill, "A Vindication of the Rights of Women to Power by Anna Komnene," *Byzantinische Forschungen* 23 (1996): 46.
92. *Alexiad*, 15.5.4, 15.11.23.
93. Darrouzes, *Tornikes*, 305.19–307.3.
94. Ibid. 307.4–309.4.
95. Ibid. 231. Here Tornikes participates in the discourse of humility, denigrating his own abilities and excusing himself for speaking. He only provides the oration because no one else has accepted the challenge. He says he expected many orators to rush to the task because of the novelty of the subject.
96. Ibid. 231.7–21.
97. Ibid. 229.21–231.7.
98. Ibid. 233.
99. Ibid. 233.13–22.
100. Ibid. 315.5–10.
101. Ibid. 315.10–14.
102. Ibid. 317.14–19.
103. Ibid. 315.20–317.5.
104. Ibid. 315.20–317.5.
105. Ibid. 317.14–21.
106. Ibid. 317.21–25.

Chapter 8

1. Ferdinand Chalandon, *Les Comnène: études sur l'empire byzantin au XIe et au XIIe siècles*. vol. 2 *Jean II Comnène, 1118–1143, et Manuel I Comnène, 1143–1180* (Paris: A. Picard et fils, 1912), 16; Charles Diehl, *Byzantine Empresses* (New York: Knopf, 1963), 191.

2. Louis Du Sommerard, *Deux princesses d'Orient au XIIe siècle: Anne Comnène, témoin des croisades; Agnès de France* (Paris: Perrin et cie, 1907), 174; Warren T. Treadgold, *A History of the Byzantine State and Society* (Stanford: Stanford University

Press, 1997), 629; Michael Angold, *The Byzantine Empire, 1025–1204: A Political History* (London: Longman, 1997), 183.

3. Barbara Hill, "A Vindication of the Rights of Women to Power by Anna Komnene," *Byzantinische Forschungen* 23 (1996): 46.

4. Tornikes describes Anna's deathbed tonsure. Anna's taking on of the "dress of perfection" is clearly presented as a prelude to her death. Jean Darrouzes, *George et Demetrios Tornikes. Lettres et Discours* (Paris: éditions du Centre national de la recherche scientifique, 1970), 313, oration number 14.

5. See page 16–17.

6. The appendix was written after the death of Eirene's daughter Eudokia and before the death of Eirene. Since neither of these dates is known with much certainty, the dating of this section of the text is difficult, but is reasonably placed in the later 1120s to 1130s. Paul Gautier, "Le typikon de la Théotokos Kécharitôménè," *Revue des études byzantines* 43, no. 1 (1985): 13–14. Skoulatos prefers 1116: Basile Skoulatos, *Les personnages byzantins de l'Alexiade: Analyse prosopographique et synthese* (Louvain: Bureau du recueil College Erasme, 1980), 149; Wolfram Hörandner, *Theodoros Prodromos. Historische Gedichte*, Wiener Byzantinistische Studien 11 (Vienna: Österreichische Akademie der Wissenschaften, 1974), 185–90, text number 2, lines 14–29; Paul Gautier, "L'obituaire du typikon du Pantokrator," *Revue des études byzantines* 27, no. 1 (1969): 249–50; Paul Gautier, ed., *Lettres et discours: Michel Italikos* (Paris: Institut français d'études byzantines, 1972), 31–34.

7. Gautier, "Kécharitôménè," 139, lines 2118–25; John Thomas and Angela Constantinides Hero, *Byzantine Monastic Foundation Documents: A Complete Translation of the Surviving Founders' Typika and Testaments* (Washington, DC: Dumbarton Oaks, 2000), 707.

8. Gautier, "Kécharitôménè," 137–39, lines 2090–118; Thomas and Hero, *Foundation Documents*, 707.

9. Gautier, "Kécharitôménè," 147, lines 2287–89; Thomas and Hero, *Foundation Documents*, 710.

10. Gautier, "Kécharitôménè," 141, lines 2170–72; Thomas and Hero, *Foundation Documents*, 710.

11. Gautier, "Kécharitôménè," 145–47, lines 2270–80; Thomas and Hero, *Foundation Documents*, 708.

12. Gautier, "Kécharitôménè," 137, lines 2104–05; Thomas and Hero, *Foundation Documents*, 707.

13. Gautier, "Kécharitôménè," 147, lines 2282–86; Thomas and Hero, *Foundation Documents*, 710.

14. Gautier, "Kécharitôménè," 139, line 2129; Thomas and Hero, *Foundation Documents*, 708.

15. Gautier, "Kécharitôménè," 141, lines 2158–63; Thomas and Hero, *Foundation Documents*, 708.

16. Gautier, "Kécharitôménè," 139, lines 2118–25; Thomas and Hero, *Foundation Documents*, 707. The transliteration has been modified.

17. Gautier, "Kécharitôménè," 139, lines 2115–18; Thomas and Hero, *Foundation Documents*, 707.

18. Gautier, "Kécharitôménè," 145, lines 2262–66; Thomas and Hero, *Foundation Documents*, 708.

19. Gautier, "Kécharitôménè," 137, lines 2090–118; Thomas and Hero, *Foundation Documents*, 707.

20. Gautier, "Kécharitôménè," 127, 1890–1905; Thomas and Hero, *Foundation Documents*, 702–3.

21. Gautier, "Kécharitôménè," 141, lines 2170–72; Thomas and Hero, *Foundation Documents*, 702–3.

22. Anna was described as living in those rooms in the appendix Eirene wrote after Eudokia's death. Since it seems secure that Eirene died before Nikephoros, Anna was resident in the monastery before the death of her husband. Darrouzes, *Tornikes*, 295; *Alexiad*, 15.11.22.36–39.

23. Hörandner, *Theodoros Prodromos. Historische Gedichte*, 382–89, text number 39.

24. Maria Dora Spadaro, ed. *Raccomandazioni e consigli di un galantuomo (Strategikon)* (Alessandria: Edizioni dell'Orso, 1998), 148–52; Charalambos Messis, "La construction sociale, les 'realités' rhétoriques et les représentations de l'identité masculine à Byzance" (PhD diss., L'École des hautes etudes en science sociales, 2006), 635–37.

25. Paul Gautier, "Kécharitôménè," 61, lines 741–49; Thomas and Hero, *Foundation Documents*, 679.

26. Theophylakt of Ochrid described Maria of Alania in her later years in terms reminiscent of monastic life, a turn which has been connected with Maria's moral stature: "There seems to have been a strong moral backlash in the popular characteristics of an imperial lady in the 1080s and 1090s: a strong tendency to *claim* a semi-monastic life is only to be expected." Margaret Mullett, "The 'Disgrace' of the Ex-Basilissa Maria," *Byzantinoslavica* 45 (1984): 208.

27. *Alexiad*, 3.6.

Chapter 9

1. The case may have been made first by Ferdinand Chalandon, *Les Comnène : études sur l'empire byzantin au XIe et au XIIe siècles* vol. 2 *Jean II Comnène, 1118–1143, et Manuel I Comnène, 1143–1180.* (Paris: A. Picard et fils, 1912), 4. Robert Browning, "An Unpublished Funeral Oration on Anna Comnena," *Proceedings of the Cambridge Philological Society* 8 (1962): 1–12, repr. in *Aristotle Transformed: The Ancient Commentators and Their Influence*, ed. Richard Sorabji (Ithaca: Cornell University Press, 1990), 398. *International Encyclopaedia for the Middle Ages-Online. A Supplement to LexMA-Online.* s.v. "Anna Komnene, historian, 1083 – 1153/4," by Alexios Savvides, Turnhout: Brepols Publishers, 2011, in Brepolis Medieval Encyclopaedias, http://www.brepolis.net.

2. The rhetorical purposes of Anna's portrait of Bohemond are brilliantly elucidated in Penelope Buckley, *The* Alexiad *of Anna Komnene: Artistic Strategy in the Making of a Myth* (Cambridge: Cambridge University Press, 2014), 195–244.

3. *Alexiad*, 12.4.4.

4. *Alexiad*, 6.8.5. Translation by E. R. A. Sewter and Peter Frankopan, *The Alexiad*, rev. ed. (London: Penguin Classics, 2004), 169.

5. Buckley, *The* Alexiad *of Anna Komnene*, 140–41.

6. *Alexiad*, 3.3.3.

7. Charles Diehl, *Byzantine Empresses* (New York: Knopf, 1963), 185; Georgina Buckler, *Anna Comnena, a Study* (London: Oxford University Press, 1929), 249.

8. Myrto Hatzaki, "The Good, the Bad, and the Ugly," in *A Companion to Byzantium*, ed. Liz James (Malden: Wiley-Blackwell, 2010), 97.

9. William of Tyre, *A History of Deeds Done beyond the Sea*, vol. 2, trans. Emily Atwater Babcock and August C. Krey (New York: Columbia University Press, 1943), 129.

10. Choniates, 51.

11. Buckler, *Anna Comnena*, 57.

12. *Alexiad*, 3.3.2, 9.9.2.

13. *Alexiad*, 15.11.17.

14. *Alexiad*, 14.4.9.

15. *Alexiad*, 14.4.9. Translation by Sewter and Frankopan, *The Alexiad*, 413.

16. *Alexiad*, 14.4.9. Translation by Sewter and Frankopan, *The Alexiad*, 413.

17. Michael Angold, "Alexios I Komnenos: An Afterword," in *Alexios I Komnenos*, edited by Dion Smythe and Margaret Mullett, Belfast Byzantine Texts and Translations 4.1 (Belfast: Belfast Byzantine Enterprizes, 1996), 406.

18. *Alexiad*, 15.11.23.

19. "In truth, it would have been better to have been transformed into some unfeeling rock . . . with shedding of tears . . . I remained . . . being so insensitive to disaster. . . . To endure such suffering and to be treated in an abominable way by people in the palace is more wretched than the troubles of Niobe." Sewter and Frankopan, *The Alexiad*, 472. cf. *Alexiad*, 15.11.23.

20. Paul Stephenson, "Anna Comnena's *Alexiad* as a Source for the Second Crusade?," *Journal of Medieval History* 29, no. 1 (2003): 41–54; Paul Magdalino, "The Pen of the Aunt: Echoes of the Mid-Twelfth Century in the *Alexiad*," in *Anna Komnene and Her Times*, ed. Thalia Gouma-Peterson (New York: Garland, 2000), 15–44; R. D. Thomas, "Anna Comnena's Account of the First Crusade: History and Politics in the Reigns of the Emperors Alexius I and Manuel I Comnenus," *Byzantine and Modern Greek Studies* 15 (1991): 269–312; John France, "Anna Comnena, the Alexiad and the First Crusade," *Reading Medieval Studies* 10 (1984): 20–38.

21. Paul Magdalino, "The Empire of the Komnenoi (1118–1204)," in *The Cambridge History of the Byzantine Empire c.500–1492* (Cambridge: Cambridge University Press, 2008), 629–46; Paul Magdalino, *The Empire of Manuel I Komnenos, 1143–1180* (Cambridge: Cambridge University Press, 1993), 27–108; Ralph-Johannes Lilie, *Byzantium and the Crusader States, 1096–1204* (Oxford: Oxford University Press, 1993), 96–141.

22. It is possible that her story did not reflect her father's actual choices all that well. Peter Frankopan, *The First Crusade: The Call from the East* (Cambridge: Belknap Press of Harvard University Press, 2012); Jonathan Shepard, "Cross-Purposes: Alexius Comnenus and the First Crusade," in *The First Crusade: Origins and Impact*, ed. Jonathan Phillips (Manchester: Manchester University Press, 1997), 107–29; Jonathan Shepard, "'Father' or 'Scorpion'? Style and Substance in Alexios's Diplomacy," in *Alexios I Komnenos*, ed. Margaret Mullett and Dion Smythe Belfast Byzantine Texts and Translations 4.1 (Belfast: Belfast Byzantine Enterprises, 1996), 68–132; Jonathan Shepard, "When Greek Meets Greek: Alexius Comnenus and Bohemond in 1097–98," *Byzantine and Modern Greek Studies* 12 (1988): 185–277.

23. *Alexiad*, 14.2–14.3.

24. *Alexiad*, 14.3.8.

25. *Alexiad*, 14.3.9.

26. *Alexiad*, 14.4.

27. *Alexiad*, 15.6.3–5; Ioannis Stouraitis, "Conceptions of War and Peace in Anna Comnena's Alexiad," in *Byzantine War Ideology between Roman Imperial Concept and Christian Religion: Akten des Internationalen Symposiums (Vienna, 19–21 Mai 2011)*, ed. Johannes Koder and Ioannis Stouraitis (Vienna: Verlag der Österreichischen Akademie der Wissenschaften, 2012), 69–80.

28. P. Maas, "Die Musen des Kaisers Alexios I," *Byzantinische Zeitschrift* 22 (1913): 343–69.

29. Diether Roderich Reinsch, "Abweichungen vom traditionellen byzantinischen Kaiserbild im 11. und 12. Jahrhundert," in *L'éducation au gouvernement et à la vie: la tradition des "règles de vie" de l'antiquité au moyen âge*, ed. Paolo Odorico (Paris: École des hautes études en sciences sociales, Centre d'études byzantines, néo-helléniques et sud-est européennes, 2009), 124; Marc Lauxtermann, "His, and Not His: The Poems of the Late Gregory the Monk," in *The Author in Middle Byzantine Literature: Modes, Functions, and Identities*, ed. Aglae Pizzone (Berlin: De Gruyter, 2014), 81.

30. Reinsch, "Abweichungen," 124.

31. Angold, "Alexios I Komnenos: An Afterword," 409.

32. Magdalino, "The Pen of the Aunt," 18; Margaret Mullett, "Alexios I Komnenos and Imperial Renewal," in *New Constantines: The Rhythm of Imperial Renewal in Byzantium, 4th–13th Centuries*, ed. Paul Magdalino (Aldershot: Ashgate, 1994), 265–66; Margaret Mullett, "Whose Muses?: Two Advice Poems Attributed to Alexios I Komnenos," in *La face cachée de la littérature byzantine: le texte en tant que message immédiat*, ed. Paolo Odorico (Paris: Centre d'études byzantines, néo-helléniques et sud-est européennes, École des hautes études en sciences sociales, 2012), 208–9.

33. *Alexiad*, 6.3.3, 12.5.3, 14.7.2; Maas, "Die Musen," 351–58, lines 106, 120, 131, 167, 283, 325, 339. The similarity is noted by Shepard, "'Father' or 'Scorpion'? Style and Substance in Alexios's Diplomacy," 70.

34. Maas, "Die Musen," 352, line 122.

35. Buckley, *The* Alexiad *of Anna Komnene*, 143, 186; Ruth Macrides, "The Pen and the Sword: Who Wrote the *Alexiad*?," in *Anna Komnene and Her Times*, ed. Thalia Gouma-Peterson (New York: Garland, 2000), 68–69.

36. Maas, "Die Musen," 351, lines 72–86.

37. Ibid. 351, lines 90–94.

38. *Alexiad*, 3.5, 5.9.3, 12.7.4, 15.7; Buckley, *The* Alexiad *of Anna Komnene*, 123, 245–77.

39. Maas, "Die Musen," 351–52, lines 105–15, 355, lines 238–44, 356, line 154.

40. Ibid. 352, lines 117–24.

41. Ibid. 328–33.

42. Maas, "Die Musen," 357, lines 322–27; *Alexiad* 1.2.2, 3.10.4.

43. Maas, "Die Musen," 356, lines 255–81.

44. Maas, "Die Musen," 357, lines 294–95. For example: *Alexiad* 9.2.

45. Maas, "Die Musen," 357, lines 294–98.

46. Maas, "Die Musen," 362, lines 71–72. For example: *Alexiad* 8.5.3.

47. Maas, "Die Musen," 352, lines 118–20, 356, lines 255–92; 361, lines 52–53.

48. *Alexiad*, 14.8, 15.8–10. For other interpretations of the roles of Alexios's heretic persecution in the *Alexiad*, see Buckley, *The* Alexiad *of Anna Komnene*, 270–77; Dion

Smythe, "Alexios I and the Heretics: The Account of Anna Komnene's *Alexiad*," in *Alexios I Komnenos,* ed. Dion Smythe and Margaret Mullett (Belfast: Belfast Byzantine Enterprises, 1996), 232–59.

49. Maas, "Die Musen," 349; *Alexiad* 3.6.4, 6.8.2.

50. Maas, "Die Musen," 352–53, lines 140–64.

51. Maas, "Die Musen," 358, lines 340–45; *Alexiad*, 2.4.8, 10.11.5.

52. Angold, "Alexios I Komnenos: An Afterword," 406.

53. Anna was called Anna Doukaina in a poem written to her by Prodromos. Her son John used the Doukas name rather than either Bryennios or Komnenos. Wolfram Hörandner, *Theodoros Prodromos. Historische Gedichte,* Wiener Byzantinistische Studien 11 (Vienna: Österreichische Akademie der Wissenschaften, 1974), 377–81, text number 38. Matoula Kouroupou and Jean-François Vannier, "Commémoraisons des Comnènes dans le typikon liturgique du monastère du Christ Philanthrope (ms. Panaghia Kamariotissa 29)," *Revue des études byzantines* 63, no. 1 (2005): 59–60.

54. Jean-Claude Cheynet, *Pouvoir et contestations à Byzance (963–1210)* (Paris: Publications de la Sorbonne, 1990), 414, note 4.

55. Peter Frankopan, "Kinship and the Distribution of Power in Komnenian Byzantium," *English Historical Review* 122 (2007): 1–34.

56. Leonora Neville, *Heroes and Romans in Twelfth-Century Byzantium: The "Material for History" of Nikephoros Bryennios* (Cambridge: Cambridge University Press, 2012), 173–93.

57. Ibid. 63–69, 75–79.

58. Ibid. 182–93.

Chapter 10

1. Charles du Fresne du Cange, *Historia Byzantina Duplici Commentario Illustrata. Prior Familias Ac Stemmata Imperatorum Constantinopolianorum, Cum Eorundem Augustorum Nomismatibus, & Aliquot Iconibus; Praeterea Familias Dalmaticas & Turcicas Complecticur: Alter Descriptionem Urbis Constantinopolitanae, Qualis Extitit Sub Imperatoribus Christianis* (Paris: Ludovicum Billaine, 1680), 175–76.

2. Ibid. 176.

3. Ibid.

4. Charles Lebeau, *Histoire du Bas-Empire,* 24 vols. Paris: Chez Desaint & Saillant, 1757–1787. The work was continued by Hubert-Pascale Ameilhon, who published volume 29 in 1817. The story of Alexios's death is in volume 18 (1775), 468–80, and John's first year is in volume 19 (1776), 1–12. My citations are to the revised edition published in Paris in 1824–1836, available through the Hathi Digital Trust at http://hdl.handle.net/2027/wu.89095907440. The text of the revised edition is the same as Lebeau's original.

5. Lebeau was assessed rather harshly in an influential early nineteenth-century biographical dictionary of significant French writers as "a cold and vague narrator who does not always write properly or show critical excellence." J. Fr. Michaud and Louis Gabriel Michaud, *Biographie universelle, ancienne et moderne,* vol. 23 (Paris: Michaud frères, 1819), 480.

6. Charles Lebeau, *Histoire du Bas-Empire,* vol. 15 (Paris: Firmin Didot Frères, 1824), 473.

7. Ibid.

8. Ibid. 474–75.

9. Ibid. 475.

10. Charles Lebeau, *Histoire du Bas-Empire*, vol. 16 (Paris: Firmin Didot Frères, 1824), 2.

11. Ibid. 3. Choniates places the conspiracy before the end of John's first year. Choniates, 10.

12. Lebeau, *Histoire du Bas-Empire*, 16:2.

13. Choniates, 10.

14. Lebeau, *Histoire du Bas-Empire*, 16:4.

15. Ibid. 3–4.

16. Ibid. 4.

17. Ibid.

18. Ibid. 5–6.

19. My references are to Edward Gibbon, *The History of the Decline and Fall of the Roman Empire*, rev. by H. Milman, vol. 4 (Philadelphia: Porter & Coates, 1845).

20. The words he has Eirene say to the dying Alexios, "You die as you have lived, a hypocrite!" are closer to those of Lebeau than to Choniates. Ibid. 230.

21. Ibid. 230.

22. Ibid.

23. Ibid. 231. I have standardized the spellings of Byzantine names.

24. Ibid.

25. Ibid.

26. Ibid. 231–32.

27. Ibid. 229.

28. Ibid.

29. He uses Anna's central Odyssean metaphor: "In the tempest, Alexios steered the imperial vessel with dexterity and courage," after providing a resumé of the dangers Alexios faced that recalls Anna's description of the state of the empire upon Alexios's ascension. Gibbon also follows Anna in admiring Alexios's "superior policy with which he balanced the interests and passions of the champions of the first crusade." Ibid. 229–30.

30. Ibid. 229.

31. Ibid. 231.

32. Johann Heinrich Krause, *Die Byzantiner des Mittelalters in ihrem Staats-, Hof- und Privatleben: insbesondere vom Ende des zehnten bis gegen Ende des vierzehnten Jahrhunderts: nach den byzantinischen Quellen* (Halle: G. Schwetschke, 1869), 300.

33. Ibid.

34. Ibid. 301.

35. Ibid.

36. Ibid. 180–81.

37. Ibid. 181–82.

38. Ibid.

39. Emil Oster, *Anna Komnena* (Rastatt: W. Mayer, 1868).

40. Ibid. 61.

41. Ibid. 66

42. Ibid.

43. Ibid. 68.

44. Ibid. 68–69.

45. Ibid. 71–72.

46. Ibid. 69, note 220.

47. Ferdinand Chalandon, *Les Comnène: études sur l'Empire byzantin aux XIe et XIIe siècles*, vol.1 *Essai sur le règne d'Alexis Ier Comnène (1081–1118)* (Paris: A. Picard et fils, 1900); Ferdinand Chalandon, *Les Comnène: études sur l'Empire byzantin aux XIe et XIIe siècles*, vol. 2, *Jean II Comnène, 1118–1143, et Manuel I Comnène, 1143–1180* (Paris: A. Picard et fils, 1912).

48. Ferdinand Chalandon, *Les Comnène: études sur l'Empire byzantin aux XIe et XIIe siècles*, vol.1 *Essai sur le règne d'Alexis Ier Comnène (1081–1118)* (Paris: A. Picard et fils, 1900), 274.

49. For example: Michael Angold, "Alexios I Komnenos: An Afterword," in *Alexios I Komnenos*, ed. Margaret Mullett and Dion Smythe, Belfast Byzantine Texts and Translations 4.1 (Belfast: Belfast Byzantine Enterprizes, 1996), 404–5; Margaret Mullett, "Tented Ceremony: Ephemeral Performances under the Komnenoi," in *Court Ceremonies and Rituals of Power in Byzantium and the Medieval Mediterranean: Comparative Perspectives*, ed. Alexander Daniel Beihammer, Stavroula Constantinou, and Maria G. Parani (Leiden: Brill, 2013), 493.

50. See page 53–55.

51. Chalandon, *Alexis*, 275.

52. Ibid. 275.

53. Ibid.

54. Ibid. 276.

55. Ibid.

56. Ibid.

57. Ibid.

58. Ferdinand Chalandon, *Les Comnène: études sur l'Empire byzantin aux XIe et XIIe siècles*, vol.2 *Jean II Comnène, 1118–1143, et Manuel I Comnène, 1143–1180* (Paris: A. Picard et fils, 1912), 7.

59. Ibid. 8.

60. Ibid. 16.

61. Ibid.

62. Ibid.

63. Ibid.

64. Ibid.

65. Chalandon, *Alexis*, 275; Chalandon, *Jean II*, 4.

66. Charles Diehl, *Figures Byzantines* (Paris: A. Colin, 1906); Charles Diehl, *Byzantine Empresses*, trans. Harold Bell and Theresa de Kerpely (New York: Knopf, 1963).

67. Diehl, *Byzantine Empresses*, 175.

68. Diehl, *Byzantine Empresses*, 175.

69. Ibid. 178.

70. Ibid. 179–80.

71. Ibid. 180.

72. Ibid.

73. Ibid. 184.

74. The currently accepted date is 1087.

75. Diehl, *Byzantine Empresses*, 185.

76. Ibid.

77. Ibid. 186.

78. Ibid.

79. Ibid.

80. Ibid. 188.

81. Ibid. 188–89.

82. Ibid. 189.

83. Ibid.

84. Ibid.

85. Ibid. 190.

86. Ibid.

87. Ibid.

88. Ibid.

89. Ibid.

90. Ibid. 191

91. Ibid. 193.

92. Louis Du Sommerard, *Deux princesses d'Orient au XIIe siècle: Anne Comnène, témoin des croisades; Agnès de France* (Paris: Perrin et cie, 1907), 173.

93. Ibid. 173

94. Ibid. 188.

95. Ibid. 188–89.

96. Ibid. 174.

97. One example among many: Barbara Hill, *Imperial Women in Byzantium, 1025–1204: Power, Patronage and Ideology* (New York: Longman, 1999), 189.

98. Joseph McCabe, *The Empresses of Constantinople* (London: Metheun, 1913), 214.

99. Ibid. 217.

100. Ibid. 214.

101. "I am afraid she was stupid. Yet it is just as well to be stupid if one is born into as doomed civilization as hers." Naomi Mitchison, *Anna Comnena*, Representative Women (London: G. Howe, 1928), 21–22.

102. Ibid. 57.

103. Ibid. 89.

104. Ibid. 90.

105. Ibid. 91–92.

106. On Buckler's own circuitous route toward history writing: Charlotte Roueché, "Georgina Buckler: The Making of a British Byzantinist," in *The Making of Byzantine History*, ed. Roderick Beaton and Charlotte Roueché (Aldershot: Variorum, 1993), 174–96.

107. Georgina Buckler, *Anna Comnena. A Study* (London: Oxford University Press, 1929), 516–22.

108. Ibid. 27.

109. Ibid. 27–31.

110. Ibid. 27.

111. Ibid. 34.

112. Ibid. 45.

113. Ibid. 45–46.

114. A. A. Vasiliev, *A History of the Byzantine Empire* (Madison: University of Wisconsin Press, 1928), 375; George Ostrogorski, *Geschichte des Byzantinischen Staates* (Munich: Beck, 1940); George Ostrogorski, *History of the Byzantine State*, rev. ed., trans. Joan Hussey (New Brunswick: Rutgers University Press, 1969), 377.

115. Kōnstantinos Varzos, *Hē genealogia tōn Komnēnōn* (Thessalonikē: Kentron Vyzantinōn Ereunōn, 1984), 184.

116. Barbara Hill, "A Vindication of the Rights of Women to Power by Anna Komnene," *Byzantinische Forschungen* 23 (1996): 46.

117. Warren T. Treadgold, *A History of the Byzantine State and Society* (Stanford: Stanford University Press, 1997), 629; Timothy E. Gregory, *A History of Byzantium* (Oxford: Blackwell, 2005), 302; Michael Angold, *The Byzantine Empire, 1025–1204: A Political History* (London: Longman, 1997), 183; J. M. Hussey, *The Byzantine World* (New York: Harper, 1961), 60.

118. Alexios Savvides, "Anna Komnene, Historian, 1083–1153/4," in *International Encyclopaedia for the Middle Ages-Online. A Supplement to LexMA-Online.* Turnhout: Brepols Publishers, 2011, in Brepolis Medieval Encyclopaedias, http://www.brepolis.net.

119. The charter of Kecharitomene was published first in 1688. See John Thomas and Angela Constantinides Hero, *Byzantine Monastic Foundation Documents: A Complete Translation of the Surviving Founders' Typika and Testaments* (Washington, DC: Dumbarton Oaks, 2000), 649. Some of the works of Prodromos were published in Jacques-Paul Migne, ed., *Patrologiae Graeca*, vol. 133, 161 vols. (Paris: Excecudebatur et venit apud J-P Migne, 1857). Others waited until the twentieth century: P. Maas, "Die Musen des Kaisers Alexios I," *Byzantinische Zeitschrift* 22 (1913): 343–69; A. Majuri, ed., "Anecdota Prodromea dal Vat. Gr. 305," in *Rendiconti della Reale Accademia dei Lincei: Classe di Scienze Morali, storiche e filologiche*, Series 5, Vol. 17 (Rome: Tipografia della Accademia, 1908), 518–54; E. Kurtz, "Unedierte Texte aus der Zeit des Kaisers Johannes Komnenos," *Byzantinische Zeitschrift* 16 (1907): 69–119; E. Kurtz, "[Monodies on Nikephoros Komnenos by Eustathios of Thessaloniki and Constantine Manasses]," *Vizantiĭskiĭ Vremennik* 16 (1922): 283–322; Paul Gautier, "Le typikon de la Théotokos Kécharitôménè," *Revue des études byzantines* 43, no. 1 (1985): 5–165; Paul Gautier, *Nicephore Bryennios histoire: introduction, texte, traduction et notes* (Bruxelles: Byzantion, 1975); Paul Gautier, ed., *Lettres et discours: Michel Italikos* (Paris: Institut français d'études byzantines, 1972); Wolfram Hörandner, *Theodoros Prodromos. Historische Gedichte*, Wiener Byzantinistische Studien 11 (Vienna: Österreichische Akademie der Wissenschaften, 1974); Jean Darrouzes, *George et Demetrios Tornikes. Lettres et Discours* (Paris: éditions du Centre national de la recherche scientifique, 1970).

120. Spyridōn Lampros, "O Biennaios kodix 'Phil. Graecus CCCXXI,'" *Neos Hellenomnemon* 13 (1916): 3–22; Robert Browning, "An Unpublished Funeral Oration on Anna Comnena," *Proceedings of the Cambridge Philological Society* 8 (1962): 1–12, repr. in *Aristotle Transformed: The Ancient Commentators and Their Influence*, edited by Richard Sorabji (Ithaca: Cornell University Press, 1990), 393–406; Darrouzes, *Tornikes*.

121. A fundamental starting point: John Marincola, ed., *Greek and Roman Historiography* (Oxford: Oxford University Press, 2011).

122. Krause, *Die Byzantiner des Mittelalters*, 300.

123. Buckler, *Anna Comnena*, 46.
124. McCabe, *The Empresses of Constantinople*, 217.

Conclusion

1. Glenn W. Most, "The Stranger's Stratagem: Self-Disclosure and Self-Sufficiency in Greek Culture," *Journal of Hellenic Studies* 109 (1989): 127.
2. Robin Wilson, "Lowered Cites," *The Chronicle of Higher Education*, March 17, 2014.

{ BIBLIOGRAPHY }

Primary Sources

Abouna, Albert, trans. *Anonymi Auctoris Chronicon Ad A[nnum] C[hristi] 1234 Pertinens II.* Vol. 354. Corpus Scriptorum Christianorum Orientalium. Louvain: Secrétariat du CorpusSCO, 1974.

Adler, A., ed. *Suda Lexicon.* 5 vols. Leipzig: Teubner, 1931.

Bekker, Immanuel, ed. *Michaelis Glycae Annales.* Corpus scriptorum historiae Byzantinae. Bonn: Weber, 1836.

Büttner-Wobst, T., ed. *Ioannis Zonarae epitomae historiarum libri xviii.* Vol. 3. Corpus scriptorum historia Byzantinae. Bonn: Weber, 1897.

Cavafy, Constantine. *Collected Poems.* Edited by Geōrgios P. Savvidēs. Translated by Edmund Keeley and Philip Sherrard. Rev. ed. Princeton Modern Greek Studies. Princeton: Princeton University Press, 1992.

Criscuolo, Ugo, ed. *Autobiografia: Encomio per la Madre: Michele Psello.* Naples: M. D'Auria editore, 1989.

Darrouzes, Jean. *George et Demetrios Tornikes. Lettres et Discours.* Paris: éditions du Centre national de la recherche scientifique, 1970.

de Catanzaro, C. J., trans. *Symeon the New Theologian: The Discourses.* New York: Paulist Press, 1980.

Duffy, John M., and Dominic J. O'Meara, eds. *Michaelis Pselli Philosophica minora* Vol. 2. *Opuscula psychologica, theologica, daemonologica.* Leipzig: Teubner, 1992.

Gautier, Paul, ed. *Lettres et discours: Michel Italikos.* Paris: Institut français d'études byzantines, 1972.

——. "Le typikon de la Théotokos Kécharitôménè." *Revue des études byzantines* 43, no. 1 (1985): 5–165.

——. "L'obituaire du typikon du Pantokrator." *Revue des études byzantines* 27, no. 1 (1969): 235–62.

——, ed. *Nicephore Bryennios histoire: introduction, texte, traduction et notes.* Bruxelles: Byzantion, 1975.

——, ed. "Theodorus Prodromos: Epitaphius in Theodoram nurum Bryennii." In *Nicéphore Bryennios. Histoire*, 355–67. Brussels: Byzantion, 1975.

——, ed. "Theodore Prodomus: Epithalamium fortunatissimis caesaris filiis." In *Nicéphore Bryennios. Histoire*, 341–55. Brussels: Byzantion, 1975.

Henry, René, ed. *Bibliothèque, Photius.* 9 vols. Paris: Société d'édition Les Belles Lettres, 1959–1991.

Heylbut, Gustav, ed. *Eustratii et Michaelis et anonyma in Ethica Nicomachea commentaria.* Berlin: Typis et Impensis G. Reimeri, 1892.

Hörandner, Wolfram. *Theodoros Prodromos. Historische Gedichte.* Wiener Byzantinistische Studien 11. Vienna: Österreichische Akademie der Wissenschaften, 1974.

Kennedy, George Alexander. *Invention and Method: Two Rhetorical Treatises from the Hermogenic Corpus.* Vol. 15. Writings from the Greco-Roman World. Atlanta: Society of Biblical Literature, 2005.

———, trans. *Progymnasmata: Greek Textbooks of Prose Composition and Rhetoric.* Atlanta: Society of Biblical Literature, 2003.

Kurtz, E. "[Monodies on Nikephoros Komnenos by Eustathios of Thessaloniki and Constantine Manasses]." *Vizantiĭskiĭ Vremennik* 16 (1922): 283–322.

———. "Unedierte Texte aus der Zeit des Kaisers Johannes Komnenos." *Byzantinische Zeitschrift* 16 (1907): 69–119.

Lampros, Spyridōn, ed. *Michaēl Akominatou tou Chōniatou Ta Sōzomena: ta pleista ekdidomena nyn to prōton kata tous en Phlōrentia, Oxōniō, Parisiois kai Viennē kōdikas.* 2 vols. Groningen: Bouma's Boekhuis, 1968.

———. "O Biennaios kodix 'Phil. Graecus CCCXXI.'" *Neos Hellenomnemon* 13 (1916): 3–22.

Lemerle, Paul, André Guillou, Nicolas Svoronos, and Denise Papachryssanthou. *Actes de Lavra.* Vol. I. Paris: Lethielleux, 1970.

Leone, Pietro Luigi, ed. *Ioannis Tzetzae Epistulae.* Leipzig: Teubner, 1972.

Maas, P. "Die Musen des Kaisers Alexios I." *Byzantinische Zeitschrift* 22 (1913): 343–69.

Magoulias, Harry J., trans. *O City of Byzantium: Annals of Niketas Choniates.* Detroit: Wayne State University Press, 1984.

Maisano, Riccardo, ed. *Niceta Coniata—Grandezza e catastrofe di Bisanzio: narrazione cronologica.* Translated by Anna Pontani. Vol. 1. Libri I–VIII. Milan: Fondazione Lorenzo Valla: A. Mondadori, 1994.

Majuri, A., ed. "Anecdota Prodromea dal Vat. Gr. 305." In *Rendiconti della Reale Accademia dei Lincei: Classe di Scienze Morali, storiche e filologiche.* Series 5, Vol. 17, 518–54. Rome: Tipografia della Accademia, 1908.

Mango, Cyril A., and Roger Scott, eds. *The Chronicle of Theophanes Confessor: Byzantine and Near Eastern History, ad 284–813.* Oxford: Clarendon Press, 1997.

Migne, Jacques-Paul, ed. *Patrologiae Graeca.* 161 vols. Paris: Excecudebatur et venit apud J-P Migne, 1857–1866.

Müller, Karl, Theodor Müller, and Victor Langlois, eds. *Fragmenta historicorum graecorum.* 5 vols. Paris: Ambrosio Firmin Didot, 1841–1938. Reprint, Frankfurt: Minerva, 1975.

Noailles, Pierre, and Alphonse Dain, eds. *Les Novelles de Léon VI le Sage.* Paris: Société d'édition Les Belles Lettres, 1944.

Oikonomides, Nicolas, ed. *Actes de Docheiariou.* Paris: P. Lethielleux, 1984.

Pignani, A., ed. *Niceforo Basilace. Progimnasmi e monodie.* Naples: Bibliopolis, 1983.

Rabe, Hugo, ed. *Aphthonii Progymnasmata.* Bibliotheca Scriptorum Graecorum et Romanorum Teubneriana. Leipzig: Teubner, 1926.

Reinsch, Diether R., and Athanasios Kambylis, eds. *Alexiad.* Berlin: De Gruyter, 2001.

Sewter, E. R. A., and Peter Frankopan, trans. *The Alexiad.* Revised. London: Penguin Classics, 2004.

Sola, J. "De Codice Laurentiano X Plutei V." *Byzantinische Zeitschrift* 20 (1911): 373–83.

Spadaro, Maria Dora, ed. *Raccomandazioni e consigli di un galantuomo (Strategikon).* Alessandria: Edizioni dell'Orso, 1998.

Spinelli, Antonio, ed. *Regii neapolitani archivi monumenta edita ac illustrata.* 6 vols. Naples: ex Regia Typographia, 1845.

Thomas, John, and Angela Constantinides Hero, eds. *Byzantine Monastic Foundation Documents: A Complete Translation of the Surviving Founders' Typika and Testaments.* Washington, DC: Dumbarton Oaks, 2000.

Van der Valk, Marchinus, ed. *Eustathii archiepiscopi Thessalonicensis Commentarii ad Homeri Iliadem pertinentes ad fidem codicis Laurentiani editi.* Leiden: Brill, 1971.

Van Dieten, Jan, ed. *Nicetae Choniatae historia, pars prior.* Corpus Fontium Historiae Byzantinae. Berlin: De Gruyter, 1975.

Waltz, Christian, ed. "Gregorius Pardus: Commentarium in Hermogenis librum περὶ μεθόδου δεινότητος." In *Rhetores Graeci,* 7.2:1090–1352. Stuttgart: Cotta, 1834.

Whitehead, David, ed. *Suda On Line: Byzantine Lexicography,* Stoa Consortium, 2000–2014, http://www.stoa.org/sol/.

William of Tyre. *A History of Deeds Done beyond the Sea.* Translated by Emily Atwater Babcock and August C. Krey. Vol. 2. New York: Columbia University Press, 1943.

Wilson, Nigel, trans. *The Bibliotheca: A Selection.* London: Duckworth, 1994.

Secondary Sources

Afinogenov, Dimitry E. "Some Observations on Genres of Byzantine Historiography." *Byzantion* 62 (1992): 13–33.

Albu, Emily. "Viewing Rome from the Roman Empires." *Medieval Encounters* 17, no. 4/5 (2011): 495–511.

Alexiou, Margaret. *The Ritual Lament in Greek Tradition.* Cambridge: Cambridge University Press, 1974.

Amelang, James. "Mourning Becomes Eclectic: Ritual Lament and the Problem of Continuity." *Past and Present* 187 (2005): 3–32.

Anderson, Jeffrey, and Elizabeth Jeffreys. "The Decoration of the Sevastokratorissa's Tent." *Byzantion* 64 (1994): 8–18.

Angold, Michael. "Alexios I Komnenos: An Afterword." In *Alexios I Komnenos,* edited by Dion Smythe and Margaret Mullett, 398–417. Belfast Byzantine Texts and Translations 4.1. Belfast: Belfast Byzantine Enterprizes, 1996.

———. *The Byzantine Empire, 1025–1204: A Political History.* London: Longman, 1997.

Barber, Charles. "Homo Byzantinus?" In *Women, Men and Eunuchs: Gender in Byzantium,* 185–99. London: Routledge, 1997.

Barber, Charles, and David Jenkins, eds. *Medieval Greek Commentaries on the Nicomachean Ethics.* Leiden: Brill, 2009.

Barzos, K. *E genealogia ton Komnenon.* Thessaloniki: Kentron Vyzantinōn Ereunōn, 1984.

Beaucamp, Joëlle. "Incapacité féminine et rôle public à Byzance." In *Femmes et pouvoirs des femmes à Byzance et in Occident (VIe–XIe siècle),* edited by Stéphane Lebecq, Alain Dierkens, R. Le Jan, and J-M Santerre, 23–36. Lille: Villeneuve d'Ascq, 1999.

———. *Le statut de la femme á Byzance, 4e-7e siècle.* Vol. 1, *Le droit impérial.* Paris: De Boccard, 1990.

———. *Le statut de la femme à Byzance, 4e-7e siécle.* Vol. 2, *Les practiques sociales.* Paris: De Boccard, 1992.

Beck, Hans-Georg. "Die Byzantinische 'Mönchschronik.'" In *Ideen und Realitäten in Byzanz,* 188–97. London, 1972.

Bernard, Floris. "The Ethics of Authorship: Some Tensions in the 11th Century." In *The Author in Middle Byzantine Literature: Modes, Functions, and Identities*, edited by Aglae Pizzone, 41–60. Berlin: De Gruyter, 2014.

Bourbouhakis, Emmanuel C. "The End of ἐπίδειξις. Authorial Identity and Authorial Intention in Michael Chōniatēs' Πρὸς τοὺς αἰτιωμένους τὸ ἀφιλένδεικτον." In *The Author in Middle Byzantine Literature: Modes, Functions, and Identities*, edited by Aglae Pizzone, 201–24. Berlin: De Gruyter, 2014.

———. "'Political' Personae: The Poem from Prison of Michael Glykas: Byzantine Literature between Fact and Fiction." *Byzantine and Modern Greek Studies* 31 (2007): 53–75.

Bravo Garcia, Antonio. "Politics, History and Rhetoric: On the Structure of the First Book of Nicetas Choniates' History." *Byzantinoslavica* 56, no. 2 (1995): 423–28.

Browning, Robert. *The Byzantine Empire*. Washington, DC: The Catholic University of America Press, 1980.

———. "An Unpublished Funeral Oration on Anna Comnena." *Proceedings of the Cambridge Philological Society* 8 (1962): 1–12. Reprinted in *Aristotle Transformed: The Ancient Commentators and Their Influence*, edited by Richard Sorabji, 393–406. Ithaca: Cornell University Press, 1990.

Buckler, Georgina. *Anna Comnena. A Study*. London: Oxford University Press, 1929.

Buckley, Penelope. *The Alexiad of Anna Komnene: Artistic Strategy in the Making of a Myth*. Cambridge: Cambridge University Press, 2014.

Burgmann, Ludwig. "Lawyers and Legislators: Aspects of Law-Making in the Time of Alexios I." In *Alexios I Komnenos*, edited by Dion Smythe and Margaret Mullett, 185–98. Belfast Byzantine Texts and Translations, 4.1. Belfast: Belfast Byzantine Enterprises, 1996.

Cameron, Averil. *The Byzantines*. Malden: Blackwell, 2006.

Cerchez, Marin. "Religion in the Alexiad." PhD diss., University of Wisconsin–Madison, 2014.

Chalandon, Ferdinand. *Les Comnène: études sur l'Empire byzantin aux XIe et XIIe siècles*. Vol. 1, *Essai sur le règne d'Alexis Ier Comnène (1081–1118)*. Paris: A. Picard et fils, 1900.

———. *Les Comnène: études sur l'Empire byzantin aux XIe et XIIe siècles*. Vol. 2, *Jean II Comnène, 1118–1143, et Manuel I Comnène, 1143–1180*. Paris: A. Picard et fils, 1912.

Cheynet, Jean-Claude. *Pouvoir et contestations à Byzance (963–1210)*. Paris: Publications de la Sorbonne, 1990.

Coon, Lynda L., Katherine J. Haldane, and Elisabeth W. Sommer, eds. *That Gentle Strength: Historical Perspectives on Women in Christianity*. Charlottesville: University of Virginia Press, 1990.

Davies, Eve. "Age, Gender and Status: A Three-Dimensional Life Course Perspective of the Byzantine Family." In *Approaches to the Byzantine Family*, edited by Leslie Brubaker and Shaun Tougher, 153–76. Farnham: Ashgate, 2013.

Dickie, Matthew W. "The Fathers of the Church and the Evil Eye." In *Byzantine Magic*, edited by Henry Maguire, 9–34. Washington, DC: Dumbarton Oaks, 1995.

Diehl, Charles. *Byzantine Empresses*. Translated by Harold Bell and Theresa de Kerpely. New York: Knopf, 1963.

———. *Figures Byzantines*. Paris: A. Colin, 1906.

Du Cange, Charles du Fresne. *Historia Byzantina Duplici Commentario Illustrata. Prior Familias Ac Stemmata Imperatorum Constantinopolianorum, Cum Eorundem Augustorum Nomismatibus, & Aliquot Iconibus; Praeterea Familias Dalmaticas &*

Turcicas Complecticur: Alter Descriptionem Urbis Constantinopolitanae, Qualis Extitit Sub Imperatoribus Christianis. Paris: Ludovicum Billaine, 1680.

Duffy, John. "Hellenic Philosophy in Byzantium and the Lonely Mission of Michael Psellos." In *Byzantine Philosophy and Its Ancient Sources*, 139–56. Oxford: Clardenon Press, 2002.

Du Sommerard, Louis. *Deux princesses d'Orient au XIIe siècle: Anne Comnène, témoin des croisades; Agnès de France.* Paris: Perrin et cie, 1907.

Efthymiades, Stephanos. "Niketas Choniates: The Writer." In *Niketas Choniates: A Historian and a Writer.* Geneva: La Pomme d'Or, 2009.

Foley, Helene P. *Female Acts in Greek Tragedy.* Princeton: Princeton University Press, 2001.

Fornara, Charles. *The Nature of History in Ancient Greece and Rome.* Berkeley: University of California Press, 1983.

France, John. "Anna Comnena, the Alexiad and the First Crusade." *Reading Medieval Studies* 10 (1984): 20–38.

Frankopan, Peter. *The First Crusade: The Call from the East.* Cambridge: Belknap Press of Harvard University Press, 2012.

———. "Kinship and the Distribution of Power in Komnenian Byzantium." *English Historical Review* 122 (2007): 1–34.

———. "The Literary, Cultural and Political Context for the Twelfth-Century Commentary on the *Nicomachean Ethics.*" In *Medieval Greek Commentaries on the* Nicomachean Ethics, edited by Charles Barber and David Jenkins, 45–62. Leiden: Brill, 2009.

———. "Perception and Projection of Prejudice: Anna Comnena, the *Alexiad* and the First Crusade." In *Gendering the Crusades*, 59–76. Cardiff: University of Wales Press, 2001.

———. "Turning Latin into Greek: Anna Komnene and the Gesta Roberti Wiscardi." *Journal of Medieval History* 39, no. 1 (2013): 80–99.

Galatariotou, Catia. "Holy Women and Witches: Aspects of Byzantine Conceptions of Gender." *Byzantine and Modern Greek Studies* 9 (1984): 55–94.

Garland, Lynda, and Stephen Rapp. "Mary 'of Alania': Woman and Empress Between Two Worlds." In *Byzantine Women: Varieties of Experience 800–1200*, edited by Lynda Garland, 91–123. Aldershot: Ashgate, 2006.

Gerstel, Sharon. "Painted Sources for Female Piety in Medieval Byzantium." *Dumbarton Oaks Papers* 52 (1998): 89–111.

Gertsman, Elina, ed. *Crying in the Middle Ages: Tears of History.* Abingdon: Routledge, 2012.

Gibbon, Edward. *The History of the Decline and Fall of the Roman Empire.* Revised by H. Milman. Vol. 4. Philadelphia: Porter & Coates, 1845.

Gouma-Peterson, Thalia. "Engendered Category or Recognizable Life: Anna Komnene and Her Alexiad." *Byzantinische Forschungen* 23 (1996): 25–34.

———. "Gender and Power: Passage to the Maternal in Anna Komnene's *Alexiad.*" In *Anna Komnene and Her Times*, edited by Thalia Gouma-Peterson, 107–24. London: Garland Publishing, 2000.

Gregory, Timothy E. *A History of Byzantium.* Oxford: Blackwell, 2005.

Grigoriadis, Iordanis. *Linguistic and Literary Studies in the Epitome Historion of John Zonaras.* Thessalonike: Center for Byzantine Research, 1998.

———. "A Study of the Prooimion of Zonaras' Chronicle in Relation to Other 12th-Century Prooimia." *Byzantinische Zeitschrift* 91 (1998): 327–44.

Grünbart, Michael. "Der Kaiser weint: Anmerkungen zur imperialen Inszenierung von Emotionen in Byzanz." *Frühmittelalterliche Studien* 42 (2008): 89–108.

———. "Prosopographische Beiträge zum Briefcorpus des Ioannes Tzetzes." *Jahrbuch der Österreichischen Byzantinistik* 46 (1996): 175–226.

Harris, Jonathan. *Byzantium and the Crusades*. London: Hambledon and London, 2003.

Hartnup, Karen. *"On the Beliefs of the Greeks": Leo Allatios and Popular Orthodoxy*. Leiden: Brill, 2004.

Harvey, Susan Ashbrook. "Including the 'Despised Woman': Jacob of Serug at the Nativity Feast." In *Byzantine Religious Culture: Studies in Honor of Alice-Mary Talbot*, edited by Denis Sullivan, Elizabeth A. Fisher, and Stratis Papaioannou, 3–18. Leiden: Brill, 2012.

———. "Women in Early Byzantine Hagiography: Reversing the Story." In *That Gentle Strength: Historical Perspectives on Women in Christianity*, edited by Lynda L. Coon, Katherine J. Haldane, and Elisabeth W. Sommer, 36–59. Charlottesville: University Press of Virginia, 1990.

Hatzaki, Myrto. "The Good, the Bad, and the Ugly." In *A Companion to Byzantium*, edited by Liz James, 93–107. Malden: Wiley-Blackwell, 2010.

Henderson, Jeffrey. *The Maculate Muse: Obscene Language in Attic Comedy*. Oxford: Oxford University Press, 1991.

Hennessy, Cecily. *Images of Children in Byzantium*. Farnham: Ashgate, 2008.

Herrin, Judith. *Unrivalled Influence: Women and Empire in Byzantium*. Princeton: Princeton University Press, 2013.

———. *Women in Purple: Rulers of Medieval Byzantium*. London: Weidenfeld & Nicolson, 2001.

Hill, Barbara. "Alexios I Komnenos and the Imperial Women." In *Alexios I Komnenos*, edited by Dion Smythe and Margaret Mullett, 37–54. Belfast Byzantine Texts and Translations 4.1. Belfast: Belfast Byzantine Enterprises, 1996.

———. "The Ideal Komnenian Woman." *Byzantinische Forschungen* 23 (1996): 7–18.

———. *Imperial Women in Byzantium, 1025–1204: Power, Patronage and Ideology*. New York: Longman, 1999.

———. "A Vindication of the Rights of Women to Power by Anna Komnene." *Byzantinische Forschungen* 23 (1996): 45–53.

Hinterberger, Martin. "Emotions in Byzantium." In *A Companion to Byzantium*, edited by Liz James, 121–34. Malden: Wiley-Blackwell, 2010.

———. "Envy and Nemesis in the Vita Basili and Leo the Deacon: Literary Mimesis or Something More?" In *History as Literature in Byzantium*, edited by Ruth Macrides, 187–203. Farnham: Ashgate, 2010.

———. "Phthonos als treibende Kraft in Prodromos, Manasses und Bryennios." *Medioevo Greco* 11 (2011): 1–24.

———. *Phthonos: Missgunst, Neid und Eifersucht in der byzantinischen Literatur*. Wiesbaden: Dr. Ludwig Reichert Verlag, 2013.

———. "Tränen in der byzantinischen Literatur. Ein Beitrag zur Geschichte der Emotionen." *Jahrbuch der Österreichischen Byzantinistik* 56 (2006): 27–51.

Howard-Johnston, James. "Anna Komnene and the *Alexiad*." In *Alexios I Komnenos*, edited by Margaret Mullett and Dion Smythe, 232–302. Belfast Byzantine Texts and Translations 4.1. Belfast: Belfast Byzantine Enterprises, 1996.

Hussey, J. M. *The Byzantine World*. New York: Harper, 1961.

Ierodiakonou, Katerina, and Dominic J. O'Meara. "Philosophies." In *The Oxford Handbook of Byzantine Studies*, edited by Elizabeth Jeffreys, John F. Haldon, and Robin Cormack, 711–20. Oxford Handbooks. New York: Oxford University Press, 2008.

James, Liz. *Empresses and Power in Early Byzantium*. London: Leicester University Press, 2001.

——. "Men, Women, Eunuchs: Gender, Sex and Power." In *The Social History of Byzantium*, edited by John F. Haldon, 31–50. Malden: Blackwell, 2009.

——. "The Role of Women." In *The Oxford Handbook of Byzantine Studies*, edited by Elizabeth Jeffreys, John F. Haldon, and Robin Cormack, 643–51. Oxford Handbooks. New York: Oxford University Press, 2008.

——. *Women, Men, and Eunuchs: Gender in Byzantium*. London: Routledge, 1997.

Jeffreys, Michael. "Manuel Komnenos' Macedonian Military Camps: A Glamorous Alternative Court?" In *Byzantine Macedonia: Identity Image and History*, edited by John Burke and Roger Scott, 184–91. Queensland: Australian Association for Byzantine Studies, Australian Catholic University, 2000.

Kalavrezou, Ioli, ed. *Byzantine Women and Their World*. Cambridge: Harvard University Art Museum, 2003.

Kaldellis, Anthony. "Byzantine Historical Writing, 500–920." In *The Oxford History of Historical Writing*, edited by Daniel Woolf, Sarah Foot, and Chase F. Robinson, 2:201–17. Oxford: Oxford University Press, 2012.

——. "Classical Scholarship in Twelfth-Century Byzantium." In *Medieval Greek Commentaries on the* Nicomachean Ethics, edited by Charles Barber and David Jenkins, 1–43. Leiden: Brill, 2009.

——. "The Corpus of Byzantine Historiography: An Interpretive Essay." In *The Byzantine World*, 211–22. London: Routledge, 2010.

——. *Hellenism in Byzantium: The Transformations of Greek Identity and the Reception of the Classical Tradition*. Cambridge: Cambridge University Press, 2007.

——. "The Military Use of the Icon of the Theotokos and Its Moral Logic in the Historians of the Ninth-Twelfth Centuries." *Estudios Bizantinos: Revista de La Sociedad Española de Bizantinística* 1 (2013): 56–75.

——. *Mothers and Sons, Fathers and Daughters: The Byzantine Family of Michael Psellos*. Notre Dame: University of Notre Dame Press, 2006.

——. "Paradox, Reversal and the Meaning of History." In *Niketas Choniates: A Historian and a Writer*, 75–100. Geneva: La Pomme d'Or, 2009.

Kambylis, Athanasios. "Zum Programm der byzantinischen Historikerin Anna Komnene." In *Dōrēma: Hans Diller zum 70. Geburtstag: Dauer und Überleben des antiken Geistes*, edited by Kōnstantinos Vourverēs and Aristoxenos D. Skiadas, 127–46. Athens: Griechische Humanistische Gesellschaft, 1975.

Kazhdan, Alexander. "Die Liste der Kinder des Alexios I in einer Moskauer Handschrift (UBV 53/148)." In *Beiträge zur alten Geschichte und deren Nachleben*, edited by Ruth Stiehl and Hans Erich Stier, 2:233–37. Berlin: De Gruyter, 1969.

Kouroupou, Matoula, and Jean-François Vannier. "Commémoraisons des Comnènes dans le typikon liturgique du monastère du Christ Philanthrope (ms. Panaghia Kamariotissa 29)." *Revue des études byzantines* 63, no. 1 (2005): 41–69.

Krallis, Dimitris. *Michael Attaleiates and the Politics of Imperial Decline in Eleventh-Century Byzantium*. Tempe: ACMRS, 2012.

Krause, Johann Heinrich. *Die Byzantiner des Mittelalters in ihrem Staats-, Hof- und Privatleben: insbesondere vom Ende des zehnten bis gegen Ende des vierzehnten Jahrhunderts: nach den byzantinischen Quellen*. Halle: G. Schwetschke, 1869.

Krausmüller, Dirk. "The Athonite Monastic Tradition during the Eleventh and Early Twelfth Centuries." In *Mount Athos and Byzantine Monasticism*, edited by Anthony Bryer and Mary Cunningham, 57–65. Aldershot: Variorum, 1996.

Krueger, Derek. *Liturgical Subjects: Christian Ritual, Biblical Narrative, and the Formation of the Self in Byzantium*. Philadelphia: University of Pennsylvania Press, 2014.

———. *Writing and Holiness: The Practice of Authorship in the Early Christian East*. Philadelphia: University of Pennsylvania Press, 2004.

Kuefler, Mathew. *The Manly Eunuch: Masculinity, Gender Ambiguity, and Christian Ideology in Late Antiquity*. Chicago: University of Chicago Press, 2001.

Kugel, James L. *Traditions of the Bible: A Guide to the Bible as It Was at the Start of the Common Era*. Cambridge: Harvard University Press, 1998.

Laiou, Angeliki. "Law, Justice, and the Byzantine Historians: Ninth to Twelfth Centuries." In *Law and Society in Byzantium: Ninth–Twelfth Centuries*, 151–86. Washington, DC: Dumbarton Oaks, 1994.

———. "The Role of Women in Byzantine Society." *Jahrbuch der Österreichischen Byzantinistik* 31 (1981): 233–60.

———. "Women in the Marketplace of Constantinople (10th–14th Centuries)." In *Byzantine Constantinople: Monuments, Topography and Everyday Life*, edited by Nevra Necipoğlu, 261–73. Leiden: Brill, 2001.

Lardinois, A. P. M. H., and Laura McClure. *Making Silence Speak: Women's Voices in Greek Literature and Society*. Princeton: Princeton University Press, 2001.

Lauxtermann, Marc. "His, and Not His: The Poems of the Late Gregory the Monk." In *The Author in Middle Byzantine Literature: Modes, Functions, and Identities*, edited by Aglae Pizzone, 77–86. Berlin: De Gruyter, 2014.

Lebeau, Charles. *Histoire du Bas-Empire*, 24 vols. Paris: Chez Desaint & Saillant, 1757–1787. Revised edition, 21 vols. Paris: Firmin Didot Frères, 1824. Page references are to the 1824 edition.

Lemerle, Paul. *Cinq études sur le XIe siècle byzantin*. Paris: Centre national de la recherche scientifique, 1977.

Leon, Vicki. *Uppity Women of Medieval Times*. 5th edition. New York: Fine Communications, 1998.

Lilie, Ralph-Johannes. "Reality and Invention: Reflections on Byzantine Historiography." *Dumbarton Oaks Papers* 68 (2014): 157–210.

———. *Byzantium and the Crusader States, 1096–1204*. Oxford: Oxford University Press 1994.

Ljubarskij, Jakov. "George the Monk as a Short-Story Writer." *Jahrbuch der Österreichischen Byzantinistik* 44 (1994): 255–64.

———. "Why Is the Alexiad a Masterpiece of Byzantine Literature?" In *Leimon: Studies Presented to Lennart Rydén on His Sixty-Fifth Birthday*, edited by Jan Olof Rosenqvist, 127–41. Uppsala: Acta Universitatis Upsaliensis, 1996.

Loraux, Nicole. *The Invention of Athens: The Funeral Oration in the Classical City*. Cambridge: Harvard University Press, 1986.

———. *Mothers in Mourning: with the essay, Of Amnesty and Its Opposite.* Translated by Corinne Pache. Ithaca: Cornell University Press, 1998.

———. *The Mourning Voice: An Essay on Greek Tragedy.* Ithaca: Cornell University Press, 2002.

Luce, T. J. "Ancient Views on the Causes of Bias in Historical Writing." *Classical Philology* 84 (1989): 16–31.

Macrides, Ruth, ed. *History as Literature in Byzantium.* Farnham: Ashgate, 2010.

———. "The Historian in the History." In *Philellēn: Studies in Honour of Robert Browning*, edited by C. N. Constantinides, Nikolaos Panagiōtakēs, and Elizabeth Jeffreys, 205–24. Venice: Istituto ellenico di studi bizantini e postbizantini di Venezia, 1996.

———. "The Pen and the Sword: Who Wrote the *Alexiad*?" In *Anna Komnene and Her Times*, edited by Thalia Gouma-Peterson, 63–81. New York: Garland, 2000.

Macrides, Ruth, and Paul Magdalino. "The Fourth Kingdom and the Rhetoric of Hellenism." In *The Perception of the Past in Twefth-Century Europe*, edited by Paul Magdalino, 117–56. London: The Hambledon Press, 1992.

Magdalino, Paul. "Byzantine Historical Writing, 900–1400." In *The Oxford History of Historical Writing*, edited by Sarah Foot, Chase F. Robinson, and Daniel R. Woolf, 2:218–37. Oxford: Oxford University Press, 2012.

———. "The Empire of the Komnenoi (1118–1204)." In *The Cambridge History of the Byzantine Empire c.500–1492*, 627–63. Cambridge: Cambridge University Press, 2008.

———. *The Empire of Manuel I Komnenos, 1143–1180.* Cambridge: Cambridge University Press, 1993.

———. "The Pen of the Aunt: Echoes of the Mid-Twelfth Century in the *Alexiad*." In *Anna Komnene and Her Times*, edited by Thalia Gouma-Peterson. New York: Garland, 2000.

Maguire, Henry. *Art and Eloquence in Byzantium.* Princeton: Princeton University Press, 1981.

———. "The Depiction of Sorrow in Middle Byzantine Art." *Dumbarton Oaks Papers* 31 (1977): 123–74.

Malamut, Élisabeth. "Une femme politique d'exception à la fin du XIe siècle: Anne Dalassène." In *Femmes et pouvoirs des femmes à Byzance et en occident (VIe–XIe siècles)*, edited by Stéphane Lebecq, Alain Dierkens, Régine Le Jan, and Jean-Marie Sansterre, 103–20. Lille: Centre de Recherche sur l'Histoire de l'Europe du Nord-Ouest, 1999.

Marincola, John. *Authority and Tradition in Ancient Historiography.* Cambridge: Cambridge University Press, 1997.

———. ed., *A Companion to Greek and Roman Historiography.* Malden: Blackwell, 2007.

———. ed. *Greek and Roman Historiography.* Oxford: Oxford University Press, 2011.

Markopoulos, Athanasios. "Byzantine History Writing at the End of the First Millennium." In *Byzantium in the Year 1000*, edited by Paul Magdalino, 183–97. Leiden: Brill, 2003.

———. "From Narrative Historiography to Historical Biography. New Trends in Byzantine Historical Writing in the 10th–11th Centuries." *Byzantinische Zeitschrift* 102 (2010): 697–715.

———. *History and Literature of Byzantium in the 9th–10th Centuries.* Aldershot: Ashgate, 2004.

Mavroudi, Maria. "Learned Women of Byzantium and the Surviving Record." In *Byzantine Religious Culture: Studies in Honor of Alice-Mary Talbot*, edited by Denis Sullivan, Elizabeth Fisher, and Stratis Papaioannou, 53–84. Leiden: Brill, 2012.

McCabe, Joseph. *The Empresses of Constantinople*. London: Metheun, 1913.

McClure, Laura. *Spoken like a Woman: Speech and Gender in Athenian Drama*. Princeton: Princeton University Press, 1999.

———. *Women in the Ancient World: A New Approach*. Malden: Blackwell, forthcoming 2017.

McDonnell, Myles Anthony. *Roman Manliness: Virtus and the Roman Republic*. Cambridge: Cambridge University Press, 2006.

McGrath, Stamatina. "Women in Byzantine History in the Tenth and Eleventh Centuries : Some Theoretical Considerations." In *Byzantine Religious Culture: Studies in Honor of Alice-Mary Talbot*, edited by Denis Sullivan, Elizabeth A. Fisher, and Stratis Papaioannou, 85–98. Leiden: Brill, 2012.

McNamer, Sarah. *Affective Meditation and the Invention of Medieval Compassion*. Middle Ages Series. Philadelphia: University of Pennsylvania Press, 2010.

Messis, Charalambos. "La construction sociale, les 'réalités' rhétoriques et les représentations de l'identité masculine à Byzance." PhD diss., L'École des hautes etudes en science sociales, 2006.

Meyer, Philipp. *Die Haupturkunden für die Geschichte der Athosklöster: Grösstentheils zum ersten Male*. Leipzig: Hinrich, 1894.

Michaud, J. Fr., and Louis Gabriel Michaud. *Biographie universelle, ancienne et moderne*. Vol. 23. Paris: Michaud frères, 1819.

Mitchison, Naomi. *Anna Comnena*. Representative Women. London: G. Howe, 1928.

Morris, Rosemary. *Monks and Laymen in Byzantium, 843–1118*. Cambridge: Cambridge University Press, 1995.

Most, Glenn W. "The Stranger's Stratagem: Self-Disclosure and Self-Sufficiency in Greek Culture." *Journal of Hellenic Studies* 109 (1989): 114–33.

Mullett, Margaret. "Alexios I Komnenos and Imperial Renewal." In *New Constantines: The Rhythm of Imperial Renewal in Byzantium, 4th–13th Centuries*, edited by Paul Magdalino, 259–67. Aldershot: Ashgate, 1994.

———. "The 'Disgrace' of the Ex-Basilissa Maria." *Byzantinoslavica* 45 (1984): 202–11.

———. "In Search of the Monastic Author. Story-Telling, Anonymity and Innovation in the 12th Century." In *The Author in Middle Byzantine Literature: Modes, Functions, and Identities*, edited by Aglae Pizzone, 171–98. Berlin: De Gruyter, 2014.

———. "Novelisation in Byzantium: Narrative after the Revival of Fiction." In *Byzantine Narrative: Papers in Honour of Roger Scott*, edited by J. Burke, et.al., 1–28. Melbourne: Australian Association for Byzantine Studies, 2006.

———. "Tented Ceremony : Ephemeral Performances under the Komnenoi." In *Court Ceremonies and Rituals of Power in Byzantium and the Medieval Mediterranean: Comparative Perspectives*, edited by Alexander Daniel Beihammer, Stavroula Constantinou, and Maria G. Parani, 487–513. Leiden: Brill, 2013.

———. "Whose Muses?: Two Advice Poems Attributed to Alexios I Komnenos." In *La face cachée de la littérature byzantine: le texte en tant que message immédiat*, edited by Paolo Odorico, 195–220. Paris: Centre d'études byzantines, néo-helléniques et sud-est européennes, École des hautes études en sciences sociales, 2012.

Murnaghan, Sheila. "The Survivors' Song: The Drama of Mourning in Euripides' 'Alcestis.'" *Illinois Classical Studies* 24 (1999): 107–16.

Neville, Leonora. "The Adventures of a Provincial Female Founder: Glykeria and the Rhetoric of Female Weakness." In *Female Founders in Byzantium and Beyond*, edited by Margaret Mullett, Michael Grünbart, and Lioba Theis, vols. 50–51:153–62. Wiener Jarhbuch für Kunstgeschichte. Vienna: Böhlau, 2010.

———. *Heroes and Romans in Twelfth-Century Byzantium: The "Material for History" of Nikephoros Bryennios*. Cambridge: Cambridge University Press, 2012.

———. "Taxing Sophronia's Son-in-Law: Representations of Women in Provincial Documents." In *Byzantine Women: Varieties of Experience, 800–1200*, edited by Lynda Garland, 77–89. Aldershot: Ashgate, 2006.

Odorico, Paolo, Panagiotis A. Agapitos, and Martin Hinterberger, eds. *L'écriture de la mémoire: la littérarité de l'historiographie*. Dossiers byzantins 6. Paris: Centre d'études byzantines, néo-helléniques et sud-est européennes, École des Hautes Études en Sciences Sociales, 2006.

Oster, Emil. *Anna Komnena*. Rastatt: W. Mayer, 1868.

Ostrogorski, George. *Geschichte des Byzantinischen Staates*. Munich: Beck, 1940.

———. *History of the Byzantine State*. Rev. ed. Translated by Joan Hussey. New Brunswick: Rutgers University Press, 1969.

Papaioannou, Eustratios N. "On the Stage of Eros: Two Rhetorical Exercises by Nikephoros Basilakes." In *Theatron: Rhetorische Kultur in Spätantike und Mittelalter/ Rhetorical Culture in Late Antiquity and the Middle Ages*, edited by Michael Grünbart, 357–76. Berlin: De Gruyter, 2007.

Papaioannou, Stratis. "Anna Komnene's Will." In *Byzantine Religious Culture: Studies in Honor of Alice-Mary Talbot*, edited by Denis Sullivan, Elizabeth Fisher, and Stratis Papaioannou, 99–124. Leiden: Brill, 2012.

———. *Michael Psellos: Rhetoric and Authorship in Byzantium*. Cambridge: Cambridge University Press, 2013.

———. "Voice, Signature, Mask: The Byzantine Author." In *The Author in Middle Byzantine Literature: Modes, Functions, and Identities*, edited by Aglae Pizzone, 21–40. Berlin: De Gruyter, 2014.

Papaioannou, Stratis, and John Duffy. "Michael Psellos and the Authorship of the Historia Syntomos: Final Considerations." In *Byzantium, State and Society: In Memory of Nikos Oikonomides*, edited by A. Abramea, Angeliki Laiou, and Evangelos Chrysos, 219–29. Athens: Hellenic National Research Foundation, 2003.

Patlagean, Evelyne. "L'enfant et son avenir dans la famille byzantine (IV–XIIe siè-cles)." In *Structure sociale, famille, chrétienté à Byzance, IVe–XIe siècle*, 85–93. London: Variorum, 1981.

Paul, Anneliese. "Dichtung auf Objekten. Inschriftlich erhaltene griechische Epigramme vom 9. bis zum 16. Jahrhundert: Suche nach bekannten Autornamen." In *Byzantinische Sprachkunst: Studien zur byzantinischen Literatur gewidmet Wolfram Hörandner zum 65. Geburtstag*, edited by Martin Hinterberger and Elisabeth Schiffer, 234–65. Berlin: De Gruyter, 2007.

Pitarakis, Brigitte. "Female Piety in Context: Understanding Developments in Private Devotional Practices." In *Images of the Mother of God: Perceptions of the Theotokos in Byzantium*, edited by Maria Vassilaki, 153–66. Aldershot: Ashgate, 2005.

Pizzone, Aglae. "Anonymity, Dispossession and Reappropriation in the Prolog of Nikēphoros Basilakēs." In *The Author in Middle Byzantine Literature: Modes, Functions, and Identities*, edited by Aglae Pizzone, 225–45. Berlin: De Gruyter, 2014.

———. "Eaten by the Moths: Dispossession and Reappropriation in Nikephoros Basilakes' Autobiography." Paper presented at Byzantine Authorship: Theories and Practices, Durham University, July 23–25, 2012.

———. "Narrating Is Not for the Weak of Heart. Some Remarks on John Kaminiates' Capture of Thessaloniki." Lecture presented at the General Seminar of the Centre for Byzantine, Ottoman and Modern Greek Studies, University of Birmingham, October 27, 2011.

Polemis, Demetrios I. *The Doukai: A Contribution to Byzantine Prosopography.* London: Athlone, 1968.

Pomeroy, Sarah B. *Pythagorean Women: Their History and Writings.* Baltimore: Johns Hopkins University Press, 2013.

Prinzing, Günter. "Observations on the Legal Status of Children and the Stages of Childhood in Byzantium." In *Becoming Byzantine: Children and Childhood in Byzantium*, edited by Arietta Papaconstantinou and Alice-Mary Talbot. Washington, DC: Dumbarton Oaks, 2009.

Quandahl, Ellen, and Susan C. Jarratt. "'To Recall Him ... Will Be a Subject of Lamentation': Anna Comnena as Rhetorical Historiographer." *Rhetorica* 26 (2008): 301–35.

Reinsch, Diether Roderich. "Abweichungen vom traditionellen byzantinischen Kaiserbild im 11. und 12. Jahrhundert." In *L'éducation au gouvernement et à la vie: la tradition des "règles de vie" de l'antiquité au moyen âge*, edited by Paolo Odorico, 115–28. Paris: École des hautes études en sciences sociales, Centre d'études byzantines, néo-helléniques et sud-est européennes, 2009.

———. "Der Historiker Nikephoros Bryennios, Enkel und nicht Sohn des Usurpators." *Byzantinische Zeitschrift* 83 (1990): 423–24.

———. "Women's Literature in Byzantium? The Case of Anna Komnene." In *Anna Komnene and Her Times*, edited by Thalia Gouma-Peterson, 83–105. New York: Garland, 2000.

Rhodes, P. J. "Documents and the Greek Historian." In *A Companion to Greek and Roman Historiography*, edited by John Marincola, 56–66. Malden: Blackwell, 2007.

Riehle, Alexander. "Authorship and Gender (and) Identity. Women's Writing in the Middle Byzantine Period." In *The Author in Middle Byzantine Literature Modes, Functions, and Identities*, edited by Aglae Pizzone, 245–62. Berlin: De Gruyter, 2014.

Roueché, Charlotte. "Georgina Buckler: The Making of a British Byzantinist." In *The Making of Byzantine History*, edited by Roderick Beaton and Charlotte Roueché, 174–96. Aldershot: Variorum, 1993.

Runciman, Steven. "The End of Anna Dalassena." *Annuaire de l'institut de philologie et d'histoire orientales et slaves* 9 (1949): 517–24.

Russell, D. A., and Nigel Guy Wilson. *Menander Rhetor.* Oxford: Clarendon Press, 1981.

Russell, James. "The Archaeological Context of Magic in the Early Byzantine Period." In *Byzantine Magic*, edited by Henry Maguire, 35–50. Washington, DC: Dumbarton Oaks, 1995.

Rutherford, Richard. "Tragedy and History." In *A Companion to Greek and Roman Historiography*, edited by John Marincola, 504–14. Malden: Blackwell, 2007.

Saradi-Mendelovici, Helen. "A Contribution to the Study of the Byzantine Notarial Formulas: The Infirmitas Sexus of Women and the Sc. Velleianum." *Byzantinische Zeitschrift* 83 (1990): 72–90.

Savvides, Alexios. "Anna Komnene, historian, 1083–1153/4." In *International Encyclopaedia for the Middle Ages-Online. A Supplement to LexMA-Online*. Turnhout: Brepols Publishers, 2011, in Brepolis Medieval Encyclopaedias, http://www.brepolis.net.

Ševčenko, Nancy P. "The Service of the Virgin's Lament Revisited." In *The Cult of the Mother of God in Byzantium*, edited by Leslie Brubaker and Mary Cunningham, 247–62. Burlington: Ashgate, 2011.

Shepard, Jonathan. "Cross-Purposes: Alexius Comnenus and the First Crusade." In *The First Crusade: Origins and Impact*, edited by Jonathan Phillips, 107–29. Manchester: Manchester University Press, 1997.

———. "'Father' or 'Scorpion'? Style and Substance in Alexios's Diplomacy." In *Alexios I Komnenos*, edited by Margaret Mullett and Dion Smythe, 68–132. Belfast Byzantine Texts and Translations 4.1. Belfast: Belfast Byzantine Enterprises, 1996.

———. "When Greek Meets Greek: Alexius Comnenus and Bohemond in 1097–98." *Byzantine and Modern Greek Studies* 12 (1988): 185–277.

Silvas, Anna M. "Kassia the Nun c.810–c.865: An Appreciation." In *Byzantine Women: Varieties of Experience, 800–1200*, edited by Lynda Garland, 17–39. Aldershot: Ashgate, 2006.

Simpson, Alicia. *Niketas Choniates: A Historiographical Study*. Oxford: Oxford University Press, 2013.

———. "Before and After 1204: The Versions of Niketas Choniates' 'Historia.'" *Dumbarton Oaks Papers* 60 (2006): 189–221.

———. "Niketas Choniates: The Historian." In *Niketas Choniates: A Historian and a Writer*, edited by Alicia Simpson and Stephanos Efthymiades, 13–34. Geneva: La Pomme d'Or, 2009.

Simpson, Alicia, and Stephanos Efthymiades, eds. *Niketas Choniates: A Historian and a Writer*. Geneva: La Pomme d'Or, 2009.

Skoulatos, Basile. *Les personnages byzantins de l'Alexiade: Analyse prosopographique et synthese*. Louvain: Bureau du recueil College Erasme, 1980.

Smythe, Dion. "Alexios I and the Heretics: The Account of Anna Komnene's *Alexiad*." In *Alexios I Komnenos*, edited by Dion Smythe and Margaret Mullett, 232–59. Belfast Byzantine Texts and Translations 4.1. Belfast: Belfast Byzantine Enterprises, 1996.

———. "Gender." In *Palgrave Advances in Byzantine History*, edited by Jonathan Harris, 157–65. New York: Palgrave, 2005.

Sorlin, Irene. "Striges et Geloudes. Histoire d'une croyance et d'une tradition." *Travaux et Mémoires* 11 (1991): 411–36.

Sourvinou-Inwood, Christine. "Gendering the Athenian Funeral: Ritual Reality and Tragic Manipulations." In *Greek Ritual Poetics*, edited by Dimitrios Yatromanolakis and Panagiotis Roilos, 161–88. Cambridge: Harvard University Press, 2004.

Stears, Karen. "Death Becomes Her: Gender and Athenian Death Ritual." In *The Sacred and the Feminine in Ancient Greece*, edited by Sue Blundell and Margaret Williamson, 113–27. London: Routledge, 1998.

Stephenson, Paul. "Anna Comnena's *Alexiad* as a Source for the Second Crusade?" *Journal of Medieval History* 29 (2003): 41–54.

———. *Byzantium's Balkan Frontier: A Political Study of the Northern Balkans, 900–1204.* Cambridge: Cambridge University Press, 2000.

Stone, Andrew. "The Panegyrical Personae of Eustathios of Thessaloniki." *Scholia: Studies in Classical Antiquity* 18 (2009): 107–17.

Stouraitis, Ioannis. "Conceptions of War and Peace in Anna Comnena's Alexiad." In *Byzantine War Ideology between Roman Imperial Concept and Christian Religion: Akten des Internationalen Symposiums (Vienna, 19–21 Mai 2011)*, edited by Johannes Koder and Ioannis Stouraitis, 69–80. Vienna: Verlag der Österreichischen Akademie der Wissenschaften, 2012.

Suter, Ann. "Male Lament in Greek Tragedy." In *Lament: Studies in the Ancient Mediterranean and Beyond.* Oxford: Oxford University Press, 2008.

———. "Tragic Tears and Gender." In *Tears in the Graeco-Roman World*, edited by Thorsten Fögen, 60–83. Berlin: De Gruyter, 2009.

Swift, Laura. *The Hidden Chorus: Echoes of Genre in Tragic Lyric.* Oxford: Oxford University Press, 2010.

Talbot, Alice-Mary. *Women and Religious Life in Byzantium.* Aldershot: Ashgate, 2001.

Thomas, R. D. "Anna Comnena's Account of the First Crusade: History and Politics in the Reigns of the Emperors Alexius I and Manuel I Comnenus." *Byzantine and Modern Greek Studies* 15 (1991): 269–312.

Topping, Eva Catafygiotu. "Kassiane the Nun and the Sinful Woman." *Greek Orthodox Theological Review* 26, no. 3 (1981): 201–9.

———. "Thekla the Nun : In Praise of Women." *Greek Orthodox Theological Review* 25, no. 4 (1980): 353–70.

———. "Women Hymnographers in Byzantium." *Diptycha* 3 (1982–83): 98–111.

Treadgold, Warren T. *A History of the Byzantine State and Society.* Stanford: Stanford University Press, 1997.

Trizio, Michele. *Il neoplatonismo di Eustrazio di Nicea.* Biblioteca filosofica di Quaestio 23. Bari: Pagina soc. coop., 2016.

Varzos, Kônstantinos. *Hē genealogia tōn Komnēnōn.* Thessalonikē: Kentron Vyzantinōn Ereunōn, 1984.

Vasiliev, A. A. *A History of the Byzantine Empire.* Madison: University of Wisconsin Press, 1928.

Vinson, Martha. "The Christianization of Sexual Slander: Some Preliminary Observations." In *Novum Millennium: Studies on Byzantine History and Culture Dedicated to Paul Speck*, 415–24. Aldershot: Ashgate, 2001.

———. "Gender and Politics in the Post-Iconoclastic Period: The Lives of Antony the Younger, the Empress Theodora, and the Patriarch Ignatios." *Byzantion* 68 (1998): 469–515.

Wilson, Robin. "Lowered Cites." *The Chronicle of Higher Education*, March 17, 2014.

Woodman, A. J. *Rhetoric in Classical Historiography: Four Studies.* Portland: Areopagitica Press, 1988.

{INDEX}

Vanity, 91, 157–158, 178
Varangians, 95, 155, 162
Varzos, Konstantinos, 170
Vasiliev, Alexander, 170
Venice, 98

Widows and widowhood, 4–5, 19–20, 38–40, 63,
  176–177, 187nn26–29
William of Tyre, 143

Xenophon, 22, 70, 103

Zeno, 119, 123
Zeus, 56, 59
Zoe Komnene (sister), 2, 137
Zonaras, John
  on death of Alexios, 115
  on Eirene's power, 93, 154
  as source for modern scholarship, 162–163,
    165, 168, 170, 177
  on succession drama, 92, 93–97, 100, 103–106,
    109, 112, 155, 202n10

CPSIA information can be obtained
at www.ICGtesting.com
Printed in the USA
BVHW031533231020
591649BV00002B/82